# WHITE SAVAGES
# IN THE SOUTH SEAS

The author with her son and Tahitian friends, Moorea, 1966

# WHITE SAVAGES
# IN THE SOUTH SEAS

◆

**MEL KERNAHAN**

## V
**VERSO**
London • New York

To the memory of
Helen Sincere Scheuer,
my mother, mentor and best friend

Nathaniel H. Freeman:
When, if ever?
Now!
Pax vobiscum

And to Tu'i,
my beloved paperweight

Frontispiece: Moorea, 1966: Mel Kernahan and son with Tahitian friends.

First published by Verso 1995
© Mel Kernahan 1995
All rights reserved

**Verso**
UK: 6 Meard Street, London W1V 3HR
USA: 180 Varick Street, New York, NY 10014-4606

Verso is the imprint of New Left Books

ISBN 1-85984-978-4
ISBN 1-85984-004-3 (pbk)

**British Library Cataloguing in Publication Data**
A catalogue record for this book is available from the British Library.

**Library of Congress Cataloging-in-Publication Data**
A catalog record for this book is available from the Library of Congress.

Typeset in Dante by NorthStar, San Francisco, California
Printed and bound in Great Britain by Biddles Ltd, Guildford and King's Lynn

# CONTENTS

FOREWORD     vii

PREFACE     ix

ACKNOWLEDGEMENTS     xi

INTRODUCTION     1

1   Striptease Comes to Tahiti     6
*New dance stuns locals*

2   Behind the Mai Tai Curtain     15
*Mystery solved*

3   Pouvanaa a Oopa     18
*Tahiti's great hero*

4   Susy No Pants     27
*Tahiti. The other side of a Quinn's Girl*

5   French Foreign Legion in Eden     36
*Tahiti. Interview with a rogue*

6   Erena     44
*First nuclear nomad in Newport Beach, California*

7   Simone     54
*Dance teacher. The shark that ate my uncle*

8   Hinano     60
*An imposter's tale*

9   What Do Naked Women Want?     67
*Man jailed for wrong answer*

10   Pepe, the Queen of Tahiti     69
*Mine from hell. What's important to women*

11   Life of an Ariki     81
*Can an Island queen find happiness with a politician?*

12   Damn You, Robert Dean Frisbie                        95
     *C.I. Interisland cargo boat romance*

13   Ghost Woman Dreaming on Aitutaki                     103
     *A teenager is a teenager*

14   The Young Unmarried                                  111
     *Aitutaki courtship in the shadows*

15   Illusions of Paradise                                114
     *A soliloquy*

16   What You Call Dat T'ing?                             118
     *King demands answer. More South Seas romance*

17   Boardinghouse, Island Style                          127
     *Fantasy and reality on Aitutaki*

18   Manuae Takeaway; or, The Great Ru Landed Where?      132
     *History through a beer bottle*

19   Some Enchanted Evening ...                           135
     *Rarotonga. Dark side of Island romance*

20   Defection to Mitiaro                                 144
     *Find untouched island. Don't make waves.*

21   Face on the Ocean                                    151
     *Found it.*

22   HMNZS *Waikato* Day                                  161
     *Start making waves.*

23   Black Tiare                                          167
     *A terrible loneliness in mid-ocean*

24   Why the Navy Had Wet Pants                           169
     *An Island CAO prevails over the Navy*

25   The Scarlet Woman of Mitiaro                         173
     *Sadie Thompson lives!*

26   And on the Seventh Day ...                           180
     *A healing Sabbath, Mitiaro style*

27   Face on the Ocean with My Tears                      186
     *The swamp. The feast. Mitiaro farewell*

EPILOGUE   Death of Three Heroes                          193

REFERENCES                                                202

# FOREWORD

I am extremely grateful to the author for allowing me the opportunity of publicly conveying my appreciation for the rekindling of memories of persons and personages that I have known so well during the past three decades.

She has taken segments of the great Polynesian nation that covers the greater part of the globe and outlined them in a perspective that those intimate with the area can say, 'this is real!' She has her finger on the pulse of the people she writes about.

The Tahiti that I knew in the mid 1930s had changed when revisited in the early 1960s. By the 1970s, it was near impossible to conjure up the places where so much enjoyment had been experienced.

The dusty Rue-de-la Pomare is now a modern highway with stop signs and lights, and the back street, Broom Road (*Ara Purumu*), where my teenaged youth vented its passions, is now covered with buildings. Similarly, Rarotonga and the Outer Islands have moved through a modernization, and it is only in old photographs that the 'as it was' can be seen.

The reader may ask, 'What has this to do with the contents of the book?'

Very few writers have been able to picture the Polynesion in a true light. They usually depict them as 'brown-skinned happy people who seem to be always laughing and loving.' This is false, and as Mel has aptly told me, '... I present our old South Seas as the hooker she is, who's been around the block a few times and suffered, and still suffers horribly from the perversions of white savages.' How true this is!

Mel has done what few European writers have. She has perceived the people as ordinary persons, the same as in any race. As a Scot, I appreciate this, as fifty-nine of my seventy-six years have been spent in and with Polynesia. I am proud that my race has assimilated into every other race under the sun by using the same yardstick that the author has used.

As a Colonial Resident Administrator of Penrhyn, Atiu, and Aitutaki Islands from the 1960s to the early 1970s, and later Judge of the Land Court and Commissioner of the High Court on Rarotonga after the Cook Islands achieved self-determination, I know well the situations depicted in this book. Although in some sense humorous, they show the true steel and independent attitude of most Polynesians.

Even though I have lived and loved through the periods so well portrayed in these pages, reading this book has brought back scenes that have lain dormant for years, and makes me so thankful for having such a full and wonderful life. All I can say is, 'Thank you, Mel, for rekindling such memories of wonderful people.'

*Judge (Rtd) John James MacCauley*
*Rarotonga, Cook Islands*

# PREFACE

Places and people in this book are real, the incidents, true. A few names have been changed for obvious reasons.

I have been as candid about my own role in these stories as I have been about everyone else's. There's a saying in the Cook Islands that translates to 'All heads are the same height.' The least I can do is stand on the same level as the Islanders I depict.

I do not presume to analyze people or cultures, to heap judgements or generalizations upon them. I offer no advice on or solutions to situations I might perceive as problems in the Islands. There's danger in that. The worst 'todays' may be the 'good old days' of tomorrow.

The only thing I have learned from all these years in and around the South Seas is that wherever we live, we are all connected and relevant, each to the other. These stories mirror distant members of our extended family. No island is an island.

# ACKNOWLEDGEMENTS

My deepest gratitude to Mike Davis. I wish there were a Mike Davis in every writer's life. Without his belief in this book and me, you wouldn't be reading it.

I also want to thank Sands Thomas, Patty Kernahan and my husband, Galal Kernahan, for reading the manuscript and giving me their invaluable input; Rene Fell and Esther Dendel for the opportunity to try out a couple of chapters in lectures on *tivaevae* for their art groups; and New York artist and favorite cousin Jill Gill for her efforts on my behalf; as well as Theodore Taylor.

I owe a special debt to my friends and teachers of Tahiti, Rarotonga, Mitiaro and Aitutaki. Ihope this book in some way helps you to better understand me and my relationship to your islands and people; I have never a found a way to express it verbally. There are so many of you: Pepe Gaultier and her family; Jock and Akateni Ariki Joseph MacCauley and their children; the Pokoati family and people of Mitiaro who took in a stranger and taught her her place in their universe.

My thanks to the people of Aitutaki whose names were changed to protect their privacy. To my beloved friend the late Pa Ariki, who will stand tall in my memory always as a model against whom I will measure all queens. To Richard, a delightful friend whom I've exploited shamelessly in this book: *meitaki maata* for laughing.

My heartfelt appreciation, too, to a generous friend of Rarotonga and Mangaia, who is not only wise, but a great humanitarian. She's asked that her name be suppressed, but she knows who she is and now she knows, hopefully, how very grateful I am for her tolerance and instruction since 1978.

I'd like to pay tribute to Susy No Pants, Simone Adams, Gene and Lea Yatlee, a certain freedom-fighter taxi driver of Papeete, Erena of Hao and Ted

Cook, legend.

I also want to acknowledge my appreciation for Dr Bengt and Marie Thérèse Danielsson, whose interviews, insights, books and articles on the French Polynesian political situation have deeply influenced my commitment to *te aho Maohi*.

# INTRODUCTION

There is a dream that paradise exists on the islands under the Southern Cross in Polynesia – that is, unless you were born there.

What image does the word 'paradise' conjure up for Polynesians? As once they explored the Pacific in great seagoing double canoes for paradise lands rumored to be just over the horizon; now they migrate in jet aircraft, seeking the glamorous life that they glimpsed in movies screened in packing sheds under the coconut palms. They settle in the US and in New Zealand, where food comes in easy-to-open packages instead of the hard way from the soil and the sea; where everyone has a television set; and where one's future isn't defined by the status of one's ancestors.

Polynesians have been packaged as stereotypes by the entertainment and travel industries. You know the women as lissome girls with coconuts on their breasts and strings of grass tassels just above the pubic hairline, grinding their hips with a fast-moving jiggle as they shake it up to an insistent drumbeat, without a troublesome brain in their flower-crowned heads. Pelvic gyrations to the drum dance of Tahiti have become a metaphor for the people of the South Seas.

Few Islanders are bothered by this. The image ensures them jobs as exotic entertainers all over the world. It's good for tourism and, at the same time, it provides them with a protective façade behind which they can shield their real thoughts, aspirations and viewpoints, ultimately hiding the inner core of their culture.

'Keep your eyes on the hands!' (Ogle those hips!) has transcended the double-entendre instruction from the master of ceremonies at a luau: it has become our only connection with the people. For communication, we're offered the voice of the drumbeat; for eye contact, the winking navel. Who are the real savages of the South Seas?

I'm going to show you Polynesians with brains, hearts and dreams. They're friends and enemies, brats and philosophers, geniuses and bimbos, lechers and preachers, laundresses, kings, queens, hookers and everything in between. The heirs to the South Sea Islands do not epitomize their gorgeous tropical dreamscape any more than you or I do.

I'll also show you scenes of brutal devastation in the Islands, where white savages have practiced domination and war rituals. As a reluctant white savage myself, I'll relate some embarrassing tales of my interactions with a civilization I should understand better after all these years of exposure to it – but don't. I've never achieved that state of grace which enables me to see only the positive and close the screen door so the flies don't get in.

I'm frequently asked how my obsession with the South Seas started. In my earliest memories, I was drawn to stories with jungle backgrounds. I didn't care if it was Africa, the Amazon or the South Pacific, my dream of perfection was the tropics. The tall tales my surrogate grandfather, Joe Eagan, used to tell me about when he was King of the Congo didn't hurt either. A retired boxing trainer, he spun these stories in serial form when I was five or so, telling me a chapter when he came for Sunday dinner, another when he took me to a bar and plied me with salted herring while he had his gin.

I acted out jungle epics with neighborhood kids; I'd costume from Mama's underwear drawer. My favorite look was a long slip slit to the thigh, a bra stuffed with paper napkins and a silk flower over one ear.

As an adult, I followed in my mother's footsteps and became a reporter, a feature writer and an editor. I fancied myself a pretty savvy, tough cookie, beyond awe. I lost all that on 14 August 1959 at 6 a.m. as the peaks of Moorea and Tahiti materialized in dawn seas which had been empty for eight days.

I was out there in mid ocean with my husband and toddler simply because we were so crazy to travel that we had borrowed money and signed on for a 38-day South Pacific cruise on Matson Line's SS *Mariposa*. We picked it because it sounded like a stress-free way to travel with a small child, the route was fascinating, the timing was right. Rotarians threw a bon voyage party for us. Whispers circulated that authentic South Sea Island beauties would entertain, which of course turned out to be us Rotary wives in cellophane hula skirts, accompanied by one ukulele (mine). From what I then knew of the South Seas from Dorothy Lamour and Yvonne DeCarlo movies, we looked about right.

Day is the same as night in a windowless inside cabin. Awake and claustrophobic, I climbed to the top deck, clawing my way forward in wind so strong it was difficult to walk. Darkness was just giving way to a lavender dawn. As the dense black smoke of night dissipated, it left a ghostly core crumpled and jagged on the horizon. The rising sun sculpted it into the volcanic spires of the island of Moorea and the mountains of Tahiti rising from a cobalt sea. I went into an open-mouthed trance, so stunned I stood transfixed for hours. I have never seen anything so beautiful before or since.

As the sun rose and the ship drew nearer, the slopes of the peaks turned to green and rust red. Individual coconut palms stood out, then flashes of orange rusty iron roofs and white church steeples. We docked at Papeete. A laughing tangle of brown people almost buried under garlands of fragrant frangipani and *Tiare tahiti* rushed on board kissing and hugging passengers and crew alike, putting leis around our necks and crowning us with flowers.

They looked right into our eyes and nuzzled our two-year-old rosy-tan son in his leopard-print bikini and crew cut. Later, ashore, they recognized us, waved and shouted greetings with smiles that hinted of shared mischief to come. To someone used to a world where people built walls around themselves by not looking at each other and not touching, this was shocking.

I grew up a dark, alienated child with a nose, thick glasses, pimples and jungle books in the North Hollywood of the 1940s, where 'blonde', 'button-nosed', 'blue-eyed' and 'ivory-skinned' described the reigning goddesses and Frank Sinatra was god of the day. Adding to my misery, teachers, parents and kids speculated openly that I was probably a bastard because my mother had a profession and a divorce, kept her maiden name, and insisted on being addressed as 'Miss'. So here was a whole island of dark people who stuck flowers in their hair, laughed at every other thing and didn't give a damn whether anyone was married.

But there was one discordant note in that first encounter. It nagged away at me for the next seven years until I could return. It was a half-told story of an incident that didn't fit, abrading my soft memories of a South Seas paradise like a hard foreign object in an oyster shell until it caused a blister.

There'd been a rumor on the beach – half-understood headlines in the French newspaper – something about rock throwing at the Territorial Assembly building by a mob. Was this possible? I asked the *Mariposa*'s purser as we sailed for New Zealand. I'll never forget his words:

'It was nothing! Forget it! Some Tahitian troublemaker was holed up in the government building and some settlers lost their tempers. A few rocks were thrown at the building. The Tahitians inside got mad and waved sticks and yelled. It was over in a few minutes.'

The smiling purser then volunteered his analysis of the Tahitian people, based on years of experience on cruise ships. 'These people are just like children. That's why the French and Chinese have to run these islands. Tahitians? They'd rather sing, dance and make love all day. Between you and me, that's all they're good for.' He tapped his forehead, implying that they really weren't all that bright.

'Tahitians are happy people, basically. Live for today, let tomorrow take care of itself. *"Aita e pe'a pe'a"*, as they say. Sometimes, like kids, they want something they can't have and they have a little tantrum. But they can't sustain it for long. Someone brings out a ukulele and a few bottles of beer and they forget the whole thing. They have a good life. They're never cold, never hungry. There's nothing left to want in this paradise.'

I first glimpsed the hidden depths beneath the 'carefree' grins six years later when I was critically injured in a motorcycle accident at the isthmus of Taravao on Tahiti. I was bloody and broken, unable to speak Maohi or French: my first lesson was that speech is only a minor method of communication. I don't, however, recommend fracturing your skull in three places, pulverising your nose and breaking your neck to know how people from other cultures relate to you and you to them.

Maybe it was lying in a dirty hospital ward among male and female Tahitians who were also suffering that made me realize we were exactly the same after all. Maybe it had to do with the young woman in the far corner who frequently moaned – when I shuffled by her bed to get to the semi-working toilet, she beckoned and handed me a big orange with 'Sunkist' stamped on it in purple. She knew somehow I was from California, where the expensive imported orange came from, and wanted to comfort me with something familiar from my faraway home. In Island hospitals, families sleep on the floor by their sick or injured kinfolk to feed and care for them. My family was thousands of miles away, yet I never wanted for anything.

Maybe it was the old ladies rolling cigarettes on the bench outside who made room for me when I first staggered out into the sunshine, clucking and pointing at the black stitches marching like millipedes over the grotesquely swollen lump that was once my face and whooping with laughter when I identified my ailment as 'Vespa' (an Italian motorscooter). They made room for me on the bench, I traded cigarettes for mangoes and we watched the mynah birds savage a papaya, blossoms fall, clouds collide and the occasional doctor amble through doors across the courtyard.

There is a myth that life is simple in the South Pacific and the people uncomplicated. The islands I've known, loved and sometimes hated most of my adult life are not easy places to live. The Polynesian culture I've collided with and immersed myself in is beyond the understanding of anyone not born into it: it's as intricate and multilayered as those of ancient China or Greece.

These are not simple people; their lives and relationships are not always easy; and they are not always kind. Their world is complex, loaded with contradictions and paradoxes, a maze of protocols and value systems radically different from those of the Western world. Casual visitors watch a hula floor show, sip a mai tai with a little umbrella in it, and go home with a tan, never seeing, hearing or knowing the people who lurk behind the mai tai curtain.

I want to lift that curtain and give you a closer look at some of the Islanders in my life, of the white savages who stalk their Islands looking for a paradise in which to play out their fantasies of love, freedom, happiness, dominance, free enterprise, war and toxic experiments. To do this, I must break certain taboos and write about politics, religion, the bomb and what women do when men aren't watching them.

Author Victor Villaseñor once told an audience that he envisioned a time when there would be no more wars. A man argued that war was inevitable. There had always been wars, there always would be wars: war was man's nature. Villaseñor pounced on the argument, declaring that history was written by men and that the record would read differently if it was written by grandmothers. Wars would fade to minor background incidents against the eternal saga of the family. As a grandmother, I see that this is so. The world history my grandmother told me was of the family and the lands they came from.

My perspective of the South Seas has been formed by my identity: I am an adventurer, a woman who watches and listens – a grandmother. In my life, people are of primary importance, overshadowing the wars of the rest of the planet.

The period we'll move through, from 1965 to 1992, is one of turbulent change in the South Pacific; a time of Western impact accelerated by the construction of international airports and the introduction of video and television. If you fear to plunge into realities that make flesh, comedy and sometimes hell of your paradise fantasies, not to worry. If living these stories hasn't shattered my dreams, it won't even bruise yours.

The real world of the Polynesian Islands still exists. It isn't as described by Robert Dean Frisbie, Pierre Loti, Nordhoff and Hall or Beatrice Grimshaw, but it's still the South Seas, lying in wait for some damned fool of a Westerner to wander into its maddening embrace. It's always the same story: the adventurer rushes forth, arms reaching out – the South Seas meets them, swaying, smiling, arms outstretched in welcome. They drift right through one another like ghosts, never really understanding, frustrated, love unrequited.

Take my hand and leap into this world with me. Why? Because it's there.

## 1

# STRIPTEASE COMES TO TAHITI

*Frangipani and vanilla! Tiare!* Inhaling a voracious gulp of scented Tahiti morning, I held it in my bursting lungs until sparkly things started whirling in front of my eyes and I felt dizzy. I released it, hoping that nine hours' worth of chilly, canned, cigarette-stained airplane air rushed out with it, never to return. Home was the lover, home from the rat race ... (apologies to RLS).

Every sensor in my body was awake now like the tentacles of a sea anemone searching for nourishment in its crystalline tidepool after the wave subsides. A cacophony of rooster crows, barking dogs and honking, beeping, rattling traffic threaded itself suddenly on a lei of song as the laughing girls walking ahead of me harmonized a few bars of an Eddie Lund country-western air with naughty Tahitian lyrics.

Papeete still had a village attitude in 1966. Strangers honk and wave. If you've returned from overseas, news flies everywhere at once on the coconut wireless: old so-and-so is back on the beach. People you might have met fleetingly on an earlier visit react as if you're a long-lost best friend. They shriek, plant joyful kisses on your cheeks, tell you that you're getting fat and swear they'll meet you later for a beer.

Thus it was on this first morning back after a year's absence that Pito, a *tinito* (Chinese-Tahitian) taxi-driver, and I were reunited. I was strolling down the road exactly as I had been trying to do when we first met. If Pito decides you are special to him for whatever mystical reason, you do not walk again, ever, if he sees you first. You ride in style and you do not pay. Never mind if he has paying customers in the cab. He screeches to a halt, greets you with a joyful hoot and stuffs you in the car if there's room. If not, he commands you to wait 'little bit', speeds away, dislodges a fare or two, careens back, screeches to a halt and shouts:

'Now! You ride!' The only way one could take a stroll in the vicinity of Papeete under the circumstances was to use back roads or slip behind a tree if one saw his cab in time.

So it was that I climbed into the front seat on this hot, sweet-smelling tropical morning in August while a backseatful of American tourists made irritated mutters. 'I'm surprised you recognized me.'

Pito's elegant, moon-shaped face, more golden Chinese than Tahitian, shatters into laughter. We kiss-kiss cheeks in the polite French way of Tahiti, then he hoots gleefully, grabs my head and kisses me full on the lips. 'You've been wasting your time at the cinema again', I chide, which he ignores.

'I know you. You face, he get small again. Las' year, you face like breadfruit. You look nice', he says admiringly. 'You okay?'

'Okay. A little crazier than before the Demon Vespa of Tahiti threw its front wheel and dropped me on my head at sixty kilometers an hour. Your doctors did a pretty good job and I kept smearing *monoi* [coconut oil] on my wounds when I got out of the hospital, like Susy No Pants said, and look, almost no scars!' I pushed my bangs up off my forehead for inspection.

He grunted approvingly, aimed his taxi into a slight ebb in the surging tide of cars, trucks and motorcycles and plunged in.

'*Monoi* good medicine. Where you go?' he asked.

'Nowhere. I just got in on the dawn plane from Los Angeles. I haven't been to bed in twenty-six hours but I'm too happy to rest. I thought I'd stroll down to the market, get a coffee, see what's going on and maybe buy a new *pareu* (two meters of island-print cloth worn in various ways as a garment).

'I no see you at airport!' he said accusingly. 'You walk to Papeete?'

'I didn't see you either. We took another taxi.' Out of the corner of my eye, I could see he was scowling.

'My husband and son came along this time, probably to see that I don't ride on any more motorcycles.'

'How big?'

'Oh, almost as tall as I am. He's eleven years old now. Or did you mean my husband?'

He barked a laugh. 'Where you husband and son now?'

'Asleep. At least, my husband is. Our son is probably trying to catch lizards.'

We pulled up to a resort, Pito dropped his fares off, stuffed francs into his shirt pocket and picked up two waving Frenchmen. 'We go out tonight', he proclaimed. 'I show you family Papeete nightlife.'

'Will you be off duty?'

'No duty', he laughed. 'Duty free. You no pay. I work. Same every night. You ride with me. I get too much passenger, you go out, wait little bit. I go drop

7

passenger. He pay. I catch new passenger. I come by. You ride one more time.'

'Won't your boss get mad?'

'Boss is me! This one *my* taxi. That one, my taxi. Got three, but one, he broke!'

Galal and I set out that night with Pito, leaving our son, Kent, in the care of a Tahitian woman, a precaution Kent assured us was quite unnecessary. As we left, he was climbing on the chest of drawers, butterfly net in hand, stalking the geckos that scuttled across the ceiling.

The evening was warm, gaudy with moon-spangled lagoon and coconut palms. We rode around in the front seat of Pito's old taxi as he picked up passengers and dropped them off. Sometimes they were boisterous locals, sometimes tourists, once a pair of government officials. When he needed more space, he'd deposit us temporarily in front of hotels or cafés out in the country. We'd watch part of a floor show or stay outside in some jungle garden, listening to guitars, ukuleles, singing and laughter, reveling in the velvet tropical night, fragrant with vanilla, *tiare Tahiti* blossoms and wood smoke, undercut with the aged-cheese smell of copra.

Traveling from Arue back to Papeete, a sign seemed to jump out of the darkness briefly, caught in Pito's speeding headlights. He was not one to dawdle, especially now that he had no paying passengers on board.

'What did that sign say back there? It looked like "Striptease tonight" in English.'

'What that?' Pito shouted over the motor. 'I don't know him.'

'There's another one! Look. "International striptease show tonight. First time on Tahiti." I'm not kidding. The sign wasn't even in French. What's striptease doing in Tahiti? Isn't Tahitian dancing sexy enough?'

The headlights raced along before us relentlessly, flashing on other signs, coconut palm trunks, groups of small, thatch-sided houses. 'I don't know striptease', Pito repeated. 'First time in Tahiti.'

'It's a dance they do overseas for men. Girls come in wearing fancy dresses, dance around the stage and take their clothes off, piece by piece.'

'What they do then? No clothes. They make boom-boom?'

'It's just a bad girls' dance they do in big cities. The men applaud. The curtain comes down. No boom-boom.'

'Jus' dance?'

'That's it. Just a dance.'

'You want stop, see him?'

'Don't you? If this is the first time here, it's a great moment in Tahitian history. You'll want to see it so you can tell your grandchildren.' My sarcasm went unnoticed.

'Okay. I stop little bit, but you no tell wife.' Making an abrupt U-turn in the middle of the road, he drove back toward Arue, swerving off finally across what looked like an empty field. His headlights picked out a track worn down in the dense, leathery grass. Ahead, a large packing shed loomed, dimly lighted from within. Motorscooters, old cars and pickup trucks were strewn helter-skelter, suggesting that half the island's population had jumped from their vehicles and rushed inside, leaving them to stop by themselves. Pito turned off the motor, we abandoned the taxi and set out through trampled grass.

The packing shed was jammed with a merry crowd of Tahitians of all ages, from newborn to great-grandparent vintage. Crowns of ferns, *frangipani* and *tiare Tahiti* made royalty out of even the most dissolute looking. A bluish haze of cigarette smoke hovered over the scene. Talk clattered like palm fronds in the trade winds, punctuated with geysers of laughter and shouts.

A portly Tahitian mama, long island-print gown topped with a woven hat almost buried under flower wreaths, blocked our path. She held up three fingers in front of a wide, toothless grin and called out in Tahitian.

'What's she saying?' we asked Pito, but he was already tucking three 100-franc notes into her hand. The matron leaned forward and whispered something in his ear that made them both laugh uproariously.

'What did she say just then? What's so funny?'

'She say, *'Popa'a* (European) lady no look like she can boom-boom two *tanes* [men].' She say, "You come wit me. I take care you."' Pito whooped again with laughter, pushed away the 300 francs we tried to tuck in his shirt pocket to repay him, and led his two slightly embarrassed tourists into the crowd.

There was no stage, no chairs. Backless old wooden benches lining the walls were already filled. Mothers and grandmothers with infants and a squirming collection of black-haired, rosy-brown children sat on the floor next to the rope, poking each other and sucking on candies and fruit. A pair of boys about seven years old shadowboxed and clowned in the center of the ring. The rest of the crowd stood or squatted on the floor.

Suddenly, a flamboyant *demi* (French–Tahitian), flower over one ear, pushed his way into the center ring and shooed the children out. Waving and shouting in French (there was no microphone), he punctuated his revelations with eloquent hands, eyebrows, shrugs and a few bumps and grinds to the shrieks of his appreciative audience.

'Big *mahu!*' grinned Pito. 'He like woman.'

'What's he saying?'

Pito, listening intently, didn't answer at once.

'He keeps saying Australia. Are the dancers Australian? I'll bet that's why the signs were in English.'

'E', he replied in the Tahitian affirmative, eyes on the gyrating compere. He pawed through his pockets, looking for papers and tobacco, rolled a cigarette without looking and offered it, first to my husband, then to me. I accepted it, he rolled another and we lit up. No more questions. The show was on.

Two women suddenly raced down a lane through the crowd, yipping and flapping their pink arms like stampeding flamingos. Bursting into the clearing, they whirled into a dance routine, one shouting, 'Lights, mate! Music!'

No spotlight picked them out from the rest of us in the gloom of that cavernous packing shed. Illumination came from a few bare light bulbs twenty feet overhead in the rafters. Somehow, the ivory-skinned women seemed to manage a luminosity of their own as they gyrated and strutted, making odd little cries.

Like an unexpected inspiration, a dance tune suddenly blasted from a loudspeaker somewhere. At the same time, a beam of light, swirling with cigarette smoke, pierced the dimness. The compere had evidently found the switches in the dark. Now, the spangled dancers glittered like sunlight on a fractured summer sea.

The born-again redhead wore her pink-orange tresses upswept in an amazing pumpkin-sized pouf. Light twinkled from jewelled metallic dust in her coiffure, embedded in enough hairspray to waterproof a boat. She was short, plump, hyper and closer to forty than thirty. The other half of the exotic dance team was a hard-faced, reptile-thin young woman with a swinging blonde ponytail that probably made every fisherman in the room salivate. Tahitians say a lock of golden hair tied to a fishing lure is the best bait there is.

We were close enough to see that both women wore heavy stage make-up and their feather-trimmed, sequinned evening gowns had bald spots and safety pins. The whole scene was so incongruous that we could only stare, mouths agape. The crowd apparently felt the same. All life outside that ring of light hung suspended.

The showgirls caught the delayed action of the beat and broke into a lewd twist, detached smiles on shiny red lips. Each danced her own interpretation of the music: slow movements at first, a sensual belly grind here, a quaking of breasts there. The beat quickened, now smacking the silence around, hard and dirty. It seemed like all hell had broken loose inside the sacred circle.

The Tahitians, who generally can't sit still if there's music with a beat, were as inanimate as woodcarvings.

The music thickened, grew intimate. The big peel began. The blonde drew off one long glove, slow and seductive, finger-by-finger. It seemed to take hours. You wondered how anyone could make such a big deal out of taking off a glove. Finally, her whole arm, her hand and then her scarlet-painted fingernails were naked and free. She began to twirl the glove, teasing the front row, which by now was a solid mass of children.

Startled wide-awake black eyes fended her off. Her blue ones blinked in a double take. She fumbled the beat. Recovering, she threw back her head with a trilling laugh like she knew all along they were only kids and lobbed the limp satin glove over their heads into the adult audience beyond. No one moved to catch it.

The eerie silence from the crowd was distracting. My eyes strayed to the faces around me. I glanced at Pito. He stared straight ahead, wooden as the rest. My wandering eyes met those of my husband, now crowd-watching too in some astonishment. He shrugged, spread his palms and raised his eyebrows, as puzzled as I was.

It seemed to take hours, but eventually, the dancers had stripped down to pasties and G-strings. Still, no man whistled, no woman muttered, no child stirred, no foot stamped, no hands clapped. The crowd was comatose. I was even starting to feel sorry for the showgirls, but my pity was wasted. The resourceful creatures had one trick left guaranteed to quicken even the dead.

Smiling coyly, the redhead began to play with her generous breasts. Was she removing the pasties? Would we get a peek at her nipples? No, she had something better than that in store for her strange, silent crowd. A scratchy recorded drum roll roared from the loudspeaker. She arched her back, loosed her breasts, flung her arms out and – behold! – golden tassels spun from her pasties. By now, the crowd was supposed to be screaming. It wasn't.

The tassels were twirling in the same direction. She stopped them and made them go in opposite directions, faster and faster, triumphant smile on lips, crescendo of drum rolls bouncing off the walls. Her blonde partner, mouth open miming a silent laughing scream of amazement, undulated around the clearing, beckoning the crowd to applaud, scream, throw coins, anything!

With a whoop, the compere leaped into the ring, dancing, goading the audience to respond, respond! Still there was no sound from those watchers, no move. Then, shockingly, a baby's cry rose in a screaming counterpoint to the thudding beat. The mother whispered soothingly, fumbled with her blouse, gave the infant her breast and a wet sucking sound replaced the wailing.

The music stopped. The performers bowed as though thunderous applause roared through the packing shed and ran waving, eyes glassy, staring straight ahead, lips drawn taut in waxen smiles through the mute canyon of flower-crowned Tahitians. 'Thank you, thank you!' they called to the silence. The audience flinched away from contact, parting to let the near-naked women pass.

The compere fossicked through the empty core of the room, harvesting sequinned, feathered jetsam from the floor. Clutching discarded costumes to his chest, he ran after them, snaking his way through the crowd as it dissipated, each member walled in a solitude of silence. What were they thinking? I tried to read eyes and expressions with no success. When a Polynesian turns off and goes inward, no one can follow. Jostled, we joined the exodus into the starry night. 'Where's Pito?' I asked my husband. He had no more idea than I did.

Spotting a familiar face among the cars and motorscooters, I called out, 'Turia! *Iaorana!*' The girl, a pastor's daughter and an old friend, halted. We kissed cheeks and exchanged pleasantries, but her eyes darted from side to side as though looking for rescue. 'Did you see the show? What'd you think?' I half whispered.

She was quiet for so long, I thought she wasn't going to answer at all. Finally, she said: 'Is new, that dance.'

'Well, did you like it? Do you think that kind of dancing will catch on in Tahiti, God forbid?'

'Is new', she repeated, politely kissed the air on either side of my face, climbed on a motorscooter and buzzed off into the night.

The waning moon cast a pale light on the scene. Pito's taxi was not where we'd left it. 'He must have picked up a cabful', my husband speculated. 'He'll be back. I wonder if he saw the grand finale?'

The few Tahitians left vanished quickly into the night. The last motor roar dwindled into silence. The field was empty except for one car. Suddenly, a babble of angry female voices flared and flickered in and out of a placating male whine. The first striptease show on Tahiti was storming toward the lonely Citroën, hunched alone in the field like a miniature army tank. The trio shoved sound equipment and suitcases in the back.

'Hi', I said. 'I'm doing a freelance article on Tahiti. Got time for a quick interview?'

The redhead waved me off, 'Not now!'

'Are you living here on Tahiti? We can set up something later.'

Both women snorted derisively, crowded into the front seat beside their compere, and slammed the door. 'Live here? Not bloody likely, mate! We can't wait to get the hell off this bloody island. There's your statement. Good night!' said the redhead.

'Madame', the *demi* said to me in excellent English over the idling motor, 'the dancers are very tired.'

Ever the diplomat, my husband went around to the driver's side, braced one hand on the car roof and spoke through the open window: 'The performance was remarkable! The audience was quiet because they've never seen anything like that before. Tahitians can be very shy. You know that. They probably loved the show.'

'That is true, *monsieur*', the compere nodded gravely. 'That is just what I was saying. We are still a shy people. I, myself, have been to Paris with my father. I know now we are very backward here. Very innocent.'

'Oh, right!' shrilled the blonde. 'Innocent! The way your women shake their arses when they dance? Go on, you bloody hypocrite.'

'He's not a hypocrite', I said. 'Tahitian dance is a language. Some of it's foreplay. Yours looks like foreplay, but nobody is sure if you mean what it looks like you mean. You're teasing. Maybe the men in the audience were confused. They probably wanted to run off to the bush with you to give you what you apparently wanted, but maybe they figured their wives might take a machete to them. I don't really know, I'm just guessing.'

The redhead exploded. 'We've danced in South Africa, Venezuela, Mexico, big cities, small towns, you name it. Everybody understands striptease is art. We've seen these Tahitian girls dance. That's *not* art. We're trying to do them a favor here and teach them a few artistic tricks. Anybody can stand there and shake their arse. You mean the only thing what stopped native guys from jumping us was their women watching them? Bloody savages!'

'It was your idea to come here, not mine', the blonde snapped at her partner.

'It was not, it was yours!'

Their voices trailed back as the car drove off into the darkness. '*Merci*' and '*bonsoir*' the driver called out over the voices of the bickering showgirls. The sounds of the Citroën faded and we stood alone in the dark silence, the last people left alive at the packing shed in the district of Arue. 'We should have asked them for a lift', I sighed. 'Let's start walking.'

As we neared the road, a pair of headlights came bumping across the field out of nowhere. It was Pito. 'Where you go? You not wait for me?' He was indignant.

We wriggled into the front seat. 'I thought you'd forgotten us', I said. 'We waited a long time. I didn't even see you leave. Did you see the end of the show? The part with the tassels?'

'*E*, I see him.'

'Is that all you have to say about it?'

He didn't reply.

'Why was everyone so quiet? Didn't they like it? Were they embarrassed? Were you? What's going on?'

'Is new. People 'shamed.'

'Why? Ashamed of the dance or because they didn't know how to do it?'

The taxi bounced over the rough ground on to the main road. Pito was silent. I tried another tack.

'Do you think striptease will replace Tahitian dancing some day?'

He would not be baited. The silence that had welled up in the old packing shed from the secretmost depths of the island now filled Pito's taxi, washing away the traces of Tahiti's first striptease like the tide.

## 2

# BEHIND THE MAI TAI CURTAIN

'Maybe you can clear up a mystery for us, Pito.' Galal changed the subject, hoping to get the conversation and relationship going again. 'It's something we've been wondering about for seven years. We first came to Tahiti on the *Mariposa* in 1959. We were just here for a couple of days, but we noticed everyone was talking about some excitement that happened. A mob supposedly threw rocks at the post office. Do you remember the incident?'

'Right!' I chimed in. 'I'm glad you brought it up. In fact, Pito, I asked you that same question last year when I was here alone. You said then that you'd tell me some day. The story I heard was that the people were rioting for independence. Do the Tahitian people want independence?

'At the time, the *Mariposa*'s purser laughed when I brought it up. He said Tahitians already have all the independence they need – they're like children: live for today, let tomorrow take care of itself. Why not? They've got everything: sunshine, food and housing materials growing wild and a sea full of fish. A few hours' work dancing for the tourists buys 'em beer and *pareus*. These natives never take anything seriously.

'I know that last part isn't true because I lay injured in a hospital ward filled with sick and scared Tahitians just like me and saw their families around them, crying, feeding them, caring for them, sleeping on the floor by their beds all night.'

It was probably not a good way to phrase the question. I was falling all over myself trying to neutralize the embarrassment of the striptease scenario and get a conversation going – a real one. Up to then, Pito and I had done little but joke and make small talk.

He frowned, struggling with an answer. I attributed his reticence to the language problem. Pito spoke fluent Chinese, Maohi and passable French, but his English vocabulary was then limited to what he had picked up from English-speaking tourists in his taxi. It didn't dawn on me then that he had to be careful about what he talked about and with whom.

'I'm sorry', I said. 'You probably don't even remember, it was so long ago. I heard the incident didn't amount to much anyway. The purser said there were just a few rocks thrown and then someone pulled out a ukulele and somebody else produced beer and everyone forgot their differences and had a party. It's just that the headlines in the newspaper here seemed to indicate it was more than that, but I don't speak or read French. Which reminds me, what do you think of these damned French Foreign Legionnaires all over the place, now?'

My husband chided me, saying it wasn't a good idea to criticize the French or the military, to which I retorted that it was all pretty damned serious if they were going to test atomic bombs here and maybe the Tahitians didn't even know what was going on. 'You ask him if he even knows about the bomb tests', I said. 'Maybe he'll understand you better than me. You speak a little French.'

Pito had been following this conversation intently, though the latter part was carried on sotto voce. We were all in the front seat, me in the middle, the engine was noisy and I was turned toward Galal. A knife-edged laugh from Pito made me jump, guiltily.

'It was long time now they throw rocks at Territorial Assembly. It was not post office. Pouvanaa he say we want independence and we make rich people pay taxes. 'Rich peoples, they get crazy. They come throw rocks. Break all the windows in Territorial Assembly and Pouvanaa house. They get big bulldozer to knock Territorial Assembly down if Pouvanaa not come out!'

'My God!' I said. 'That doesn't sound like Tahiti!'

'Is Tahiti!' Pito shouted.

'Who threw rocks? Tahitians?'

'I say rich peoples, I no say Tahitian peoples. *Papa'a* mans have big store, little store, plantation.'

'Did the Chinese storekeepers throw rocks too?'

'Little bit. Chinese stay out of it.'

'What happened to this Pouvanaa? Did he get away?'

'He get away that time. Another time, they come get him. Take him away to French prison. Long time he not come Tahiti.' Pito stared ahead at the road.

'Was he a Frenchman?'

'No. No *Farani* (French). Mother, he Huahine woman. Father, some kind *Papa'a* (European) sailor. Pouvanaa born Huahine. Live Huahine. Then he fight war overseas. Pouvanaa a Oopa, that him.'

'Did he die in prison?'

'He no die. I wait for him. Many Tahitian people, he wait. Pouvanaa come back. We fight for independence again. He come back little bit. He got fifteen years' exile.'

'What on earth did he do? Did he kill somebody?'

'In war, maybe. In Tahiti, no. He say, "We want independence. We want rule ourselfs." All the peoples come listen him talk on this island. *Farani* say you not talk on radio. You no go on boat to talk on other islands. They arrest him.'

We had reached the hotel. 'Pito', I begged, 'please can you come up and tell us the story about Pouvanaa a Oopa? The whole story? Maybe some day I will write about it, tell people in the outside world. We don't know anything about what the Tahitian people think and want, really. The French tourism office and Americans say, 'Oh, Tahiti is paradise. All the Tahitians have it made. They are happy as kids.

'I tell American people in my club, Friends of Tahiti, the French are going to test an atomic bomb near Tahiti, what do you think of that? And they say, "*Aita e pe'a pe'a*! [No problem]. The French know what they're doing. Don't worry. You're too serious."'

Pito's working day was long over, but he showed no sign of tiredness. Another taxi pulled alongside and he shouted something to the other driver in Tahitian. The man grinned, tossed his head in assent and sped off. 'He tell my wife I with American man and wife.' he explained. 'My wife he get mad, think I with womans.'

Our son was asleep. The only sound was the frantic scratching from geckos trapped in a box, the occasional slap of a fish jumping in the lagoon and the surf gently shushing on the distant reef. I produced a few bottles of Hinano, the local beer, and we settled into chairs on the terrace in the warm night. The moon had set, but the lagoon seemed like a dark luminous mirror, reflecting a million brilliant stars. Pito 'talked story' until the sky lightened behind Moorea and its peaks began to strike the sky like a drumbeat. There was another Tahiti behind the mai tai curtain and behind that, another and behind that, still another and another. I pulled off my glasses and rubbed my tired eyes. The *tiare Tahiti* behind my ear fell to the deck, wilted and brown, its soft gardenia fragrance already turning sharp and sour.

## 3

# POUVANAA A OOPA

Pouvanaa Tetuaapua Oopa was born to a Polynesian woman of Huahine, 10 May 1895, but his fair skin and blue eyes were a legacy of his father, a Danish sailor.

He grew up like any island boy around the turn of the century, catching land crabs, fishing, climbing coconut trees and wielding a machete to split nuts for copra. He learned to handle and navigate an outrigger canoe, which served him well in later life in escaping from *gendarmes*. His formal schooling was sketchy. He knew only one book, the Bible, but he knew it well. His aptitude for quoting the right Scripture at the right time became legendary.

When World War I broke out in Europe, the young half-caste was shipped overseas along with scores of other Island boys to fight for France. He left in 1914, a youngster who had known nothing but village life on a remote South Sea island. He came home in 1918, a war hero, uniform blooming with medals, head stuffed with progressive ideas. Other Islander soldiers, too, came home wide awake with exciting concepts they never learned in Tahiti's schools: labor unions, income taxes, the rights of all people to self-determination.

Pouvanaa was too restless now to settle for a life of fishing and hacking coconuts on remote, rural Huahine. He moved to Tahiti. He wasn't alone; hundreds of other war veterans opted to look for opportunities in the capital rather than return to their villages in the outer islands and atolls of French Oceania.

The Huahine war hero took up carpentry as a trade. Business was plentiful. Already a charismatic character, he never seemed to lack an audience for his progressive ideas. He could usually be found after work, surrounded by cronies, debating, discussing, dreaming, politicking.

The first time he was jailed for his radical speeches was in 1941. Free French leader Charles de Gaulle sent a Corsican air force colonel named Orselli to take over as governor of Tahiti. Orselli turned the economic affairs of the colony over to the French- and Chinese-controlled business community to manage without government interference. The result was a black market trade that priced everything from basics to luxuries out of sight for most Polynesians. Pouvanaa was vocal and eloquent in his criticism of the setup.

Jail only increased the war hero's popularity. As soon as he was released, he was making speeches to growing crowds of Tahitian malcontents. The next time he was locked up would have reduced a less focused man to a whimpering neurotic. In those days, a horror chamber of an insane asylum stood on Tahiti that was said to be one hundred years old. If jail wouldn't humble him, perhaps a period in this rotting institution would. Pouvanaa was declared insane and committed. When he was finally released, he was physically weakened but mentally stronger than ever. The attempt to discredit his sanity backfired. His popularity soared.

Orselli was smart enough to figure that killing Pouvanaa would make a martyr of him and set off a massive native Maohi insurrection. He had to get him away from the capital; he exiled him to Huahine and ordered him kept under guard twenty-four hours a day. The Islander slipped away easily, paddled an outrigger canoe nineteen miles to another island, boarded the interisland schooner and sailed back to Papeete. Orselli was replaced at the end of World War II. His successor left Pouvanaa alone, rightfully concluding that further harassment would only endear Pouvanaa to the new crop of returned war veterans.

Like their predecessors, most were not content to return to planting and fishing on undeveloped islands. In Europe, they'd learned, among other things, that the French government was far more democratic in France than it was in Tahiti. One of these malcontents was Pouvanaa's own son, Marcel. Wounded in action, he was the most decorated soldier in the Tahitian battalion.

Marcel and the new crop of Maohi veterans, most of whom had been seriously wounded and maimed, flocked to Pouvanaa's movement. Another brilliant half-caste, Baptiste Céran Jérusaléme, who was later to play a key role in the downfall of Pouvanaa, was among them. The dynamic pair united. Their skills complemented each other. The younger, well-educated Céran could read and interpret the ever-changing menu of French regulations that so confused the Tahitians; Pouvanaa had never become fluent in French, but he could read and write in Tahitian. Céran had strong organizational skills; Pouvanaa was an effective orator. Together, they made an impressive political machine in days when political activism was unheard of for Tahitians or half-castes.

Government jobs were plentiful for the French in their island colony after World War II. Little but menial work was available even to educated Maohi. The first major uprising occurred in 1947. Three civil service jobs became available. Ignoring applications from qualified Maohi war veterans who'd risked their lives in battle for France, the governor in Tahiti looked to metropolitan France to fill the openings.

As the steamship carrying the trio of new civil servants entered the pass through the reef into Tahiti's harbor, thousands of Tahitians, including most of the able war vets, formed a living wall on the Quai to prevent anyone from disembarking. The masterminds behind the massive demonstration were, of course, Pouvanaa and Céran.

A state of martial law was declared. Troops marched forth. Pouvanaa and six collaborators were arrested and charged with conspiracy against the security of the state. The charges could not be proven. Nevertheless, the seven men spent five months in the old Papeete City Jail, a squalid, dirty, poorly ventilated dump. They were shaky and ill when they were finally released.

Two years later, Pouvanaa had the effrontery to run for a seat in the French National Assembly. He won, 10,000 votes to 5,000, over his closest opponent. Céran organized a Polynesian political party, the Rassemblement Démocratique des Populations Tahitiennes (RDPT). The RDPT candidates won eighteen out of the twenty-five seats in the Territorial Assembly.

Now in his fifties, Pouvanaa was not only a local hero but a father-figure to the Maohi. He was referred to deferentially as *metua*. Tahitians of all ages came to him with their problems or looked to him to arbitrate disagreements. Always the master storyteller, he used every opportunity to use the parables of Jesus to guide his people in working out their difficulties.

The *metua* was reelected to the National Assembly in 1951, this time with 70 percent of the votes cast. Despite the numbers, however, the title held little power. In the National Assembly, he was in competition with all of the French metropolitan deputies for government attention to their problems. Obviously, distant Tahiti got little. As for the Territorial Assembly, it too was impotent, unable to discuss or vote on political issues.

Rumors reached Tahiti from Paris about discussions of a decolonization process of some sort in the wind for the Islands. It was more wind than decolonization, however. It started with a name change. French Oceania became French Polynesia in 1957, and something called the Government Council was created. This latest body only added to the growing maze of political divisions confronting the Islanders. The existing Territorial Assembly would elect seven ministers to the new Government Council, but there was a catch. The man who would preside as governor would be appointed by Paris. It was he who would decide what items would be on the agenda for discussion and action. If the elected ministers didn't suit him, he had the power to fire them. He took his orders from Paris, not Papeete. The Territorial Assembly was expanded from twenty-five to thirty seats and given broader economic powers, but substantive politics were taboo. If the French government decided that the elected Polynesian representatives had exceeded their powers, they could simply dissolve the Territorial Assembly.

Pouvanaa was somehow less than impressed with these highly touted first steps toward decolonization, but he decided to give the reforms a chance. Surely these changes were somehow an indication that France was readying its piece of Polynesia for a voice in its own affairs.

The RDPT won seventeen of the thirty seats in the elections for the new, expanded Territorial Assembly. Like players in a board game, the newly constituted body elected Céran president. They voted Pouvanaa and six others in as Government Council. Pouvanaa was elected vice president and minister of the interior, as high an elected post as a Polynesian could gain.

With this victory behind him, our *metua* was not one to settle down to a life of compromise to ensure himself a long career at the top. A title with intrinsic political power was the tool he'd been waiting for to improve the condition of his people, which brings our story to the stoning of the Territorial Assembly building.

French colonial rulers had reduced the concept of Maohi ancestral tribal lands to real estate that could be bought and sold. Speculation and fraudulent land deals were rampant as overseas settlers moved in. Pouvanaa passed a decree suspending further land sales while existing land deeds were examined. Acting in concert, the RDPT, with Céran at the helm, proposed an income-tax bill. Pouvanaa was at the bottom of this one, too. In Tahiti in those days, everyone, rich and poor, paid the same taxes. They were indirect and levied mostly on customs duties and imports. The new bill called for a tax on incomes over 100,000 Pacific francs a year, increasing on a graduated scale from 5 to 20 percent for incomes of 2,000,000 francs and over. The only island residents earning incomes high enough to be affected were the approximately 600 merchants, traders and planters, none of whom were Maohi.

There was little protest recorded from the Chinese sector, but the French business community declared war. They hired Rives-Henry, a Paris 'fixer', as their advisor. He arrived in April 1958 and made a speedy analysis of the situation. It was quite obvious, he pointed out. Pouvanaa and the RDPT were going to use the tax money they collected to make the colony self-sufficient. That accomplished, they would demand independence! He exhorted the French settlers to refuse to pay these 'treasonous' taxes. That was the news they had been waiting for. A protest was mounted.

Pouvanaa and his people ignored the demonstrators and went about their business until the morning of 29 April 1958 when a mob that could not be ignored gathered outside the Territorial Assembly building. They came with a bulldozer, firearms and a truckful of sticks and rocks. Leaders screamed an ultimatum: Abandon the income-tax plan or they'd raze the fragile old building and beat and stone the politicians inside to death.

Papeete's police force was predominantly Polynesian. They arrived on the scene and blocked the staircase entrance so the mob couldn't get into the building. French gendarmes stood by, awaiting orders.

The mob surged forward. The police beat them back.

Demonstrators appealed to the gendarmes. They merely wanted to discuss problems with the assemblymen inside. How could they do that if the police would not let them enter their own government building? The gendarmes ordered the police to allow mob spokesmen in.

Céran received the delegates and heard them out. Their terms were straightforward: Give up the income-tax proposal and the demonstrators would leave. Refuse and they'd bulldoze the building and stone everyone inside to death. Céran had them thrown out.

Rocks and molotov cocktails pelted the building, shattering windows. The men holed up inside doused and stamped out fires before damage was done. Suddenly, Pouvanaa appeared at an upstairs window and tried to address the angry demonstrators. Their loudspeakers drowned out his words. Frustrated, he picked up stones from the floor and hurled them back at the mob. Assemblymen now appeared at other windows and did likewise, pitching rocks back at the crowd. When they ran out of rocks, they threw ashtrays and boxes.

The bulldozer began to move toward the rickety old building. Marines intervened: stalemate. The bulldozer driver signaled to the crowd, made a U-turn and sped off to the governor's office. Demonstrators followed.

It was a new French governor and an overwhelmed one at that. He wrung his hands. He begged for twenty-four hours to study the situation. The mob agreed and took up posts outside the Territorial Assembly to make sure no one escaped. Even with the building under siege, assemblymen inside managed to smuggle a message out to their constituents.

Pouvanaa's house was attacked with a barrage of stones after sunset. Every window was smashed. In the meantime, the first wave of trucks and buses filled with Tahitians began rolling to the rescue down the crushed coral road through the palm groves. The defense force had armed themselves with whatever they could find: wooden clubs, fishing spears and hunting rifles. Their opponents had the latest in modern firearms. The two sides hovered in the shadows, waiting for dawn and the governor's decision.

Overseas, France was on the brink of civil war after the loss of the war in

Algeria. Paris had no time for silly street battles on one of their little South Sea Islands. The governor was on his own. He issued a proclamation. The populace must show respect for law and order in the name of France! He then convened the Government Council, which referred the matter back to the Territorial Assembly, asking that it postpone the new tax law. For some reason, they complied.

Céran was livid. On his own, he boycotted the Assembly meeting. The governor retaliated by changing the word 'postpone' to 'cancel', killing the income-tax bill. Pouvanaa blamed Céran's rash maneuver for the defeat, and the rift between the two was never healed.

Shortly after this stormy incident, General de Gaulle made a surprise announcement from Paris. Before the year ended, all French colonies that wanted independence would be granted independence. The stunning proclamation was posted on public buildings throughout the Islands. There were two options: vote yes and France would allow her colony to decide the form and degree of 'independence' it wanted *within* the framework of the new French commonwealth; vote no and France would cut its island colony off from any further moral or material help.

Independence within the French commonwealth was not even close to Pouvanaa's definition of independence. His response was swift. The only vote possible was no. He would have nothing less for his people than full and complete independence as it existed in the Islands before France occupied them. The amount of 'moral' and 'material' help trickling into the Islands from France since its occupation was of questionable value to the native Maohi. While foreigners profited, the heirs to the Islands were losing their lands, received only minimal education and had few job opportunities other than as servants and laborers. They were self-sufficient before the French came, they could be so again. Céran balked at such a radical step. He prophesied a black future without French economic aid. The split between the two leaders was a death blow to Tahitian political unity, from which it still has not recovered almost forty years later.

Pouvanaa must carry on without Céran. If he could reach voters in the outer Islands, he could sit down with them and explain why Paris was pushing a yes vote and the great potential he foresaw for the Islanders if they had the courage to opt for real independence by voting no.

The colony's population outside of the island of Tahiti itself had no way of knowing what was happening in the capital. The only political information to which they were privy came from shortwave radio broadcasts in French from the French government. The *metua* might well have influenced these voters had he been able to reach them – and the French evidently realized this. Pouvanaa's every move was blocked.

The territory of French Polynesia covers four million square kilometers of ocean and includes the Society Islands, Australs, Tuamotu Archipelago and the Marquesas. Pouvanaa needed a ship and three months to cover the distances. He could paddle to Moorea in an outrigger canoe to educate the people, and he did, but four million square kilometers was too big an area to cover by canoe in time for the election. By law, the French were obliged to put the government schooner at his disposal. Even this distant South Sea colony of islands was an honored part of the French democratic system, was it not? The government representatives apologized profusely when Pouvanaa presented his request. Alas! The government vessel needed a complete overhaul! Even as they spoke, it was en route to the Navy shipyard!

Determined, Pouvanaa walked the picturesque Quai. There were plenty of private ships in port. He laid his case before captains and ship owners, but they were all French or Chinese businessmen who strongly disagreed with Pouvanaa's views on taxation and his advocacy of independence. They felt no personal sense of obligation to see that the *metua* exercise his right to present his position to his constituents in time for the election.

Pouvanaa didn't give up. He could still reach his people by radio. 'But of course!' the governor agreed. 'One would think you could broadcast, but we have discovered an obsolete decree that probably should have been repealed long ago but wasn't. Terrible thing! It prohibits local politicians in the colonies from using the government radio. Only de Gaulle and metropolitan French party leaders can speak on the radio before a referendum. What can I do? My hands are tied. It is the law.'

After Pouvanaa left his office, a nervous governor relayed his anxiety to Paris about this troublesome island politician from Huahine. De Gaulle made short work of the problem. He ordered Pouvanaa and all ministers on the Government Council fired, effective immediately. It was the morning of 11 October 1958. Pouvanaa and his regime had fallen. Murderous, armed anti-income-tax agitators moved in for the kill. The horde marched through Papeete, gathering merchants as they moved toward Manuhoe. The old *metua*'s followers formed a solid human barrier around his little house. It looked like the end for Pouvanaa. Abruptly, sounds of disciplined marching feet and sharp commands came nearer and a great battalion of marines, gendarmes and police broke through the crowd. Was this rescue?

Stillness fell. But the order that shattered the quiet was not for the crowd to disperse; it was for Pouvanaa to come out. The *metua* emerged from his home without the slightest idea of what was to come. His followers parted to make a passageway. His head held high, he marched forward and faced the commander. Immediately, he was surrounded and arrested, to be taken away along with thirteen of his supporters in police vans. News bulletins were issued by the government. Pouvanaa had been arrested on suspicion of hatching a plot to burn Papeete to the ground!

Pouvanaa and his colleagues wasted away in the city jail for a full year before the trial opened 19 October 1959. It was two months after we'd sailed away on the *Mariposa* to the chuckles of the ship's purser over what 'carefree children' these Tahitians were, who had 'everything that they wanted.'

Pouvanaa appeared in court, his spirit unbroken. He denounced the frame-up and maintained his innocence. The trial was a farce. The *metua* was sentenced to fifteen years of banishment, eight of which would be in solitary confinement. In addition, he was slapped with a fine of 36,000 Pacific francs (about US$360).

Pouvanaa a Oopa was sixty-four years old when he was sentenced. With his exile, he would not be able to return home until he was seventy-nine, if he lived that long under the harsh conditions in Baumette Prison in Marseilles. A few nights after he was sentenced, the *metua* was driven to the north coast of Tahiti in a police van. A power launch was waiting to transfer the prisoner to a French ocean liner that had sailed from Papeete hours earlier. As the passengers slept, he was taken aboard and locked in a cabin.

There was no retaliation from Pouvanaa's followers. De Gaulle had recently dispatched troop reinforcements from Paris equipped with modern machine guns. An armed French navy vessel patrolled the coast.

There was more at stake to France than the inconvenience of an income tax and examination of land deals. It was evident, even to the most unsophisticated Islander, that something big, something sinister was building up, and it was. Secret arrangements were under way to prepare a military and scientific infrastructure for atomic bomb tests in French Polynesia. Pouvanaa's followers made up three-fourths of Tahiti's population. The powerful *metua* had voiced strong opposition to rumors that France would use her island colony for nuclear weapons tests. The French feared his popularity too much to kill him outright. Better to let him moulder silently in prison and die an undistinguished death from old age.

In the years between Pouvanaa's exile and my return to Tahiti in 1966, the Tahitians showed how they felt about their *metua*. His son, Marcel, was elected to his vacant seat on the French National Assembly, his daughter-in-law to his seat in the Territorial Assembly by sweeping majorities. Hopes of keeping Pouvanaa's leadership alive through his family soon flickered out, however. Marcel showed little of his father's political acuity, and it was soon apparent that he was dying of cancer. His wife had neither schooling nor political experience.

During the years that followed, Pito and hundreds of Pouvanaa's supporters met secretly and planned for the day their *metua* would come home to lead them to a sovereign future.

Outside the hotel, the sun had fully risen and another Tahiti carried on its business. Pito went home to sleep until his shift started in late afternoon. I slept fitfully for a few hours until the morning warmth changed to the sticky heat of afternoon. I woke up crying for an old man I'd never met and in shame over the savagery of my own white race, which seems to invest itself with godlike powers over everything it touches. I stood under the shower, hot tears mingling with the cool water. Finally, gathering all my forces of denial around me, I put on an island-print sundress and tucked a *frangipani* behind my left ear. Outside, the colors that had drenched Paul Gauguin's palette saturated the senses with strokes of red, purple, yellow, brown, blue and green in shades not yet named. Brilliant whites intensified the joyous fragrant tropic extravaganza.

I sought out Susy No Pants in Quinn's. I needed laughter and jokes while I tried to figure out what to do with the pain of this new side of Tahitian reality.

# 4

## SUSY NO PANTS

Susy No Pants was not a whore. Being a whore requires a certain amount of business acumen or, at least, a pimp who takes care of his girls. Susy had no business sense, no pimp and no pants. If you asked her where she got her name, she'd flip up her skirt and show you with a whoop.

Susy No Pants was the most famous of the 'Quinn's Girls' of the 1960s, and Quinn's Tahitian Hut was probably the raunchiest, most notorious bar/dance hall in the South Pacific. It clung to this distinction until 1974, when it was torn down by the French as part of an urban renewal to 'beautify' Papeete's water-front. With it died the most venerable sorority in the South Seas.

It's easier to say what a Quinn's Girl was not than what she was. They weren't dance hall hostesses because they danced with whomever they pleased, whenever they pleased. They frequently went home with customers, but it was their choice. If they were paid, it was usually a new dress, shoes or some knick-knack. Susy's loves included beachcombers and businessmen, sea captains, travel writers and at least one American politician. She followed her heart and the gods of uproarious good times.

I first met Susy in 1965. I'd returned without my family after a seven-year absence. I shared a room with a young woman, out for a last fling before her wedding. Reckless with our unaccustomed freedom, we took on Quinn's.

The place was filthy, noisy, crowded and, for some reason, funny. Fights were funny, dancing was funny, drunks falling on your table were funny, step-ping on live cigarette butts with your bare feet was funny. We found a vacant table next to the dance floor. It soon became apparent why such a fine table was available on a Saturday night. It was blocking a traditional drunk crossing. Soon there was beer in my shoes, beer on my dress, beer in my purse. Whenever we got wrung out and refilled our glasses, another drunk would stumble into our table or sprawl across it.

Quinn's Girls lined the bar, shouting, laughing, occasionally lurching onto the floor with a partner. As the beer flowed and the evening advanced, some became wild women, others retreated into almost catatonic states, slow-dancing robotically.

Two stood out from the rest, unquestionably the queens of the outrageous. Charmaine, a tall, thin French-Tahitian, affected bawdy sophistication. She wore tight pants and a high-crowned island hat almost buried under wreaths of shells, ferns and flowers. She wore the narrow brim cocked so low, only one eye was visible, but that one eye missed nothing.

The other was Susy No Pants, a big-framed Marquesan from the island of Uapou, a country girl almost six feet tall. She was not pretty in the European sense. Her beauty was larger, more generous, more powerful than that. She was all Polynesian woman, no holds barred. Her thick black hair hung midway down her back, starred with a *tiare Tahiti* behind her left ear and a circlet of them on her head. Her eyes were black and opaque, heavy lidded, either dancing with reflected lights when she laughed, which she did frequently, or dark two-way mirrors which gave back nothing but the viewer's reflection. She could not have been unaware of her striking appearance but its effect on her was not conceit but hilarity.

Susy and Charmaine were masters of the 'Tahitian handshake', that notso-secret handshake of Quinn's 'sorority sisters.' It was a very low handshake. Strangers as well as friends were the target. The element of surprise was essential. The girl would rush forward, all Tahitian smiles and sweet-smelling flowers, the man, seated or standing, would spread his arms wide to receive the customary hug and two-cheek kiss. This left him wide open for a hard grab between the legs and the triumphant scream: "allo, you sonofabitch, goddammit. Whassa mattah you?' If he could still walk, he'd usually be dragged immediately out onto the dance floor amidst hoots of laughter.

There was even a little song Quinn's Girls sang:

> 'Allo, capitaine, 'ow are you?
> 'Allo, capitaine, 'ow are you?
> I love you, yes I doooo,
> Goddamsonofabitch, whassa mattah you?

Quinn's Girl–English was acquired, for the most part, from sailors and beachcombers. It was rich in phonetic obscenities for which there was no equivalent in the Maohi language. Susy and her sisters loved these combinations of sounds. They were great 'ice-breakers'.

That first night in Quinn's, Charmaine decided she wanted to dance with a man sitting at a table behind ours. Tables, chairs and people were packed solid. *Aita e pe'a pe'a!* (What the hell!) She reached across us, toppling bottles and glasses, seized the fellow, dragged him across our table and stood him up on the dance floor. Either the man couldn't dance or said something Charmaine didn't like. 'You no goddamn good!' she shrieked. With a rowdy laugh, she shoved him back in the direction of our table, where he sprawled between us in a puddle of beer.

A Quinn's bouncer pushed through the dancing crowd and bawled her out in French. She scooped up a beer bottle and brandished it, screaming back. He shouted something over the din, she changed her mind abruptly, put the bottle on our table, said '*Bonsoir*' politely and strolled back to the bar, hips revolving fluidly with the beat.

The cavernous, smoke-filled room was jammed with French Foreign Legionnaires, civilians, yachties and Tahitians. Men outnumbered women almost two to one with the population explosion of military personnel sent to French Polynesia to prepare the infrastructure for French atomic bomb tests. The scattering of Tahitians diffused the grim intensity of a military bent on loosening up.

The band played rolicking two-steps, waltz tempos, tangos and, periodically, the *upaupa*, a fast, wicked, hip-swinging Tahitian dance in which I was gaining some skill. As young, unattached women, we were almost mobbed. I growlingly rebuffed the Legionnaires and danced only with the sweet-smelling, laughing Tahitian men. Alice, impressed with my outraged lectures on the evils of nuclear bomb testing and the French occupation of Polynesia, went along with my boycott for awhile. She finally succumbed, first to one insistent Legionnaire, then another. Catching her eye, I signaled I was leaving. That brought her back in a hurry. 'Would you abandon me here in Quinn's?' she asked, blue eyes wide, speech slurred.

'You bet', I said. 'I don't like your friends.'

'Then let's go to Zizou's. I hear it's better than this filthy dump.'

'Okay, but first, I want to go to the ladies'. There must be one here.' We started to circumnavigate the room, laughing off dance and other invitations. The Goddess Susy was suddenly before us, blocking our path.

'*E*, you want *fare iti*?' I looked back blankly.

'What's she want?' Alice asked nervously. 'Are we doing something wrong?'

'*Fare iti*?' I repeated. Susy laughed boisterously.

'*Fare iti, fare iti*', she said, pushing us firmly toward a back corner of the room where a *pareu*-print curtain concealed a doorway. In front of it, two French sailors surveyed the dance scene, absently buttoning their pants.

'Oh wait, *fare iti* means little house. Yes, outhouse, that must be it, but this is the men's *fare iti*. *Aita fare iti tane'*, I said, stretching my tiny Tahitian vocabulary almost to its limit. *'Fare iti vahine?'*

'What'd you say, what'd you say?' Alice asked, now even more worried.

'I think I said, "No men's outhouse! Women's outhouse", but maybe not. She's laughing her head off again.'

Susy, one hand on each of our backs, propelled us forcibly through the curtain. *'Fare iti!'*

'Oh God, we're in the men's room', Alice gasped. 'Wait. There are women in here too! Oh my God, my mother would die!'

We were in a long room with a grate running down the center of the cement floor. On one side were two stalls, but men and women urinated together unconcernedly, the men standing over the grate, the women squatting. The stench was suffocating.

Susy hiked up her skirt and squatted, calling out greetings to friends. We backed out so fast we nearly knocked an old man over as he pushed through the curtain.

We found Zizou's and decided to investigate the sanitary facilities first before ordering more beer. This waterfront dive was less crowded, with no raucous Quinn's Girls to add to the evening's danger and hilarity. The sound of Papeete's power plant nearby drowned out the music.

The *fare iti* had a real door. This was promising. We pushed it open and a man immediately followed us in. Alice took him by the collar, turned him around firmly and shoved him out. We had captured the loo.

This one had several stalls with doors. There was still a grate down the middle and that pervasive smell. The U-joint was missing from under the sink. We turned on the faucet and a torrent of water cascaded over our feet and down the floor drain. Alice leaped back with a squeal to protect her shoes. My feet were unspeakably filthy and wounded from my barefoot dancing, so I kicked off my sandals and plunged in.

'Now I know how they train for the firewalk. They send you to Quinn's to dance barefoot on live cigarette butts. After a few hours, you don't even feel the pain anymore.' I flaunted my blisters proudly. Alice was no longer having any fun. The beer, the stench and now my dirty blistered feet. She was vomiting. Such was the lot of the fastidious pub crawler on Tahiti.

Before we left the island, we returned for one more dose of Quinn's, now as veterans. We found a table near a fast escape route to the street, should fights break out. 'Look at that!' I nudged Alice. 'Susy waved at us!' Pleased, we waved back.

As the senior member of our team, I laid down the law: 'No dancing with anybody but Tahitians and just one beer each so we don't have to rush off to

Zizou's to go to the loo. Okay?' Alice nodded meekly.

The crowd was sparse. The music seemed almost sedate. A few Quinn's Girls dozed at the bar or chattered quietly. Susy wandered over to join friends at a table across the dance floor. The American cruise ship *Monterey* was in port, disgorging a scattering of blue-haired men and women in polyester to sample Papeete's wicked nightlife.

The band revived, ukuleles started pounding out 'Tamure, Tamure', and immediately a Tahitian I'd danced with on my last visit pulled me to my feet and away we went. Alice jumped up, wiggling her hips to the beat, and a handsome Tahitian, *frangipani* behind one ear, whooped and joined her. I gave Alice a thumbsup sign of approval. She still insisted on wearing shoes, but I felt she was showing enormous progress.

The music stopped and the band took a break. A pair of portly cruise ship matrons rose and moved hesitantly around the room. 'Looking for the ladies' room, I'll bet', I told Alice. 'Watch and see if Susy's going to initiate them.'

Spying us, however, the Americans headed straight for our table. 'Do you speak English?' one asked.

Hardly able to contain my glee, I replied, 'A little.'

'Thank goodness', she sighed. 'Could you please tell me where the ladies' room is? The WC. The toilet.' She turned to her companion. 'Is there any other word for toilet? I'm not sure she understands.'

'Toylet', repeated Alice slowly.

'The ladies' toilet', the woman repeated, raising her voice.

'Ah, laydee toylet', I said as though a light had dawned. I rose smiling, beckoned and proceeded to lead my two tourists toward that curtain from hell, hips swaying to the music in my slinky new Tahitian dress.

'She knows where it is. Come on', called one of the women to a third, across the room, who joined us cooing, 'How nice. You speak English, do you, dear?'

Pausing at the curtain, I stepped aside and bowed. The women strode confidently through. There was no one else inside. Nuts, I said to myself. That's no fun. But it was, because immediately, a sailor shoved past followed by a couple of burly Tahitian dock workers. The screams rang out behind me as I walked slowly with dignity back to the table. Alice was laughing so hard, tears were streaming down her face. 'Wait', I begged, trying to keep my face straight. 'Ten, nine, eight, seven ...' The women raced through the room and out the door in a flying wedge.

It grew late and more cruise ship passengers strayed in. We repeated our performance. Then Alice, smitten with her new Tahitian friend, decided to go off with him to Lafayette's, an after-hours place outside of town. As the couple left on his Vespa, Susy appeared at my side. 'You come', she said.

Puzzled, I followed her across the room. Grabbing a chair vacated by some-one on the dance floor, she motioned me to sit and join her party.

'Susy No Pants', she said, pointing to herself. 'You gonna ask why?'

I shook my head. 'I *know* why.'

She guffawed. 'These my friends. What you drink?'

'Hinano', I said. She insisted on paying for it.

We made stilted small talk until a thickset sandy-haired man strode up. He tossed his head, indicating Susy should follow him. Instead, she laughed and patted an empty chair. Again he made an insistent motion, this time pulling on her arm. Snatching her arm away, she yelled at him in Tahitian, French and English. Two of the other women joined in. The man backed off, stopped by the bar and glared at her.

'That one no good. No good', Susy said emphatically.

'What was he, German?'

'No. Russian sailor. No good! Always want to fuck in ass. That hurt!' She sprang to her feet, revolved her hips in a fast *ami*, rubbed her behind and hooted with laughter. An older, heavier mama joined in, trying to outdo Susy with graphic Tahitian dance movements. Behind the bar, the band took up the beat. Soon the whole room was rocking and dancing again. The Russian slunk out.

Susy was quite an education.

Now, I was back with my husband and eleven-year-old son. A year had passed. As I headed for the market to buy new *pareus*, my men stayed behind, indolently lingering over breakfast in the Hotel Tahiti. 'I'll meet you at Quinn's at noon', I called over my shoulder. 'You can't miss it. It's right downtown on the Quai.' I picked Quinn's because it was easy to find. I didn't expect them to go inside.

Noon came and I scanned the sidewalk in front of the old landmark. There was no sign of my family. I waited around for a few minutes, then ambled in to get a Coke. There they were, lined up at the bar drinking orange sodas and having an evidently hilarious conversation with none other than Susy No Pants. My mouth gaped.

'Dis one you wife?' Susy cried, sweeping me into the group with one muscular brown arm. 'dis one? I never know dat! Dis one my *sister*!' Engulfing me in a great Marquesan hug, she kissed me on both cheeks, as enthusiastic as if I really were her long-lost sister. Paralyzed, I stared at my husband over Susy's shoulder. Later, he asked sweetly, 'When are you *really* going to tell me what you did at Quinn's last year?'

Susy No Pants seemed completely dazzled by my husband. Here was a man with a book and a little boy, drinking soda pop in Quinn's. Now on rare occasions in Quinn's you might run into a man who didn't drink, but never one with a little boy and a book. He was equally dazzled by Susy. He'd never met anyone like her. I had to explain to him later that she was making passes at him: book, child, orange soda and all. 'No', he said. 'She was just being friendly.'

'He's a good man', Susy No Pants told me later. 'Good man, like priest. How you get that little boy, eh?' Had she given up on him so quickly or did she have something else in mind?

Late that evening, as we strolled along the waterfront, we met Susy No Pants with a date, a giant of a Norwegian sailor from a boat anchored out in the harbor. He must have stood at least six and a half feet tall and was as fair as she was dark. Lurching and weaving, he had his arm around her, head bent as he whispered in her ear. They'd obviously had several beers.

Disentangling herself, she rushed over and greeted each of us with hugs and kisses. 'These my friends', she said by way of introduction. 'This one my sister! They come home with us. Eat some food.'

We protested, but it did no good. Tipsy, the sailor glared at us. He neither spoke nor understood English, but he understood that he no longer had Susy to himself. When Susy No Pants made a decision, there was no appeal. She herded us all, two men, a boy and a woman, upstairs to her cubicle of a room in an old house near the waterfront. The only furniture consisted of a double bed and a wooden ladder-back chair. The bed was covered with a magnificent red and white Tahitian *tifaifai* (appliquéd coverlet) heaped with heavily embroidered pillows glowing with every known color.

Galal sat on the high, soft bed, pulling Kent up beside him. He beckoned to the sailor, but the man withdrew to stand sulkily against one wall. I took the chair.

Susy prattled on and on, every inch the proud hostess. A *pareu*-print curtain hid a wardrobe from which she pulled dress after dress to show me, insisting on giving me two. Mute and furious, the sailor sat rigidly on the edge of the bed next to Galal, who looked at him compassionately.

'It's getting late, Susy, we must go. Kent's falling asleep', he said tactfully.

'I'm not tired', our son said, missing the whole point, and slid off the bed. 'There's a gecko!' he said. 'A big one. Have you got a jar?'

Susy laughed and said, 'Mo'o. Him, *mo'o*.'

'What's that mean, mom?'

'She's telling you the word for lizard.'

'It's not a lizard, it's a gecko', said our precise son. 'What's the word for jar?'

'Honey, I don't know. We have geckos in our room. Don't go off on one of your hunts now. Be polite.'

'You want cold *taro* in coconut cream? I got some. You like?'

'Oh yes, we love it, but it's too late now. Maybe tomorrow. We must go.'

'No. You stay. Eat. I get *taro*. She ran downstairs and outside and disappeared. The silence in the tiny room was intense. Galal tried to make small talk with the sailor, who kept shaking his head and saying something dark in Norwegian, over and over. He stretched out on the bed, finally, lying on his side, glowering.

Susy returned with a bowl of sliced bluish gray *taro* mottled with congealed coconut cream. She passed it around proudly like a plate of cookies at a tea party, urging everyone to eat. 'Is good for you.'

As we snacked, Susy began pulling out still more objects to show us, including two blankets she had won on Bastille Day. 'What are you going to do with blankets on Tahiti, Susy?' I asked in amazement.

'Maybe I send to Uapou', she said. The sailor now reached boiling point. Furious, he struggled out of the cloying soft embrace of the bed and lurched out.

'He come back pretty soon', Susy shrugged nonchalantly and carried on with her show and tell. He did, but the romance seemed to be wearing thin. The next morning, Susy hailed us as we passed her rooming house. The Quinn's Girl glamor was gone. Her hair was in a single side braid, her full lips devoid of lipstick. She wore a faded *pareu* tucked about her solid frame. Her broad feet were bare. She looked older and rather matronly in the morning light, a palm leaf midrib broom in her hands like any respectable island mama.

'*E*, Papa', she said. 'Where you been? I wait long time. I wash clothes now. You walk my fren, okay?'

Barely able to stifle his laughter, he said: 'Walk your friend? You mean take your friend out for a walk?'

'*E*. You walk him. Now I get my work done.'

She meant exactly what she said. Her obviously lovestruck Norwegian sailor wouldn't leave her alone and she had chores to do. 'Does he need a leash?' I muttered snidely.

Ignoring me, Galal gave Susy a slight gallant bow and told her he'd be honored to walk her friend for her. Turning, Susy called out sharply and the giant blonde sailor emerged, blinking in the brilliant tropical sunlight, hawked and spit in the crotons, trotted meekly over to the older man and the pair set out.

'Good man, you husban'', Susy said approvingly. 'He like priest. I like him stay with me, walk my friends.' She went inside, brought out a bundle of dirty clothes tied in a *pareu*, squatted on the grass, turned on a hose and proceeded to do her washing in a small bucket, oblivious to the traffic roaring by on the road a few feet away. She withdrew behind her black eyes, as placid as if the hose were a mountain stream, the battered frame building behind her, the towering

spires of lonely Uapou, and the street noises of Papeete, the murmur of her
village almost 800 miles away across the ocean to the northeast.

Susy No Pants was not a whore. She was a Quinn's Girl. She was my sister.

# 5

# FRENCH FOREIGN LEGION IN EDEN

Like Tahiti, the French Foreign Legion has been highly romanticized. The very name conjures up gentlemen with a secret, condemned to wander the face of the earth to forget, exiles with assumed identities joining forces in the world's hellholes to fight battles too dangerous to risk the lives of the Establishment, adventurers whose deeds would later be dramatized by the likes of Errol Flynn and Richard Burton.

The Legion itself perpetuated the myth with such books as *The Bugle Sounds* by Major Zinovi Peckhoff, who describes his organization as '... a refuge for men of any nationality who cannot adapt to conditions in their own countries or who simply must get away for reasons of conscience ... mistakes they have committed, griefs they can't bear ... a refuge for all those whom Dostoevski calls "The insulted and injured".' Euphemisms aside, the Legion, for many, was an alternative to prison. Adventurers and jilted lovers undoubtedly joined forces with this polyglot of mercenaries, but mostly their ranks bulged with thieves, rapists, murderers and other deviants.

Therefore, their sudden appearance in Papeete, Tahiti shocked me. I first noticed them in 1965. Stinking and sullen, they were anachronisms in this naive, dizzy little South Seas town sweet with laughter and the fragrances of vanilla and flowers. They lurked on street corners, in sidewalk cafés, bars and, of course, Quinn's, leering at the *Tahitiennes*.

You could find them in the hot tropic night by their body odor. Accustomed to hard duty in Algeria where, apparently, water is too precious to waste on bathing, this lot scorned the considerate Polynesian custom of frequent daily showers or dips in the lagoon followed by rubdowns with *tiare Tahiti*–scented coconut oil.

Why were they in Tahiti in the first place? It didn't take a wizard to figure that out. The ill winds from the Sahara had dropped them like weed seeds with the 'secret' atom bomb test conglomerate. They were sinister, even in their short tropic pants. Dance-hall fights now seemed the rule rather than the exception. Tahitian women, unaccountably, were pairing up with these newcomers, even marrying them. Frustrated, their men retaliated, raping French women and occasionally a tourist on islands where rape was unknown.

To a writer, there was a wealth of stories here. Unfortunately, hopes of marketing them in the US were dim. Only a handful of underground newspapers would print negative pieces about nuclear weapons testing, especially if they'd harm the burgeoning Pacific tourism industry. One publishable angle occurred to me: an 'innocent' interview giving insight into the paradox of the French Foreign Legion in 'paradise', told through the story of one typical man and his island sweetheart.

I could have found an interpreter with Pito's help, cornered Legionnaires in Quinn's or at sidewalk cafés and simply started interviewing until I found the perfect subject or gathered enough information to form a composite. Instead, during a temporary lapse from sanity, I went through 'channels'. Letter to Gerard Gilloteaux, Bureau of Tourism, Papeete, early 1966: 'I am greatly interested in writing a magazine article based on a day (and perhaps an evening) in the life of a member of the French Foreign Legion stationed in Papeete. ...'

Gilloteaux replied some months later: 'I have transmitted your request to the competent military authorities. I shall not fail to communicate the answer of these authorities.'

'Oh God!' I said.

Two months later, I heard from Louis Vorms, Deputy Consul General of France in Los Angeles: 'Some weeks ago you sent to the governor of French Polynesia a request to visit the Foreign Legion. I would like very much to discuss this project with you. We could meet at this office, where you can call me ... after 28 July in order to make an appointment.'

I was leaving for Tahiti on 6 August. I could have eluded the great French Public Relations Steamroller I could see looming to flatten any creative story angles I might develop. I could ignore the summons, fly off to Papeete and do random interviews on the Quai. If challenged by authorities, I could say innocently, 'What letter? I didn't get it. Perhaps it arrived after my departure.' Not me. Instead, I set up the appointment, donned my only suit and drove to the French consulate in Los Angeles days before my flight to Papeete.

I announced myself to the receptionist and sat down uneasily, facing a huge portrait of Gen. Charles de Gaulle in full military regalia. The afternoon dragged on. A group of chattering French tourists burst into the lobby, hung with cameras. A woman with her elderly mother peeked in, Americans getting visas. Finally, my name was called. Any hope of a dignified first impression vanished. My foot was asleep. I limped in like I'd been shot. I tried to joke about it; Vorms was not amused. A tall, slender, imposing bureaucrat, he questioned me with unnatural attentiveness, searching my face for signs of insurrection.

I explained what I had in mind, all very simple, very innocent: an interview with a typical Legionnaire in Eden who'd fallen in love and was living with a Tahitian girl – just human interest stuff, nothing political.

What had I published recently? I handed him a copy of an article on Tahiti in a leading American magazine. Impassively, he scanned it. 'But this is not your name!' he cried. I explained that sometimes I use a pen name. 'Oh, but I will need some proof that the author of this article is yourself!' His tone was triumphant.

'But I leave in three days!'

He shrugged, 'I must have proof, madame.'

I drove home, wired my agent asking her to verify my pen name, packed and left for the airport.

In just a year, the change in the slightly naughty, sleepy little port was disturbing. Thirty thousand French servicemen including Legionnaires in a country of eighty-five thousand are bound to have a negative impact. The majority were on Tahiti, which had a population of only forty-five thousand, mostly Polynesians. Traffic that had simply been erratic the year before was now demonic. There was nowhere you could go to escape the military presence.

I fled to Moorea, across the 'Sea of the Moon' on the inter-island boat. Young servicemen jammed every deck. An aircraft carrier squatted in Pao Pao Bay, framed by leaning palms and serrated mountain peaks. On the dusty coral road between the Bali Hai Hotel and Pao Pao Bay, where once chickens pecked and Tahitians ambled and gossiped, now sweaty servicemen jogged and snorted like boxers in training.

'It isn't happening', I said, put on bikini, mask and snorkel and fell face down into the lagoon in front of the hotel. As I drifted in the turquoise waters, I became aware first of a strange vibration, then an audible growl, which built to a roar. Tidal wave? Frightened, I groped for a foothold on the coral heads below and stood up, shoving my mask back. A massive military helicopter hovered low overhead.

'Bastards!' I returned to Papeete raging. Slitty-eyed, voice dripping with poisoned treacle, I called Gilloteaux in the tourism office. Of course he remembered me, he enthused in English better than mine. Yes, he had not only received identification from my agent via the consulate in Los Angeles but copies of my last article. He was so enthusiastic about my project! Yes, he understood perfectly that all I wanted was a warm, human story, an adventurous French Foreign Legionnaire, heart captured by Tahiti and a beautiful *vahine*. These were very sensitive times in French Polynesia, but of course, madame was not interested in political affairs.

How very perceptive he was, I cooed. The only affairs I was interested in writing about were affairs of the heart. (Like hell! I said to myself.)

'Madame is *so* sensible! I am pleased to report good news. It just so happens that I know a Legionnaire personally. The naughty boy is living with a *Tahitienne*. He sleeps in a *fare*, a humble little grass shack, at night instead of on the base. There is only one tiny thing you must attend to first and that, madame, is military clearance, even though your request is so innocent.'

A drizzling rain was falling the next day as I darted from the market to rue du General de Gaulle for my appointment with Commandant L'Ancien, propelled like a ball in the pinball machine of military bureaucracy. Late, I rushed past Pomare's Palace. Something on the periphery of my vision made me stop as abruptly as if a hand had closed on my shoulder. What was wrong? I took a second look at the palace. It looked broken. The red-roofed tower, once so cocksure and proud, now tilted at a 45 degree angle, where it hung foolishly, guyed by ropes. This historic building, relic of the last queen of Tahiti, was being demolished. By nightfall it would be rubble. New government buildings would someday rise where it had stood.

Tears streaming, I watched the tower come down. Depressed as well as angry, I reported for my interview. I described my mission tersely. It didn't even sound credible to me anymore. Finally, I was instructed to report to the Legion Outpost to make an appointment. I was warned that I could not speak to any Legionnaire, even a personal friend of Monsieur Gilloteaux's, without an official appointment.

'Impossible!' I said testily. 'I leave for Bora Bora and Ra'iatea in the morning. I won't be back for ten days.'

It was still raining as I left with vague assurances that if an appointment could be made on my behalf, word would be left at my local address, Hotel Tahiti.

I needed cheering up. I headed for Vaima on the waterfront and there, like a gift, was a table with four chairs and three totally disreputable looking Legionnaires. The hell with protocol, I said to myself, strode over, smiled and they rose in unison, offering the empty chair. Two spoke no English. The third, a German, spoke enough to be understood. We exchanged names, small talk and many smiles. I mentioned L'Ancien and my difficulties in setting up interviews. Could we talk for awhile?

'They think I'm a spy', confided the German, gesturing toward his friends.

The non sequitur caught me off balance and left me momentarily speechless. 'Okay, I'll bite', I said. 'Why do they think you're a spy?'

'Because I speak English.'

'I don't understand.'

He tried to explain, but his vocabulary wasn't up to the task. Finally, he shrugged at the hopelessness of it all, leaned toward me and whispered: 'They are watching us.'

I couldn't talk to the military and I couldn't escape it, even by fleeing to the Isles sous le Vent.

From high atop a ridge dividing Bora Bora, I watched with my husband and son while a hulking white computer ship that would monitor the nuclear tests in the Tuamotus glided over the sunset-stilled lagoon. Gunboats nestled in the bays of sparsely populated Tahaa and Ra'iatea.

In Uturoa, Ra'iatea's women spoke contemptuously of the French military 'invasion' but few could resist the novelty of a French boyfriend. 'With a Tahitian man', one confided, 'you get a beating on Saturday night. With a Frenchman, you don't even have to do the housework.'

Polynesian men were angry and humiliated. Sex had always been a relatively uncomplicated game. If one girl said no one night, maybe she'd say yes the next, or someone else would be in the mood. Now, frustrated Maohi men prowled the coconut groves along the road, even in remote Uturoa, looking for girls. Where once anyone could walk alone at night, now one ran fast and carried an empty beer bottle as a weapon. French-looking women especially were the target. Stories of vicious gang rapes were reported in the press.

We returned to Papeete, troubled by the ominous changes. In keeping with the new, sinister French Polynesia, I'd managed to complicate septic mosquito bites with coral poisoning. My hugely swollen legs looked so gruesome, the flight attendant tried to argue me into accepting a stretcher from plane to taxi to clinic. I made it upright, stubbornly stumping along on treetrunk appendages that seemed directly connected with my fattened toes without benefit of ankles. I managed forward motion with a sort of hip-and-thigh roll. 'It's elephantiasis, isn't it?' I asked miserably, as the doctor examined me. Fresh from Paris, he spoke no English. Someone in the clinic was found who did, after a fashion, and the phrase 'yellow coral' came up. Had I been swimming around any on Ra'iatea with open wounds? Well, yes, there was yellow coral, but I didn't have any open wounds, unless you count infected mosquito bites. 'Ah, madame, that is open wounds!'

'Oh.'

They assured me I did not have the dread elephantiasis, gave me a shot and told me to come back for a second one the next day. I retreated to Hotel Tahiti and there, awaiting me, was a note from Commandant L'Ancien: 'Tomorrow morning at 8:30 a.m. there will be two Legionnaires who come to the hotel for interview.' The effect was magical. The impossible had happened.

I reported to the clinic early the next morning for my second shot and ampules for the trip home. Several women were ahead of me, waiting on the wooden bench or squatting on the cement with small children. I'd almost given up hope that I'd be called in time, but then I was, the shot was administered, a taxi called and I was back at the hotel, stumping through the lobby.

'Have the Legionnaires arrived yet?' I asked the desk clerk, scanning the handful of people in the area. He gestured with his chin. Simultaneously, two immaculate gentlemen in crisp uniforms rose smartly.

'*Oui, madame*', he gestured in their direction.

'Oh, my God', I said, sagging against the counter as they approached. There was no relationship between this elegant pair and the Legionnaires on the streets. They greeted me in French. Evidently, the older, more distinguished of the two was the adjutant himself. He wore sunglasses and a neat little moustache, was graying exquisitely and exuded charm from every pore. His youthful companion was clean-cut with short-cropped blond hair and an Open Boyish Grin. He looked like a candidate for Boy Scout of the Year.

Instead of refusing my request, I had been provided with professional spokesmen and no interpreter, just in case I got around the first obstacle. It was a public relations way of saying, yes, you cannot write a story on the French Foreign Legion in French Polynesia. I had two options. I could send them away, which would verify any suspicions they had about my real motive, or I could go through the motions of an interview with as much grace as possible, pretending I was talking to exactly the sort of Legionnaires one saw hundreds of all over Tahiti. The first option was unthinkable in a foreign country to which I wanted to return.

'I will try to find an interpreter', I said slowly, raising an index finger in what I hoped was a 'wait a minute' gesture. I turned to the desk clerk who was also the manager. Could he interpret for me? Perhaps later, if I could find no one else.

We found a table in the dining room and sat down. We smiled. We looked serious. We stared into space. Around us, people buzzed contentedly in several languages, eating breakfast. Waitresses rippled by, Tahitian hips swaying. Suddenly, the adjutant stood up. He said something I thought was related to getting an interpreter. Instead, he got us a larger table.

I ordered coffee. They looked amazed and ordered beer. We stared some more. Inspiration struck. I went to the phone and called Gilloteaux. He wasn't in yet. No, his secretary could not suggest an interpreter. Mr G. would call me when he got in. Grimly, I returned to the table. 'No interpreter yet?' the manager asked as he passed.

'None!' I sighed. 'Can you spare a waitress?'

'Perhaps, for thirty minutes. Would that help, madame?'

'Anything would help', I replied.

A slim *Tahitienne* named Colette joined us. She gave the men a dazzling smile. To me, she said: 'Please to speak slow. I do not speak much English.'

Slowly, carefully I phrased and rephrased a question. No luck. She didn't understand. I tried another. She didn't get it. In twenty minutes, the only useful information I learned was that the younger man was named Berselli.

Then, my husband, also a writer, strolled over, fresh, rested and breakfasted. 'You're interviewing!' he said. 'I'll see you later. I don't want to interrupt.'

'Stay', I said desperately. Introductions were made. Somehow, it came out that the adjutant spoke Spanish. Spanish is Galal's second language. Elated, I thanked Colette warmly and she kissed us each goodbye politely first on one cheek, then the other.

Shoulder to shoulder, my husband and I faced down the French Foreign Legion and conducted an interview guaranteed to fire the imaginations of readers everywhere – the story of a boy who joined the French Foreign Legion to escape some dark secret past, a *Tahitienne* who outshines Rarahu, the bride of Pierre Loti. A magical meeting of two people from different worlds, she rushes to his arms offering love, he rushes to hers, they consummate their passion, then he irradiates her island, her seas and her food supply with poisonous nuclear fallout.

I ask a question in English. My husband translates it into Spanish for the adjutant. He, in turn, translates the Spanish to French for the young officer, who replies in French which is then translated into Spanish, then into English.

Q. 'Where were you stationed before Tahiti?'

A. 'Algeria.'

Q. 'How long?'

A. 'Six years.'

Q. 'How do you like Tahiti?'

A. 'Very much.' Then, after some thought, he volunteers: 'I hope to live here.'

Q. 'Why did you join the French Foreign Legion?' (A loaded forbidden question.)

A. (Glances nervously at adjutant. Adjutant nods. Go ahead. Confess. We can trust this woman with the answer.) 'Because – It is the Finest Branch of Service in the world!' (Shoulders a bit straighter, firm chin a tad higher, eyes ablaze with pride. Adjutant flicks the tiniest of smiles.)

Q. 'Shit! No, don't translate that. Try this: Are you married to a Tahitian girl?'

A. 'Yes.'

Q. 'How long?'

A. 'Two months. We have one boy, two years old and one seven months old.' (We four join in a chuckle.)

Q. 'What is your assignment in the Legion?'

A. 'I drive a gravel truck.'

I glare at my husband. 'A gravel truck? Are you sure you translated that right? A goddam gravel truck?'

'A gravel truck', he repeats, mouth working, tears of suppressed laughter almost spilling. Obviously, he's on the verge of falling off his chair and rolling around on the ground howling. Peevishly, I snap: 'Try this:

Q. 'How did you meet your wife?'

A. 'I waved at her.'

'And she just waved back? That's it? See if you can get some details here. Ask him where? Was she washing clothes in a stream? Dancing in Quinn's? Paddling a canoe on the lagoon? Getting shellfish in the shallows?'

The minutes tick by as the three men explore this puzzling nuance in French and Spanish. Finally, the committee agrees on an answer:

A. 'I work from 6 a.m. to 11:30 a.m. and again from 1 p.m. to 4:30 p.m., so I used to drive past her house four times a day and I waved each time.'

I end the interview with effusive thanks, point to my ghoulishly swollen legs and say I must take my medicine and lie down. I am too ill to continue, alas.

We all kiss cheeks and say adieu.

# 6

# ERENA

Erena was an atoll woman, daughter and granddaughter of atoll women who in turn were children of atoll people. Her first light was sunlight flickering through the crevices in walls made from pandanus leaves, woven by her mother and aunties. Her first bed was a mat woven from the same materials, which she shared with family members. When awake, she was carried and petted until she could walk on her own.

Her first foods besides mother's milk were the jellylike meat of the green coconut and fish from the sea. She never tasted cow's milk. At her mother's side, she learned to find edible shellfish and seaweed in the lagoon shallows as soon as she could toddle. Her wide feet grew tough, flexible and utilitarian so she could move about easily on the sharp coral boulders of the reef where food grew in abundance.

One by one, she mastered basic atoll survival skills. She learned to use a machete, climb trees, open coconuts, catch fish, raise food crops, make fire without matches, cook in a pit oven, weave mats for a floor or a house wall, plait a watertight roof from pandanus leaves or the great fronds of the coconut palm, sew, and deliver and raise babies. She was well versed, too, in fending off monotony. She sang, played the guitar and, by the age of puberty, excelled in the arts of gossip and lovemaking.

Erena received the average formal education most atoll kids of the 1940s got. She knew the names and significance to the food chain of every daily phase of the moon in her rich language. She read weather signs and practiced medical arts with herbs and massage. She could probably recite her genealogy back to ancestors who navigated by the stars and ocean currents and who colonized the islands of the Pacific before white men ever sailed out of sight of land, but of what use was all that in Newport Beach, California?

It was worthless. It was there that Erena began to die as she had been taught through ancestral lore whispered by her tribal elders. She was not yet thirty.

A few months before Erena began her short California life, a catastrophe occurred over an atoll called Moruroa out in the Pacific near her former island home of Hao. A French admiral, more afraid of angering French president Charles de Gaulle than of raining radioactive fallout on Pacific Islanders living west of Moruroa, detonated a plutonium bomb of 120 kilotonnes with the wind blowing the wrong way. It was 11 September 1966.

The Big Bang was a day late. The morning it was actually scheduled, winds which usually blew that time of year were coming from the wrong direction. A strong westerly blew all the way up into the highest altitudes.

De Gaulle had flown out from Paris on a tight schedule for the big occasion. He changed planes on Tahiti and continued on to France's newest military base, which sprawled where Erena's village once stood on Hao in the Tuamotus.

Now Hao had been of no significance to anyone but its inhabitants until the 1950s. Its hardy Polynesian population was left alone to fish, raise food and families and bury their dead. It was a lovely atoll, not much above sea level, with a clear turquoise lagoon and the usual resources: coconuts, seafood, pearl shell for the button industry and some pearls to trade with passing ships for luxuries such as sugar, coffee, white flour, scented soap, beer and cigarettes.

Its early history was unremarkable. The first European to see and land on Hao was probably Pedro Fernando de Quiros, judging by the location he logged in 1606. He named it La Conversion del San Pablo and reported that he was treated with utmost hospitality by its inhabitants.

It was apparently untroubled by further tourists for 162 years, until French explorer Louis Antoine de Bougainville studied the land mass in some astonishment. 'Is this land, so extraordinary, nascent? Is it in ruins?' he wrote in his ship's log in 1768. He had probably never before seen an island made up of the rim of an exploded undersea volcano covered with luxuriant vegetation. He named it La Harpe for its shape and commented on its tall, well-proportioned peoples. A year later, in 1769, British explorer Lt James Cook sailed through the neighborhood, spied the atoll and named it Bow (as in bow and arrow) Island.

The atoll and its people managed quite well for the next two centuries, visited only by war parties from other islands, hurricanes, traders and missionaries, all of which had similar impacts. France added it to its Polynesian island collection around 1853 along with the rest of the Tuamotus. These were rather insignificant acquisitions until Algeria achieved independence and sent the French packing, closing down their nuclear bomb test site in the Sahara Desert.

France had a long way to go to catch up with the USA, Great Britain and the Soviet Union in the nuclear arms race. Despite its size, it was determined to become a major world nuclear power – if not number one, at least number two or three. It was imperative that the lost Sahara test site be replaced immediately, but where in their world could they carry on such research? Exposing French people to these dangerous tests by conducting them at home was unthinkable.

The British and Americans had already set the precedent in the 1950s with nuclear bomb tests in the Pacific; the British on Christmas Island, the US on Bikini and Enewetok in the Marshall Islands. Henry Kissinger validated the choice of using Micronesian islands with his immortal rationalization: 'There are only 90,000 people out there. Who gives a damn?'

There were, of course, considerably fewer people in France's South Pacific possessions, and it was there they turned for 'disposable' islands. The winners chosen for the dubious honor were part of the Tuamotu Archipelago. Hao proved ideal for a hightech military base because there was land enough for a jet airfield plus space for living and recreation areas for military personnel. Moruroa and Fangataufa were picked for test sites since their only use was to supply occasional fishing and food-gathering expeditions from other islands.

Hao's 'hospitable, tall, well-proportioned' heirs were dispersed to the four winds to join the small, bewildered bands of other nuclear nomads, made landless in an island world where survival is dependent on ancestral land rights that guarantee food, shelter and identity.

President de Gaulle landed on Hao on 9 September and boarded the *De-Grasse* to sail the 200 nautical miles to the bomb test site at Moruroa. He was eager to catch up, having missed the first blast on 2 July because he couldn't work it into his schedule.

According to Bengt and Maria Thérèse Danielsson in their book, *Moruroa Mon Amour*, the president was not pleased to be informed the next morning that the scheduled test was cancelled. The admiral explained delicately that if the bomb were detonated in contrary wind conditions, radioactive fallout would rain down on all inhabited islands downwind, including French Polynesia, New Zealand, the Cook Islands, the Samoas and Fiji.

The following day, the contrary winds still blew. De Gaulle was fuming. He had pressing matters to attend to in Paris. He couldn't just cruise around the Pacific endlessly. As the Danielssons tell it: 'The poor admiral was in a terrible quandary. If the bomb did not explode soon, the general would. Having weighed these two risks against each other, he decided the latter disaster would be the worst ... before the day was over, the plutonium box was detonated.'

In ancient days, when Moruroa was known as Hiti tautau mai, it was guarded by the god Otu'u ha'amana a Ta'aroa. When disturbed, according to local lore, he would manifest himself as a great fearful storklike creature and challenge passing canoes. Now his slumber was shattered by forces even greater than those of the volcanoes that created the islands and atolls of Polynesia. He underwent a violent metamorphosis. Rising to the skies as the deadly apparition of a mushroom cloud, he scattered radioactive fallout on all the canoes, ships and islands west of Moruroa. Readings taken soon after the blast by the National Radiation Laboratory of New Zealand substantiated the admiral's prediction.

A few months later on a cold California night in late December, depressed over news bulletins from French Polynesia, I drove down to the ocean to brood. Impulsively, I turned onto the narrow Balboa Peninsula bordered by some of the best surf in California on one side and Newport Bay with its shoals of yachts and fishing boats on the other. A block or two from the Fun Zone I saw a sign on a restaurant that read 'Vaima's'. The only Vaima Restaurant I knew of was the one on the Quai at Papeete.

I drove around the block for a second look. The sign definitely read 'Vaima's'. Now I was aware of the complex smells of Chinese food on the cold wind blowing in from the sea beyond. With Tahiti heavy on my mind, I left the car in the first parking place I saw and walked back to investigate this interesting coincidence.

A large Gothic arched window took up most of the front of the building facing the street. Inside, tables covered with bright *pareu*-prints filled the room. Red hibiscus blossoms lay at intervals on the bar along the right wall. Except for a beer-drinking man in a baseball cap, there were no other customers. An aloof brunette behind the bar hailed me. Did I want a drink? They weren't open for dinner yet. 'Do you have burgundy?' I asked. 'I'm freezing!'

She brought me a glass and a decanter. 'You look cold', she said, 'and sad, too. This will fix you up.'

She grinned then and the effect was like sunlight. 'Are you from Tahiti?' I had to ask.

'E, you know Tahiti?' She laughed delightedly and introduced herself as Lea from Papeete, daughter of a French father and a Tahitian-Chinese mother. 'My grandmother, she come Papeete from little island in Tuamotu, name Hao. She live with Chinese man, get my mother.'

'Hao. Isn't that the island the French took over for a military base for the bomb testing?'

'How you know that?'

'It's been in the news. I'm so sorry. You must feel awful. Is there anything left of your village?'

'I don' know', she said. 'I never been to Hao. Very far from Tahiti. Nice place for fish, but no cinema, no cafés, no cars, my grandmother tell me.'

'Plenty of cars there now', I said. 'Jet planes, earth-moving equipment, maybe cinemas and cafés.'

She looked interested. 'Maybe I go there someday.'

'Is your grandmother still living?'

'She dead. Long time now.'

Lea was somewhere in her mid thirties then and kept up a pretty urbane façade. But sometimes late at night, she would talk about Tahiti and the old days. Then the island girl inside would surface, no longer so sure of herself in a world of pavements, processed foods, freeways, plastic flowers and incomprehensible rules.

Lea and her Papeete-born Chinese husband owned Vaima's. He had the unlikely name of Eugene – Gene to his American customers. Skinny, quick and smart, his darting eyes were always searching and evaluating, his hands busy. Weekends, Vaima's drew a crowd of local yachties, fishermen and Tahiti aficionados from a fifty-mile radius. Instant musical groups would erupt. Someone would produce a guitar or ukulele, another a pair of spoons and Gene would trade his dishtowel for drumsticks and beat out Tahitian tempos on an empty five-gallon can. Lea usually danced on those nights. She remembered old *aparimas* or story dances her grandmother had taught her that were sometimes funny, sometimes so sad tears would spring to our eyes, quickly dissipated by the ever-ready ribald joke. Everyone laughed at almost everything those nights in Vaima's, even at the bomb or jokes in Tahitian no one could understand but the Tahitians.

I had picked up a bit of the dancing in the Islands to Lea's apparent delight. 'You got dark hair. You take off your glasses, you look like French-Tahitian. She taught me one or two *aparimas* and I danced beside her for my supper some mirth-filled weekends. She decided I should have a Tahitian name and christened me Moemoea after her sister. It was an apt choice. It means dreamer. She said I spent too much time reading old books on the Pacific and worrying about the Bomb, which nobody could do a thing about! Better to sing, dance and forget.

Southern California's small community of Tahitians burgeoned after the filming of Marlon Brando's *Mutiny on the Bounty*. Numerous actors and extras hired on the beaches of Tahiti and Moorea followed the film crew home for the adventure of it. Some succeeded in getting bit parts in movies. Most ended as dancers and musicians in the South Seas–themed bar/restaurants that flourished in the 1960s in Los Angeles, Torrance and Long Beach.

The best nights at Vaima's were the nights the Tahitians showed up. There was never any warning. They'd arrive about closing time after they got off work.

No Chinese-Tahitian fare was good enough for these reunions. Gene would rush to the kitchen and cook up massive pot roasts or meatloaves, mashed potatoes and gravy and corn on the cob to impress his countrymen with his authentic American cuisine. Then the beer would flow freely and the gossip, jokes, singing and dancing would go on until sunup. Occasionally, there would be songs from the phosphate-mining days on Makatea in the Tuamotus or rollicking old *utes* and *hivanaus* that rattled the great glass window as the basso grunts and chanting of the men pounded and boomed against the keening counterpart of the women. These parties would end when the last guests staggered upstairs to Gene and Lea's living quarters to sleep a few hours before revving up battered old cars for the long drive home.

Life in the Chinese restaurant was demanding. Before dawn, there were trips to the produce market in Los Angeles. Days were spent cleaning and chopping mountains of fresh vegetables, scrubbing down the restaurant and cooking. As business improved, the workload reached such a pitch that the couple worked seven days a week and still couldn't keep up. That's when Erena entered the scene.

Erena was a cousin of Lea's from her Hao grandmother's side. She'd been drifting from relative to relative on Tahiti, a misfit who spoke little French and an obscure Tuamotu dialect. Eventually, she moved in with Lea's older sister and her large family.

What little money Erena had of her share of the small settlement the French distributed to the people of her village quickly disappeared. She bought gifts and food for her kinsfolk, squandered a good portion on high heels and dresses, which she also gave away, tickets to the cinema and beer which she shared.

Cash doesn't replace lost Polynesian island lands that fed generations. Money, as any Polynesian can tell you, is for sharing with the extended family. But it isn't like food crops. It doesn't grow back. She had no land on Tahiti. She had given birth to two children but relatives had asked for them and she'd given them away, as is Polynesian custom. The novelty of citified Papeete disappeared with the money. She began to yearn for the familiar patterns of her village, built on the bones of her ancestors. She grew withdrawn.

Lea's sister called her one day from Tahiti. She was at her wits' end with Erena. She couldn't send her back home because there was no 'back home' anymore. She was drinking, miserable – maybe a change of scene?

Gene paid for the airline ticket and Lea's sister painted a glowing picture to Erena of what her new life would be like with her rich sister and brother-in-law who owned a fine restaurant in a seaside village just outside Hollywood. 'It will be just like in the cinema!'

My first impression of Erena was of a rather plain, broad-featured, dark-skinned Polynesian woman about five feet seven with the sturdy build of someone who had worked hard all her life. She was still young: we guessed about twenty-eight. Her legs bore the purple brands of healed coral wounds and septic mosquito bites. Her wide, educated, splay-toed feet evolved for reef walking were not the feet to stuff into high-heeled shoes, but she managed, somehow, at least for the early part of her evenings at the bar. She seldom smiled, but when she did, you wondered how you got the idea she was homely. Those rare flashes transformed her face like a shaft of morning sun transforms a whirling column of dust motes. She was dazzling. It made you want to stand on your head or do anything just to make her smile – to dispel that terrible sadness that inhabited her eyes.

During her days at Vaima's in Newport Beach, Erena did much of the heavy work: scrubbing, cleaning, washing tablecloths by hand, island style, squatting on the cement kitchen floor over a tub. When she wasn't slaving in the kitchen, she was sitting at the bar, drinking. As weeks passed, her thirst for beer became insatiable.

One night, a customer brought in a guitar. She put down her glass and stared at the instrument with such lust, he held it out to her. She cradled it, tuned it and all shyness disappeared. Strumming the insistent beat of the Tuamotus, she played fast rollicking songs so infectious, she was soon the center of a yipping, hip-swinging mob. Her contralto voice was melodic, true and powerful. After that, evenings at Vaima's were joyous with the sound of her unfettered singing and laughter.

Still, it wasn't much of a life for Erena. She was lonely. She was a healthy woman, young and unaccustomed to going for long without sex, which for her was an uncomplicated appetite and pleasure. A few months after her arrival, she began going home with first one customer, then another. It wasn't long before the police picked her up ready to book her for prostitution.

They brought her in to Vaima's first because 'Vaima' was the only word she said they could understand. I pleaded her case to the officers: 'She's not selling herself. She comes from a little South Seas Island you've never heard of that's just been commandeered by the French for a military base. She's lost her home, she's a refugee, she hasn't learned our ways yet and she's very lonely.'

Skeptical, the officer asked a few more questions. Finally, he agreed to let the matter drop this time, but he warned Lea not to let her cousin wander the streets of Newport Beach late at night with a bottle in one hand, her shoes in the other, accosting men.

I was away after that for a month, working on a story assignment. When I burst back through the door at Vaima's finally with a merry 'Iaorana!', three tables of very tense-looking customers glared at me like I was crazy. I went back to the kitchen. Dodging around Gene's chef's hat as he worked, I kissed him on the cheek in greeting. 'Where's Lea?' I asked. 'Where's Erena?'

Gene growled that he'd tell me later, couldn't I see he was busy? He slammed his pots around to illustrate his point. 'Do you need some help?' I yelled over the din. He paused, looked me over with open skepticism, then shrugged, evidently deciding I was better than nothing.

It is not as easy as it looks to deliver a large tray stacked with bowls and platters heaped with Chinese food. The gravy slops out, the tea spills, the catsup in the tiny saucers gets on the stomach. Somehow, we got through the dinner hour and then the regulars started calling for entertainment. Gene asked me if I would dance if he'd play the guitar. I was tired, my dress was a study of abstract designs in soy sauce, catsup and Chinese mustard. 'No', I said. 'I'm beat and I look like hell.'

'Just sing, then', he pleaded. 'It's Friday. They want a little music. I'm tired too.'

He looked exhausted. 'You know I'm no singer', I muttered. 'Just make a lot of noise so they don't notice.' I got the ukulele from behind the bar, tried to tune it with his guitar, got fairly close and we started playing as loud as possible, making singing-like noises.

Our efforts weren't very impressive. Customers began walking out before we'd finished our first number. 'Okay, I'm gonna try dancing', I whispered. 'Play "Takaroa".' His nimble fingers picked out the melody and he began to belt out the *aparima*.

Suddenly, Lea appeared at the back door. She was ashen, her hair greasy and in disarray. Not even the red print dress she wore or the bright artificial flower in her hair could detract from the fact that she had a nasty looking 'shiner'. She glared dismissal at me, bloodshot eyes blazing in her bruised, swollen face and swayed out on the dance floor, hips and hands taking over the story line from the music. I backed off to the bar. Gene's eyes were fixed on the floor as he beat out the tune on his guitar. Embarrassed, I slunk out.

I returned a couple of nights later. Lea looked much better. She greeted me with kisses and a fond stroke of the cheek. 'How are you, Moemoea?' she cooed.

'What happened to you? Did your husband hit you?'

'Nothing happened. I don' know what you mean. Come, you must dance with me.'

'No way! I don't feel like it after what happened.'

'You must! We have no entertainment if you don't!'

'Where's Erena? Why doesn't she come down and sing?' Angry tears pooled in Lea's dark eyes. 'What's wrong? Is she sick? In jail?' Lea slammed out of the room.

There was only one table going and that couple was finishing up. Gene hurried out of the kitchen, gave them their check and slipped behind the bar to draw a pitcher of beer. 'I can take care of the bar', I said. 'I think I can handle pouring beer and wine okay.'

The evening dragged on in dreadful silence. No one else came in to eat. One customer, a lonely old derelict who came in nightly, ordered a pitcher of beer, parked his industrial-sized flashlight on the bar and talked to it, was the only one left. Gene wadded up his apron. 'Slow, tonight', he said, suffering drawn all over his very scrutable Chinese face.

'Gene', I said, 'what is going on? Did you and Lea have a fight? Where's Erena?'

Sighing, he sat down beside me at the bar. 'You see Mama's eye? Erena did that to her.'

'My God, why? Poor Lea!'

He laughed in a short burst. 'Not poor Lea, poor Erena. She not going to sing for us for long time, not until her face, he get small again.'

'They fought? But why?'

He sighed deeply. 'Erena no like this life. All the time, work in kitchen. Nothing grow here. No time for fish. Cars, crowds, crazy people, you know this place. Mama and me, we get crazy here too sometime. Erena get new boyfriend with house in Santa Ana. He say she stay with him, he take care of her, give her garden, bring her fish. Then, something happen. I don' know what. Policeman find her downtown in Santa Ana. They speak Mexican to her and she no under-stan' nothing. She get real quiet. They think she on drugs and lock her up. Ver' bad, that jail. Long time before we find. We take her home but she *fiu*.

*Fiu* is a Tahitian word that rhymes with flu and covers everything from 'I'm fed up and I won't go to work!' to 'I am burned out and will now die!'

Erena took to her sleeping mat upstairs on the floor and proceeded deliber-ately to die in Newport Beach, California, amidst the yachts, boutiques, movie stars, business tycoons, hippies, surfers, hot dog vendors and tourists, within blocks of the birthplace of the frozen chocolate and nut-covered banana, be-cause she was *fiu*.

Two weeks passed as she lay there, visibly fading, waiting for her life force to flicker out. 'She dying, all right. Her eyes, they all funny. I feel death in that room', Gene said grimly.

I had heard that seemingly healthy Polynesians once had the ability to die when they chose, simply by ceasing to live. I don't know anybody personally who's done this or witnessed it, but I've read that people were doing it well into the early twentieth century.

The more Lea thought about it, the madder she got. Here she'd paid all that money for plane fare to bring the girl to California where she could live for nothing! Ungrateful, lazy, stupid bitch! As she watched the atoll woman fade, day by day, her resentment grew until finally something snapped. Dragging Erena from her deathbed by the hair, she punched her in the face, screaming in fury. Erena revived with a bang and gave Lea a black eye, after which Lea gave her a thorough beating.

Would Erena live? Gene was sure of it. 'Lea should have done that a long time ago', he said.

Erena came downstairs eventually to work sullenly in the kitchen. After a few weeks, she again picked up her guitar, but now her singing was soft and personal. She slumped on a barstool over her guitar and a bottle, night after night, unresponsive even to admiring young men. Her soft singing would grow fuzzy and discordant as the evening wore on. Finally, she'd lurch out and climb the stairs to the shabby living quarters overhead. Finally, Lea shipped her back to Papeete in disgust.

The heart was gone from Vaima's. Business dwindled and the café finally closed. At a luau years later, I tried to find out what had happened to the family. 'Gene and Lea? I heard he made a bundle in Tahiti – introduced the American hamburger!' said a yachtie who'd once been a regular. 'Erena? I wish I knew. She was the real thing, you know? I was half in love with her myself.'

Timi Turi, a Tahitian drummer who used to stop by Gene's late parties, had news of the girl. 'Erena? She go home', he said. 'She back on Hao in the Tuamotu.'

'No!' I said. 'Her village is gone.'

'She no think so. She steal a canoe from big Tahiti resort, put some green coconuts in and she go.' He tapped his head. 'Erena, she *maa maa* [crazy]. *Fiu!*'

Erena was an atoll woman, daughter and granddaughter of atoll women who in turn were children of atoll people. She was nobody anywhere else.

# SIMONE

There's a faceless duplex in an anonymous apartment complex in Costa Mesa, California. It squats among its sisters in a cul-de-sac where screaming children play baseball on warm summer evenings. Cars line the street. The sky is white hot. A few young trees stand listless, dusty leaves dangling. A dog sniffs at one, then raises his leg.

A pregnant mother sits on a blanket scratching grass flea bites while her baby sits nearby in its little wooden cage, fondling whitened dog doodoo scooped out of the grass through the bars. A woman in bright pink shorts with mottled blue-cheese thighs stands balancing a laundry basket on one hip, talking to a young girl whose slender neck seems scarcely able to support her sixties tribal headdress of fat, pink rollers.

Sounds fill the air: traffic noises, sirens. A baby cries. Rock and roll screams for attention. A TV quiz show drones and explodes in countermelody from one of the duplexes. Underneath this cacophony, a thumping beat pounds away, tying together all life in the complex. It goes on day and night. Most of the neighbors are so used to it they don't question what it means or why it exists any more than they do the sound of their own pulse. Mostly, it's skin drums, deep and base with a high counterpoint clatter of stick against hollow log. Sometimes the terrible tinny roar of sticks on empty five-gallon cans makes a third voice, almost unbearable except for the beat, the constant rattling beat that unifies everything in this percussion symphony.

They can point out its source. It comes from behind the second peeling door, rear house, front duplex. 'Some kind of a savage lives there, no kidding', they'll tell anyone who asks. 'Ugga bugga.'

Behind this weathered door, Simone holds court for a steady stream of housewives, teenaged girls, an odd child or two, sometimes a swarm of brown-skinned people in highly colored clothes talking excitedly in some foreign language. She greets then all impartially with a ceremony of kisses and hugs, though Californians practice only the handshake and the back slap.

Strangers get a glimpse of her through the door, red-lipsticked pouting mouth, protruding eyes, brown wavy hair coiled in a topknot loaded with hairpins and decorated with a spray of bouganvillea, a circlet of leaves or plastic flowers. Mostly, one notices her dress, or lack of it. She wears a scant island-print brassiere, full breasts surging over the top and sides, matching sarong around her hips, tied well below her navel, exposing an ivory mound of belly. She stays out of the sun, cultivating pallor.

This is Simone, born in Papeete forty-something years ago to a French-Jewish harbor pilot father struck down in his prime by pneumonia, and a Tahitian mother. 'There wasn't a goddam doctor in Tahiti the day he died!' she spits. 'They were all on some other island making love to the girls.'

Simone was brought up as a French girl in Tahiti, forbidden to dance with common Tahitian girls. To make sure of that, she was sent to a convent school with broken glass on the walls. When she graduated, she was shipped off to Noumea in New Caledonia to study medicine. Between that point and her arrival in California, her history is a bit cloudy. There were numerous men, some of them husbands. The United Nations came in somewhere along the line. She lived in Mexico and various countries she dismisses with an airy 'here and there' and freshens up her morning vodka. She still thinks of herself as something of a doctor.

'I had a man living here once with me', she tells a spellbound group of Tahitian dance students. 'He was dying of cancer. They just sent him home from the hospital to die! I took care of him night and day, I mean to tell you. Sometimes he just raved all night and his fever, it was so high you couldn't take it with a thermometer. I kept putting two aspirin up his rectum every two hours.' She stops for effect, drains her vodka and fruit juice and pours another. 'I mean to tell you, that man recovered!' Her student-audience, wearing *pareus* and bras like Simone's, sits around the kitchen table in stunned silence.

Suddenly, the bedroom door opens bang against the wall and Hiro walks in. He's a handsome fellow in his early twenties, raised in San Diego by his Tahitian mother and Caucasian father. Young lover or just friend? The women look him over, speculating. His normally tanned face is pale and ill-looking. Despite the summer heat, he has a blanket wrapped around his shoulders.

Simone greets him with concern and makes a place for him at the table. 'Hiro's got the flu', she explains. He mumbles something to her about fixing him some soup. She pads across the threadbare linoleum to the refrigerator, her bottom tracing almost a complete circle with every other step. This is just the way she walks.

A woman gets up and wanders around the small living room cum dance studio, picking up objects on lace doilies on the sidetable, studying shell lei-draped pictures and artifacts on thinly paneled walls. 'Simone, where did these shark's teeth come from? Not around here, I hope?' Costa Mesa is less than a mile from the ocean. Everyone turns to study the huge bleached jaws and double row of teeth gaping at least two feet apart at the apex. Hiro suddenly comes to life.

'That's from Tahiti', he answers for Simone. There's a silence.

'Well, aren't you going to ask who caught him?'

'Yes. Did you catch him, Hiro?' asks a pretty high school senior with a white plastic hibiscus in her hair.

'Certainly', Hiro responds complacently. There's another silence while Simone stirs the soup. 'Well, don't you want to know how I caught him?' he asks finally.

'You shouldn't talk so much with your sore throat, Hiro', snaps Simone.

'Well, I'll tell you anyway', he says, ignoring her. 'We were in a canoe and he was cruising around and around us. Twice, he seemed like he was going to leap right in with us. I got ready. Then he jumped. He came straight for us. As he passed over the boat, I took two aspirin and poked them up his rectum with my little finger, like that!' and he makes a jabbing motion in the air. 'He was dead before he hit the water.' he says solemnly and begins to blow on a spoonful of soup while the room roars with laughter. Simone spits something venomous at him in Tahitian.

Simone ostensibly made her living as a Tahitian dance teacher in this duplex apartment. She attracted a strange assortment of students: precocious children, one a whip-thin Chinese girl of thirteen whose elderly mother came with her each time, watching the girl intently as she taught her body the disciplined motions of Tahitian dance. Her mother had her studying every type of exotic dance available with eight different teachers. 'Then she will support the family', mother said. There was a tawny, sunbleached blonde housewife who looked as if she'd be more at home on the tennis courts. Four months pregnant, she continued her punishing lessons, trying to pick up speed with her *amis* (pelvic rotations) to the recorded drumbeat. In contrast was a tall hawk-nosed girl, so thin and angular she looked as if she'd shatter if you bumped her. She would spend hours practicing, practicing. She never tired and she didn't sweat, even when everyone else was streaming. One student was a teacher of Hawaiian hula with dyed black hair, heavy makeup and long white arms, who fancied turquoise polish on her finger and toenails. Well into her fifties, she was a quick study, analyzing every movement, memorizing with her body motions she'd soon be selling to her students. But Simone's real pets were the sexy, teenaged girls with beautiful bodies and show business aspirations who came and went.

Simone's treatment of the dance form was more Las Vegas Showgirl Tahitian than traditional and ethnic. Her pelvis, driven by strong pumping thighs, played riffles and scat with the drumbeat, always with it, but improvising in ways that defied duplication. Her arm movements and style were strictly her own. Independent of her expressive hips, her hands would make coy gestures and she'd glance over her shoulder with a little simper.

She loved to tell stories of her girlhood in Papeete. 'Down the road from us', she related once during a break, 'there was a Chinese baker, a *tinito*, and every morning he would put his rolls out on racks to cool. I mean to tell you, that smell could drive you *wild*!

'He was an old, skinny man and ugly, ugh. My cousin and I used to sneak out in our *pareus*. We didn't wear pants underneath. We would stroll down the road to his house and then my cousin would just sit down under a tree and look at a flower or something. She would put her legs up so he could see right down her *pareu*.

'Pretty soon, he'd stop working and just stand there looking at her. She wouldn't pay any attention. Then I would sneak behind him and steal as many rolls as I could hold in my *pareu* and we would run like crazy down the road with him pounding after us screaming!

'My mother would let us in and we'd throw anything we could get our hands on at him out the windows until he went away. He fell for it every time we did it.' She'd hug herself in glee, remembering.

Simone was frequently in a rage about something, usually some wrong someone had done her. People always seemed to be stealing from her. While the records thumped out their Tahitian rhythms, she would storm up and down the small studio, shrieking curses on some friend who had crossed her. Despite that, she was Mama Simone to an ever-changing mob of houseguests, usually needy Tahitians, fresh from the Islands, who had not yet learned that in California, possessions are private, not free for the taking of any extended family member or friend.

The first time I met her, she was on the rampage, livid with fury. 'Some damned thief stole my necklace!' she screeched. 'My shark's tooth necklace. I had it since I was a little girl. Now somebody has stole it.'

'Do you have any idea who would do such a thing?'

'No. I don't have no idea, but I mean to tell you, when I find out who did it, I am going to ...', she finished in a burst of Tahitian.

'Was it valuable?'

'Was it valuable!' she repeated with a snort. 'It was from the shark who ate my uncle!'

'How sad. And that was all you had left of your poor uncle? Oh, that's really awful.'

'It was all I had left of that shark. I mean to tell you, that was one big shark. I hated my uncle. My cousins hated my uncle. Everybody hated my uncle. He was one sonofabitch. One day he was out fishing. That's when the shark got him. When we heard the news, I mean to tell you, my cousins and me had one big party, we were so happy.' Her bright red lips twisted into a mean little smirk and she flexed her thinplucked eyebrows.

'How old were you then?' I asked.

'Oh, ten, maybe twelve, I don't know. I just had my first period. Anyway, one day, we saw this big shark in the lagoon. Sometimes they get over the reef. My cousins and I killed it. It couldn't get away from us. We drove it into the shallow water. We had spears and bush knives. Well, we dragged it up on the beach and we cut it open. It was the shark who ate my uncle!'

'How do you *know* it was the same shark?'

'There were parts of my uncle still inside.'

'But how could you tell whose they were?'

'How could I tell? You think I don't know my own uncle's parts? It was him, all right, I mean to tell you. Well, my cousins and I had a big fight on the beach to see who got to keep those shark's teeth.'

'And you won.'

'You bet I won! I made them into a necklace and now somebody's stolen them from me. I wore those teeth every day of my life since I was a little girl.'

Life wasn't easy for Simone in California. Too old and overweight for the island-theme nightclub circuit, she coached an endless succession of students, but the money she earned went quickly when members of her extended Polynesian family visited. Sometimes she had to borrow for the bare essentials: rent, telephone and vodka. A born fighter, she survived using her wits. Woe to anyone who crossed her, for her traditional Polynesian coup de grace could haunt a man forever.

Living as noisily as she did, boxed in by non-Tahitian neighbors, it was no surprise that there were a few complaints. Her greatest critic and enemy was an old man who lived alone upstairs in an apartment overlooking her little weed-choked backyard.

'I don't know his name. I don't want to know his name. He got nothing to do but stand on his balcony all day and all night screaming *"Quiet!"* Sometimes he swears. He even called me a whore! He tells lies to my manager. He tries to get me kicked out. Listen! Hear that? There he goes again.'

A male howled 'Shut up down there, you goddamned bitch!' almost drowning out the insistent drumbeats.

'See how he talks to me?' she screeched, hands on her hips, bare belly puffed full of air, globular breasts spilling over a skimpy Tahitian bra. 'Me!' She pounded her chest with her index finger. 'Me, Simone! That pig dare to call *me* a bitch!'

Simone chose a bright sunny day to deliver her coup de grace. Her dissident neighbor could be seen through the sliding glass doors of Simone's studio, glaring down in the direction of her duplex. Turning the music up to full blast, she slid the glass door open and strolled insolently into her yard, hips revolving dangerously, red hibiscus bristling behind one ear.

She took up her stance in the center of the weed patch. Their eyes locked. Elegantly, she turned her back, bent over double, flipped up her red and white *pareu* and mooned him, waving her bare bottom round and round, back and forth to the music. He never appeared on his balcony again as long as Simone lived in Costa Mesa. 'Maybe he moved, maybe he had a heart attack', she said indifferently.

Simone's story has a happy ending. One day, this aging Tahitian, French, Jewish princess retired from the battlefield and tried marriage one more time. He was a quiet type, the president of his own small electronics company, a man with a furrowed face and white hair. He had just returned from his first, long delayed fantasy trip to Tahiti, where he'd had some sort of personal conversion experience. 'I'm a born-again Tahitian', he declared to sympathetic friends at a Friends of Tahiti luau in Long Beach. It was there he met Simone.

To Simone, he represented wealth, stability and kindness. He was the sort of man who would give her diamonds if she wanted such rubbish but who would never steal treasures from her like the teeth of the shark that ate her uncle. He was a trophy to exhibit proudly to relatives in Tahiti, he was someone to grow old and fat with comfortably. She was ready.

To him, she was the Tahitian sex object of his dreams. Nothing she could say or do offended him. She taught him to defy gravity and laugh. He moved her into his 2,000-square-foot house, where there was plenty of room for her ever-changing cast of extended family members and Tahitian parties and they lived happily ever after for a few years.

# 8

# HINANO

Hinano is the name of the flower of the pandanus tree or screw pine; it's the brand name for a Tahitian beer; and it's the only name by which we remember the dead girl. At least, the Tahitians think she's dead. Some of the rest of us wonder.

Hinano was about nineteen when we knew her. Her skin was the color of mocha ice cream, but warmer and smoother. She was small, with a perfectly proportioned body. Her waist-length, black wavy hair was probably a wig. That wasn't so unusual in show business, especially on the luau circuit of Southern California. Many Tahitians cut their hair when they emigrated to L.A. so they wouldn't look so 'different'. A lot of them then had to rush off and buy long-haired wigs because the only marketable skills they had were singing, dancing and looking decorative like South Sea Islands props.

Hinano described herself as a *demi* (Tahitian–French mix) from Papeete – at least, that's what we think she was trying to tell us in her fractured English. Her feet were a dead giveaway that this was no village girl. Narrow and elegant, they had not grown strong and wide on the rugged coral reef looking for shellfish or from clutching rough trunks of coconut palms. These were European feet, shod since infancy, attached to shapely brown legs unmarred with the purple scars of healed septic mosquito bites, coral and machete wounds.

Where she learned to dance like she did is a mystery. It wasn't Tahiti. She didn't clamp the floor with her feet like limpets on rocks when her hips went into their spin-dry cycle the way village-trained girls did. She danced on the balls of her little tan feet. When the *tamure* beat took over, she'd go until even her Tahitian partners dropped. She never seemed to tire of dancing or singing. She was crazy with energy.

She had a special style. The male members of Friends of Tahiti went wild when she walked into a room, scarlet hibiscus over one ear, wearing one of her slinky, long, fitted *pareu* print gowns. They'd clap and hoot and pound the tables until she'd ravish them with Tahitian songs in a husky, raucous voice that sounded like she couldn't wait to tear their clothes off.

Those fortunate enough to sit near Hinano during those F.O.T. luau nights had a riotous time trying to communicate with her. She turned everything into a bawdy joke. You couldn't understand most of the words but you had to laugh anyway just to keep up with her.

Calling members of this newly formed club Tahiti aficionados would be an understatement. Fanatics would be more like it. A typical member (and 70 percent were male) had been to Tahiti more than once, knew Susy No Pants, was 'almost kicked out of Quinn's', saw Marlon Brando's *Mutiny on the Bounty* a minimum of three times, could dance the 'Tamure' after a fashion and spoke fluent broken English whenever a Tahitian was present. In fact, communications at those Friends of Tahiti meetings in the 1960s made broken English sound like a language you could learn at Berlitz. This wasn't much help to the immigrants who were trying to learn our language.

It wasn't easy to get a lot of Tahitians to show up at these monthly meetings, even with the offer of a free, all-you-can-eat buffet. Most of them had to work nights as entertainers or as restaurant kitchen help. The assortment of doctors, dentists, engineers, aerospace types and travel industry people who made up the hard core membership would stake out tables, saving seats and watching the door so they could claim the few Tahitians before their fellows did. Competition was fierce with these middle-aged schoolboys as they shouted Tahitian names and entreaties in an acquired gibberish one could call Tahinglish. 'E, you, Tehani, you come sit with me, baby. Okay?'

Wives of these men, and many had them, were often just as bad, screaming out Tahitian names, begging men and women to sit next to them. A table with no Tahitian was a table with no status. A couple of times the F.O.T. president intervened, making short speeches about 'sharing in the real spirit of Polynesia – one or two Tahitians per long table, please!'

The South Seas fad swept Southern California in the 1960s. Two factors caused it. The first was the partial filling in of the lagoon at Faa'a, Tahiti and construction of a runway capable of taking jet aircraft. This, of course, was to enable France to ship supplies and personnel for the infrastructure of their nuclear bomb testing in the Tuamotus. The second was the publicity surrounding the filming of *Mutiny on the Bounty*, introducing the exotic Tarita, who was the prototype of America's South Seas wet dream.

Before the airport, Tahiti was a fantasy, known only through the word pictures of novelists and poets, recreated in films. From Los Angeles, it was an eight-day trip by cruise ship, and several weeks by yacht. But in the 1960s Tahiti was redefined by the Brando movie and offered up on a macadam platter to jet airliners stuffed with tourists from all over the world: instant gratification.

A number of Tahitians who worked, mostly as extras, in the movie followed the crew home to Hollywood hoping for more film work and a glamorous life where they'd never again have to plant taro or climb coconut trees to eat. Los Angeles was paradise! Tahiti? A deadend of poverty and hard manual labor just to survive in a subsistence economy. Employment and education opportunities were almost nonexistent for the Polynesian contingent of French Polynesia. Paradise is in the eye of the beholder with a return ticket.

There wasn't much work for Tahitians in Los Angeles either. Most were undereducated, unskilled and fluent only in French and Tahitian. As the South Seas craze gathered momentum, however, nightclubs seized the theme and for a couple of years, Islanders who sang, danced or played musical instruments were the center of attention.

Hinano, with a Tahitian dance troupe, got a contract to work the luau circuit from San Francisco to Las Vegas. We were deprived of her gorgeous company for months. American expectations that every member of the troupe show up on time and entertain whether they felt like it or not lay heavy on these spontaneous people. The Tahitians mutinied, one by one, some simply going home with customers to stay. These were replaced by whichever exotic-looking dancers were available. Finally, it got down to Hinano, a Tahitian drummer, a Filipino girl, a Japanese-Hawaiian and two Mexicans who seldom smiled. When the drummer left too, the group fell apart.

It wasn't all bad, though. Somewhere along the line, Hinano met a 35-year-old bachelor Beverly Hills investment banker named Howard. She gave him the scarlet hibiscus she wore in her hair. Nobody, man, woman or child, had ever given Howard a flower before. Fortunately, the night they met, she was wearing a real one.

They became lovers. Male faces fell when she first walked in to an F.O.T. luau with him. The sparks between them were evident. They were quite a contrast, she with her glowing pale-brown skin, full sensuous lips and brown eyes, he with his sandy crew cut, pale blue eyes, rather prim mouth, navy blue tie and gray suit. One of the F.O.T.'s took him aside and threatened to cut off his tie. He never wore a suit to luaus again. He acquired an admirable wardrobe of gaudy polyester Hawaiian shirts that had to do until he could make his first trip to Tahiti and put together a more distinctive wardrobe. He always looked odd, somehow, as though he were in costume. Maybe it was the sharp crease in the white trousers and the white shoes and socks. It was hard for him to relax.

After a few meetings, the dentist from Pasadena cornered Howard and said in Tahinglish: 'Hey, buddy, when you go Tahiti, meet Hinano family?'

Howard had a hard time speaking broken English. He'd seen *Mutiny*, of course, but only once, and he couldn't seem to get into the role yet. 'I don't know. Every time we get ready to go over there, something happens. Now she says her father is building a new house on Taravao and would be mortified if we arrived before it's finished. Before that, her mother had to go over to Bora Bora to stay with her sick grandmother. Very complicated, these Tahitians. I said, let's just go to Bora Bora then. She said no, there'd be no place for us to stay except in a little grass shack in a remote mountain village with no plumbing. I said I could deal with that for a limited time. No, she says, she'd be too embarrassed for me to live at the level of her poor relations.'

The dentist groaned. 'Oh, man, I'd give anything to go stay in a grass shack in some unspoiled village. That's the only way to meet a real island girl who hasn't been corrupted with civilization.'

'I already have my real island girl', Howard said with a sly grin. 'She's corrupting me!'

It was a little awkward for a Boston-bred Beverly Hills investment banker to have a mistress in those days. His only living relative, an older sister, was quite taken aback when she met Hinano. 'She's awfully dark, isn't she, Howard?' she remarked later on the telephone. 'Surely this isn't a serious liaison?'

He closed the door to his study before replying. 'She's much lighter than her Tahitian friends and her features are considerably more refined. She doesn't have the broad flat nose, for instance. Her French blood comes out in all the right places.'

'Howard, love, I'm not saying she's not beautiful. She's the most beautiful girl I've ever seen, but half of her is one of the dark races. Suppose you married and had children? Suppose they were throwbacks and came out like little black Tahitians?'

'I'm going to tell you something about Tahitians', he said to his sister archly. 'They are not Negroes, they are Polynesians and Polynesians are Caucasians.'

'Who told you that, Howard?'

'A client of mine, a Mormon from Honolulu. Hinano and I went out with him and his wife. Afterwards, he said to me, "You know, if I were you, I'd marry that little goddess before someone comes and takes her away from you!" and I told him it had certainly crossed my mind. But I wanted a son some day to carry on the family name. I told him I didn't think it would work out so well, light as she is, she's still one of the dark races. I said the same thing to him you just said to me. That's when he told me, Polynesians are Caucasians.'

'I didn't know that', Howard's sister said, sounding relieved. 'I'm sorry. I didn't mean any insult.'

The engagement was announced. The diamond was three carats. The couple missed several meetings after that. Then, Hinano showed up alone. She wasn't her usual bubbly self. She sang a few old Tahitian songs, sad ones, like 'Tahiti Nui', accompanying herself on the guitar.

Later, I went to the ladies' room and heard someone crying in the next stall. The door opened and out came Hinano. It was rather shocking to see this exotic creature broken and sobbing. Awkwardly, I asked if there was anything I could do. She took some toilet paper, blew her nose and shook her head. She looked awful. Her flower was cockeyed, her face was streaked with mascara and her skin was bluish gray. 'I got the cramps', she said. 'I have trouble with my periods sometimes.'

'Jeez, Hinano, do you want me to call a doctor?' I could see now that there was blood all over her dress. I was so shocked, it didn't register then that she was talking like an Anglo.

'No!' she choked out, lurched away from my stroking hand, slammed her hip on the porcelain sink so hard it made my teeth gri,t and passed out on the dirty floor.

I didn't have to go farther than the bar to get a doctor. Our esteemed president was an internist. He worked on her while I stood back with the crowd outside the bathroom door. 'Hinano, is he sick?' one of the Tahitian women asked me. 'I go help him?'

'I don't know. She looked awful. She was hemorrhaging so bad, she didn't even sound like herself. Maybe you'd better go in there in case she needs an interpreter.'

'Hinano no need interpreter', said the woman with a cock of her eyebrows. 'What that mean, hemor …? What he doing in there? Too much beer?'

'She's having trouble with her menstrual period, I think. Too much bleeding.'

'*Aue!*' she cried and lapsed into excited Tahitian with her friends who cried, '*aue!*' frequently and chattered animatedly, tragedy twisting their expressive faces.

The doctor opened the door a crack just then and barked: 'Somebody call an ambulance, please.'

We never saw Hinano again. Years later, I pieced her story together with the help of Tahitian friends. Hinano had never set foot on an island, not even Catalina, twenty-seven miles across the channel from Los Angeles. She was born in East Los Angeles. Her mother was a Black prostitute, her father, unknown, except that he was white, obviously. Her mother named her Peaches because of the color of her skin and she grew up on the streets of Los Angeles. She grew up beautiful too soon and dropped out of school in the tenth grade.

The only jobs she ever managed to get standing up were in the kitchens of various Los Angeles and sometimes Beverly Hills restaurants. One night, she was part of the cleanup crew for a fancy luau in then all-white Brentwood. Each member of the female staff was issued a hibiscus to wear over one ear for that South Seas effect. When Hinano went out front to pick up the dirty dishes, several guests asked her if she was Hawaiian. She got a rush of attention from the males.

As luaus became the 'in' thing for backyard parties, she was in demand because of her looks. She was promoted from cleanup to serving. The hibiscus over one ear became a fixture. Working out front now, she could watch the floor shows critically. She decided she liked Tahitian dancing, but Hawaiian was too sedate for her.

She met a fat white woman in a muu-muu with dyed orange hair and turquoise eyelids at one of the luaus who called herself Auahi Manu. 'That's Tahitian for firebird, dear, and that's what I was, in my prime.' It was her dance students who were doing the entertaining. Alas, she had gained seventy-five pounds due to 'a glandular condition', and now her life was her 'sweet' students. She became Peaches's teacher and mentor. She was probably the only non-Tahitian who knew the girl's secret. She should: she helped her create every nuance of her new persona.

From that first meeting with Auahi Manu, Peaches's life seemed enchanted by a fairy godmother. A bright mulatto with no education, no future, who didn't fit in with Blacks or whites in the 1960s, she'd been given a new way to define herself that could bring the world to her feet. Magical! All she had to do was remember to stick a flower in her hair, speak broken English, learn a few Tahitian words to throw in for authenticity, memorize songs, dances and a few place names.

She watched the Tahitian immigrants wolfishly, devouring their mannerisms, their English speech patterns, their rhythms. Here were women darker than she was who were the darlings of the white establishment, even marrying into it. The main difference between her and them, as far as she could see, was a flower and an accent. While the Islanders struggled to become Americanized and get a piece of the American dream, she struggled to metamorphose into an exotic import so that she, a half-Black child of Los Angeles, could get a piece of that American dream, too.

The Tahitians, for the most part, were delighted with the game and remarkably unjudgemental. If Peaches wanted to be Tahitian, she could be Tahitian, as far as they were concerned. She was renamed Hinano because she was strong like Tahitian beer and made the men crazy. Word got out on the coconut wireless. As far away as Las Vegas, Tahitians knew the story and took great delight in perpetuating what, to them, was a very funny joke on the likes of Friends of Tahiti members.

Her affair with Howard seemed destined for a Hollywood movie ending until the day she realized she was pregnant. She went to see her mother for the first time in four years. Her mother heard the story with disgust. 'You bettah get ridda that baby, girl', she warned. 'That baby be Black like me, you lose your rich white man.'

Her mother gave her $500 and put her on the bus for San Diego. From there, she got to the Mexican border and crossed over into Tijuana. Abortions were illegal in California in those days. The desperate girl found a dirty little clinic on a back street. The so-called doctor told her it would cost $300. She counted out the money. He had her get up on a table, gave her an injection, raped her, then aborted her foetus.

He drove her to a noisy motel on the outskirts of Tijuana to recover. The next day, a woman entered the room. She spoke no English but seemed to have some nursing skills. She helped the girl clean herself up, pronounced her 'okay' and left. Somehow Hinano made it back to Los Angeles and Howard. She couldn't very well tell him where she'd been and what she'd done. Unfortunately, the only feasible explanation for her two-day disappearance, as far as the investment banker was concerned, must be that she was having an affair. He told her to get out, he never wanted to see her again!

Sick and angry, she went to the F.O.T. monthly luau alone, hibiscus blazing defiantly in her black hair. Was she not the Tahitian goddess men dreamed of? Forget Howard! She could have any man she wanted! Instead, she had a hemorrhage.

After Hinano was released from the hospital, the president confided her problem to his wife, who leaked word that she'd had an illegal abortion which was so butchered she'd never be able to have children. 'But don't waste any sympathy on her. She wasn't even a real Tahitian! She was a Negress! I wondered about that girl from the start.'

'Come on! She's some kind of Islander! I'll bet she's Jamaican!' said a dentist who adored her.

'Not even that!' she said. 'She's just from around here in L.A. somewhere. Her mother came to pick her up. Horrible looking woman!' She shuddered.

A few of us Anglos languishing with the wannabe virus were pretty impressed that a person could just cross over and *be*. We talk about her sometimes. After all, was her fantasy to be someone else all that different from ours, immigrant Tahitians included? Tahitians say, 'Hinano, dead.' Do they mean their game or the woman? We're more inclined to wonder, who is she now?

# 9

# WHAT DO NAKED WOMEN WANT?

The explosion of French civilian and military workers demanded urban renewal in Papeete. By the early 1980s, its once picturesque waterfront was transformed by glass buildings glittering like costume jewelry on a hooker.

Gone was the snarl of jovial maniacs maneuvering and socializing on bikes and motor scooters and in old cars. Freeways complete with rush-hour gridlock brought Papeete into the twentieth century. Suburbs defaced the jungle-green and earth-red foothills spreading for miles, like acne.

Exotic resorts catered to an international set which came in packaged tours to act out South Sea fantasies. But the fantasy fulfillment promised in shimmering blue lagoon brochures was not to be for the likes of the Maohi heirs to these tropic isles.

A lei of barbed wire encircled a certain resort on the island of Moorea and guards patrolled twenty-four hours a day. Across the Sea of the Moon on Tahiti, a fisherman grew old in jail, berating himself not for what he did but because he didn't do it well enough. A planter named Vili gave me a lift to the dock and told me the story.

'Last year, a woman, not young but not old either, came here from Paris and stayed at that big resort. She walked down the beach, took off her *pareu* and lay down on the sand. She had no clothes on at all. Nothing! Along comes a fisherman from a little village near Papetoai. He sees her lying there. He stops. Is she dead? No, her breasts rise and fall. She breathes. He is confused. Why is she lying there naked? In all his life he has never seen a totally naked woman. The sun is hot. She is not even in the shade. Is she unconscious? No, she sighs and spreads her legs apart. "She's waiting for me!" There is no other explanation. He puts down his fishing net and does what any man will do when a woman has this need. But she is not satisfied. She screams and screams at him!

'The gendarmes lock him up in jail in Papeete. Terrible place, terrible! He does not speak French, only Tahitian and he is illiterate. Even the court's translator can't explain the charge. He's too ashamed to raise his head when he's sentenced. "She needed me and I did not satisfy her" is all he understands.

'With our people, when a Tahitian girl goes alone to a lonely place, it's a signal she wants boom-boom. This lady was far from her friends and she was naked!

'He got six years for rape, but he thinks he's in prison because he's a terrible lover. Maybe he will never be able to make love to a woman again!'

The French tourist was not chided for flagrant disregard for Polynesian standards of decency or ignorance of local customs, though one did not need a course in anthropology to grasp the basics. Even artist Paul Gauguin wrote of his difficulties in persuading Tahitian girls to pose with their genitals exposed. She received effusive apologies from the resort manager and the promise of a complimentary all-inclusive week if she'd only return to 'paradise' next year. He assured her of her complete safety. She had a right to sunbathe as she pleased on French soil. If the natives could not respect French standards of decency, they could go paddle their absurd canoes off to some other islands to live – or rot in jail!

And so it came to pass that the first barbed wire coiled around 'Eden'.

## 10

# PEPE, THE QUEEN OF TAHITI

Since the genesis of European contact, men have glorified the women of the South Seas in novels, poems, songs and travelogues as simple, uncomplicated children of Eden to whom the white man is god. They peer out at us with dreamy smiles from violet shadows of purple prose, the personification of Eve, asking nothing but to laugh, sing, dance, have babies and be nursemaid, mother, daughter, servant and whore to their men. What of this languor Paul Gauguin immortalized? His female figures rest so deeply in violet shadow they could be stone *tikis*.

What do we really know of the lives of Polynesian women? What do they value in themselves and in each other? If Tahitian women chose a Woman of the Year to be rewarded with a trip to Paris, rich prizes and television appearances, what criteria would they use?

Pepe was fifty-six when we first met in California in 1981, in a motel across the street from Disneyland. Born in the Cook Islands during the harsh New Zealand colonial era of the 1920s, she spent little time dreaming in the violet shadows of the Paul Gauguins or frolicking in the jungle pools of the Pierre Lotis.

As a child on Rarotonga, she was one of fifty servants toiling for a white man who owned movie theaters. Pepe's job was to care for his children. He prevented her from going to school because it would interfere with her work. Finally, the authorities intervened.

She was twenty-six before she finally managed to run away to Tahiti, 600 miles distant. There she made connections with the *Oiseau des Iles*, a 500-ton schooner which made the regular 120-mile run from Papeete to Makatea in the Tuamotus where her sister lived with her phosphate miner husband. It was there that Pepe met her Tahitian husband and bore him two children, Frederick and Juliette.

Pepe and her man were ambitious. Their one hope of carving out freedom and the good life was cash. For men such as Gautier, there were jobs only as laborers on ships or in the phosphate mines; for their women, servitude. He signed a contract and for the next few years, the pair belonged to the Compagnie Française des Phosphates de l'Oceanie on the island of Makatea.

This small upthrust bit of coral real estate, measuring five miles by four by 350 feet at its highest point, had literally been transformed into a huge factory for mining and crushing phosphate rock to be sold overseas as fertilizer. During the early 1940s, over 300,000 tons were exported annually. The devastation of this islet started in 1908 and continued until the 1960s.

Once Makatea was an independent kingdom, described by Teuira Henry in *Ancient Tahiti* as densely wooded with good soil in which coconuts, breadfruit and other fine timber trees flourished along with a sturdy population of humans and birds. The latter, of course, predated the humans by thousands of years and, having splendid bowels, were responsible for the massive phosphate deposits. A Dutchman named Roggeveen, the first European credited with sighting the island (1772) ironically named it Recreation Island.

The original Polynesian discoverers and settlers were as warlike as any in the Tuamotu Archipelago. After King Pomare I annexed Makatea and abolished cannibalism in the late eighteenth century, the inhabitants had to rely solely on fish, birds and the occasional turtle for protein to supplement their diet of fruits, tubers and vegetables.

The Makateans were in for another dietary change when the French and British discovered they could make millions by selling the ancestral land out from under them to fertilize the crops of strangers overseas. They agreed to pay the Islanders a small royalty on the phosphate exported and trees destroyed so they could purchase imported foods and building materials, now that they could no longer feed and house themselves. They could stay and work in the mines or migrate to other islands.

Pepe and her husband labored on Makatea for years: he as a miner, she as a laundress, forever wet, squatting over pools and tubs, beating dirty clothes clean on stones with sticks for miners and white administrators alike, for a few francs a day.

The population in the mine's heyday was over 2,000, including Polynesians, Chinese, Japanese, Annamites and the European staff. When the phosphate ran out in 1966, the mine was closed, the workers dispersed to Papeete or their own islands. The population shrank to fifty-five.

Pepe, now a widow, is frequently racked with gut-wrenching coughing spasms that she says are a souvenir of her Makatea years when she was constantly wet, doing laundry with no air to breathe that wasn't thick with phosphate dust. She was a pretty thing in those days, a Polynesian woman who might have inspired romantic European writers or artists, had there been such on Makatea to miss the point of this picturesque slice of South Seas life – Pepe at the pool, thick black hair piled high on her head, tendrils tickling brown cheeks flushed rosy with exertion.

Her face is deeply lined now, black hair shot with gray, body thickened somewhat but not with fat. She's an energetic woman bordering on hyperactive, smoking incessantly. 'No, that is *not* why I cough all the time!'

She picked me up at the airport at Faa'a when I returned to Tahiti in 1982. In the sixteen years I had been absent, thousands of French settlers and military personnel had poured in. The rich red earth and jungle-clad hills of a thousand shades of green were now encrusted with the scabs of their housing tracts. Slum settlements huddled in valleys and on the outskirts of Papeete. Crude shacks of tin, cardboard and discarded junk housed landless Tahitians and Outer Islanders.

Urban renewal had rendered downtown Papeete almost unrecognizable. Picturesque wooden buildings with fancy iron grillwork had been replaced with glassy modern structures. Traffic was no longer a quaintly mad affair with good-natured maniacs darting in and out on anything with wheels and a horn to blow. Now it was a grim mayhem of rush hours and jammed freeways, L.A. style.

Mercifully, the ever-present trade winds flush traffic pollution away, leaving Papeete fragrant with *tiare Tahiti* and growing things. The pungent Roquefort cheesy odor of copra that once hung heavy on the air on the waterfront is gone, but so too is the scent of vanilla beans that in certain areas made Tahiti smell like a fragrant cookie.

One can still sit in a waterfront café, people-watching, and never be bored. Chic French, Chinese and Polynesian blends saunter by amidst businessmen and tourists from all over the world. On the bustling Quai, a Maohi woman squats, cleaning a big fish. 'Some people here, if they no fish, they no eat', says Pepe.

We stroll about, getting me oriented to this new Papeete. The afternoon deepens. We spy Pito, my old taxi driver friend with whom I'd seen the first striptease on Tahiti. His grinning ChineseTahitian face is uncreased by time. He owns a fleet of taxis now and has traveled all over the world. The three explosions of French Polynesia, Nuclear Bombs, European Population and Tourism, have brought him prosperity.

Pepe lives on a large parcel of land in the district of Arue, about seven miles outside of Papeete. Mangoes, papayas, *tiare Tahiti*, *frangipani*, anthuriums, crotons and hibiscus compete for attention with flowers and trees I can't name, against a backdrop of lush green lawns.

There are two houses, one behind the other, looking as if they'd been transplanted intact from California's suburbs. The rear house belongs to Juliettete, Pepe's aristocratic-looking daughter, now thirty-two. Her handsome, rotund son Frederick, twenty-eight, lives in the front house with Pepe. Other residents include caged doves, six fat little dogs who are the babies of the household, and two teenaged girls from Rarotonga, Maeva and Luisa, granddaughters of Mama Ruta Tixier, considered by many the greatest *tivaevae* designer in the Cook Islands. Watching Mama Ruta once as she made detailed flower sketches for future designs, I asked her where she'd studied art. The old woman frowned in annoyance. 'I no study arting. I just make the pictures for the *tivaevae*.'

I am assigned the entire rear house while everyone crowds into the front one with Pepe. Mine is hardly a bachelor apartment, having four bedrooms, living room, two baths, dining room and kitchen. The unwritten laws of Polynesian hospitality overrule my objections. 'Take a nap before dinner', orders Pepe. 'You been on the jet all night and downtown all day.'

Resigned, I sigh. 'I can't sleep in the daytime but maybe I'll just lie down for awhile.' Fourteen hours later I awake at sunrise, confused. Where am I? The air is warm and rich with the scent of gardenias mixed with the smell of burning leaves. Roosters crow. The puttering clucks of chickens scavenging for breakfast mix with the rasp of rakes and brooms searching for every fallen vagrant leaf or blossom. Doves coo, sad and haunting. Mynah birds chatter and mew. Now I remember. Wrapping myself in a *pareu*, I slap over to the window barefoot in time to see Frederick coming up the drive with loaves of fresh French bread from the bakery. The whole family is already hard at work.

Breakfast is waiting on my wide verandah: scrambled eggs with pungent onions, a loaf of French bread, *pamplemousse*, the sweet Tahitian grapefruit that's as big as a cantaloupe, sweet rolls and coffee laid out on a *pareu* tablecloth overlooking the verdant gardens.

To my right is a huge spreading mango tree some fifty feet tall, to my left, a papaya laden with orange globes of fruit. As I look in astonishment at the movie-set loveliness, I catch a shivering motion out of the corner of one eye. Turning my head, I'm just in time to see an old lady in a magenta dress climb up the big mango tree. She's hidden in the leaves before I can even move. In no time, she climbs down friskily, clutching mangoes in her skirt and scampers off out of sight. Soft trade winds ruffle the petals of the flower arrangement of hibiscus and anthuriums on the table. Had I really seen what I thought I'd just seen?

Dazed, I sit down to breakfast, in state, alone. The gardens, blustering with activity earlier, now stand silent and deserted, dreaming in the fresh morning air.

Nothing stirs but the leaves, whispering in the breeze. I wait, thinking perhaps someone will join me. The house in front looks deserted. Surely sophisticated, well-traveled Pepe doesn't revert to Outer Island ways at home and treat white visitors like colonial 'royalty'? We'd see about that! I eat my lavish breakfast hungrily, then load my empty dishes on an ornately carved Tahitian tray and carry them down to Pepe's house.

The family is at breakfast in an airy kitchen, seated on benches at a long wooden table. As I enter, Pepe begins to scold me for carrying my dishes down.

'I was getting lonesome. Can't I join you?'

Flustered, she apologizes for what looks to me like an immaculate kitchen and says she hopes I won't be too shocked and disgusted by her humble family's ways. Baffled, I look around the big room that is obviously the real heart of both households.

Off to one side are two cots covered in bright red and white *pareu*-prints, opulent as harem couches with embroidered, appliquéd throw pillows. At one end of the room, a massive, old-fashioned stove reigns. There's a sink, a work table and tropical-style open-front cupboards where no roach can hide. The whole room is almost painfully clean and orderly.

Juliettete makes room for me on the bench at the table. There's no cutlery in sight except for a machete for the bread. There's no silverware, either. Everyone eats with fingers. There's fruit, some sort of meat I can't identify that is probably fish and glass bowls of hot tea. Everything is first dunked in the tea.

'Would you like another cup of coffee?' Pepe asks.

'Tea's fine. Whatever you're having.'

'I no think Americans drink tea.'

She busies herself at the stove, then brings me tea in a china cup with saucer. 'A bowl like yours would do, Pepe. I'm not fancy. You should know that!' There's a tension between us that hadn't existed in California when she visited with a tour group of Islanders. Did ghosts of colonial masters still dictate how Polynesians must treat white guests in the Islands?

'Where's the older lady I saw in the mango tree?' I ask curiously, trying to diffuse the awkwardness.

They look at me strangely. 'What lady?'

'An old lady. She was wearing a purplish dress.'

Pepe raises her eyebrows and says nothing.

I tentatively poke at the wall between us with small talk and jokes. Finally, Pepe, a great *raconteur*, is laughing and chipping away at her side, too. She's outraged over topless beaches and nudity in Tahiti.

'Can you wear the *pareu* downtown now?' I ask.

'Yes! Not just *pareus* but the bikini!'

'I was asked to leave Vaima's downtown in the sixties for wearing a *pareu* as a skirt with a tee shirt. How times have changed!'

'Maybe now you be arrested for wearing too much clothes', she snorted. 'I went to that Club Med on Moorea one time to see a friend. There were two ladies from my own Federation there, beeg, fat, sitting on the beach with their beeg teetees just hanging there, bare! And their husbans were there too! And I ask them, "Do you think that's nice, you sit there, everybody can see your teetees and you all fat and old?" They say, "When you here, you do what everybody else does!"'

Pepe has two passions. One is traveling. The other is her Women's Federation. There are several throughout French Polynesia. In Pepe's, each woman pays about CFP1,000, roughly about US$10 a year plus 10 percent of their crafts sales, which goes into a general fund for maintenance and electricity for their building. If a woman hasn't got the funds to buy materials to make things to sell, according to Pepe, she can borrow up to CFP5,000 from the Federation as long as she repays it in three months. The Federation serves as club and marketing outlet. Hers is one of the largest in French Polynesia.

She escorts me excitedly through the houses to see her wares. There are Cook Islands hats from the atolls, white, soft and flexible, made from *rito*. There are heaps of the less precious *pandanus* hats of Tahiti with high crowns and wonderful shapes, circled with shell headbands of often lavish design. There are rolls of mats, some elaborate and multicolored; bags; woodcarvings; hatbands of fiber flowers and intricate plaiting; fat hassocks upholstered in checked gingham tuckwork piled ceiling-high; appliqués of all sizes from pillow covers to kingsized bedspreads. In addition, there are crocheted tablecloths, lampshades and just about anything the human mind can devise with cloth and fiber except traditional *tapa* or bark cloth. That art had completely died out in Tahiti.

In one week, Pepe's Federation selects their Woman of the Year, who will reign as their queen. This isn't a beauty contest, it's an achievement contest. She's judged on her *tivaevae* and on the quality and quantity of her output of crafts for the year. Pepe's determined to win the crown. Since she lost last year by a narrow margin, she's scarcely stopped working to eat.

'Please, Pepe', I say urgently, 'May I see your main *tivaevae* entry?'

'We no say *tivaevae* here. That Cook Island way. In Tahiti, we say *tifaifai* and I no have time this morning', she says, then seeing my eagerness, she shrugs. 'Okay. If you gotta see it!'

Juliettete takes one end of the long roll of cloth, Frederick the other. Reverently, the three unroll it. The creation leaves the senses reeling. Vivid giant purple orchids fill each corner, reaching toward the center. The design is embellished with embroidery in brilliant colors following every cut of the appliqué, mostly in a fishbone stitch. It's taken three months, even with the help of her nieces. Mama Tixier herself had created the design for Pepe. 'How can anybody compete with this? It's magnificent and it links the finest artists of Rarotonga and Tahiti. You're gonna win!'

Everyone laughs. The girls unroll another *tifaifai* designed by their grandmother and executed by Pepe for the show. This is covered with gigantic red poinsettias. Seeing my enthusiasm is still strong, they show me antique *tifaifais* made by the grandmother of Pepe's late husband. These are not of floral or leaf designs, but patchworks of tiny pieces, meticulously sewn together from scraps of childrens' clothing that had traveled to Tahiti as donations from missionary societies over one hundred years ago. The colors are still surprisingly strong.

Like plants and songs, *tifaifai* patterns travel throughout the islands of Polynesia, interpretations of one culture blending into or changing that of another, until the art would scarcely be recognized by the early missionary women who had so earnestly taught their first converts. Colors lean toward the flamboyant. In the Cook Islands, embroidery embellishments are favored. In Tahiti, emphasis is on strong appliqué design elements. Hawaiians quilt theirs. The creations are seldom made completely by one woman but by many working together. Even so, most take at least a month to complete.

Pepe says a Cook Islands woman revolutionized *tifaifai*-making in Rurutu in the Austral Islands. Marama Rangi Makea of the powerful Makea Ariki dynasty of Rarotonga married a man from Rurutu and went to live there. She took the secret of the patchwork with her, where only flower and leaf motifs were known. Now, according to Pepe, Rurutu women make patchwork *tifaifais*, Cook Island–style with a Rurutu innovation: they sew portraits of people composed of hundreds of tiny patches.

'Enough talk of *tifaifais* and the Federation', says Pepe, rolling up the last design. 'Now, you must get completely out of the way because we have much work. We have guests for dinner tonight.'

'Can I help?'

'Most certainly *not!*'

Tables, chairs, cushions, mats, everything portable is carted out and dumped on the lawn. The houses are scrubbed and polished until every surface, which already gleamed, gleams more. The grounds are pruned and raked. Mountains of food are prepared. I almost run out of places to which I can retreat. In the midst of it all, I am summoned to lunch, and there, magically, on 'my' terrace is stew, French bread, salad and tinned pears. Dinner is a feast of roast beef, roast chicken, string beans, poi, breadfruit, marinated raw fish, pork and cabbage. 'How do you *do* all this in this heat?'

The next morning, after my obvious distress over the white princess treatment, I'm allowed to eat breakfast in the kitchen with the family. Forks materialize. Juliette spears a piece of papaya with one. I ignore mine and pick up a slice of papaya with my fingers. 'E, you have a fork!' Pepe says. 'Use it!' She hands me a special plate. 'This for your bread and butter.' My coffee is stubbornly poured into a little teacup, which is placed on a saucer. The rest of the family dunk big chunks of bread into their wide bowls of coffee, sugar and milk. I try to follow suit with my little cup. Coffee sloshes over into the saucer. 'See!' I point out the mess I'm making to Pepe. She ignores me.

The next day, everyone has forks. My rejection of them is viewed as patronizing. 'We all eat like "civilized" Europeans!' Pepe's decree is absolute. She's probably borrowed the silverware from her Federation. Obviously, I'm getting to be a real pain in the neck.

That week for Pepe and her family was one of ceaseless labor starting just before sunrise. Juliette and Frederick have jobs downtown, she in a bank, he in the post office, but they work with their mother every spare minute. Pepe goes from project to project. When she tires of one, she picks up another. Sometimes she crochets, sometimes she embroiders with her work stretched tight in a large embroidery hoop, glasses low on her nose, seated on the floor crosslegged on mats she's woven. One afternoon, everyone works on 'my' terrace, including Frederick, cutting and tying fringe on a white double bedspread Pepe has crocheted. I am not allowed to help. Sometimes Pepe irons, standing in her carport to catch a breeze, sweat streaming down her weathered face. When she isn't working toward the show, she's raking, sweeping, burning leaves and cooking.

In the evenings, we get together and swap adventures, solve world problems or come to grips with our histories. Sometimes Pepe talks of Makatea days, a harsh life of endless toil and nothing but tinned food to eat on that sweltering, denuded island.

'What happened when the phosphate petered out?'

'The people left', says Pepe. 'Some got work at the bomb tests at Moruroa and Hao.'

'Did you?'

'No, I go to my husband's land on Tahiti.'

'That's good. I think nuclear bomb tests are the worst thing that's ever happened to the Pacific!'

A flash of anger darkens Pepe's eyes. 'If they not got the bomb, where the people work? We go to school now. We eat the white bread. We want to wear nice clean clothes, work in the office and drive cars like you people.'

'But Pepe', I interrupt, 'very few Tahitians have office jobs and not that many work on the bomb. Your family is doing very well, but you're the exception. It's mostly the French and other expatriates here who have education and good jobs. Tahitians have slums!'

'Whole world has slums!'

'You never had them before in Tahiti. The bomb made those slums. People left their land in the Outer Islands to come here to work, but when the construction was finished, there was no more work. They got hooked on the excitement and stayed, you know that! They didn't have land to grow food or make shelters and they didn't have trees to make boats to go fishing. There are no slums in the Cook Islands, Tonga, Samoa, Niue, no place in Polynesia except for Tahiti! You call that progress?' Disregarding all niceties, I pounded the table. 'This is the only European colony left in the Pacific. All the rest of the Island groups are running their own affairs. They're doing just fine without European administration *or* the bomb!'

'I don't know about that but everybody must have slums some time!' she claimed angrily. 'What you want us to do? Stay backwards? Dig taro? Lissen this. There was a meeting of all Island chiefs and young boys and these chiefs making the meeting say to these boys, "Go back to our old ways!" And the young boys say, "Okay. But first *you* go home to your own island and plant!" Even the chiefs don't want to do that. The young don't respect what they say anymore. Childrens these days won't even pick up your rubbish. They want to work for money. Everybody wants to work for money. They want clean hands and white shirts like your people have.'

'Okay. But there's no jobs because most of your people don't have enough education or training. Why is that? Has the bomb helped that? And what about cancer? What about pollution? What about contaminated fish? Don't you care about your childrens' health?'

'Fish already poisoned before bomb! One fish, *maito*, black fish, poison. Doctor give you milk, make you throw up. Give you shot. *Rui* fish also poison. You eat, you have to run to doctor, get injection. Iron and rubbish in lagoon make reef go bad for fish.'

'Pepe, where does the iron and contaminated rubbish come from? It's dumped in the lagoon and on the reefs by the military. What about Mangareva? The people can't eat the fish from their lagoon because they've been poisonous since the bomb tests started in 1966. If they do, they get sick with fever, vomiting and they ache all over. Sometimes they get paralyzed. A lot of women there give birth to deformed babies, according to what I've heard. What do you think about that?'

'How you know?'

'I read about it. Scientists from all over the world except France seem to be concerned. What if fish are contaminated with radiation and you eat them? They swim all over, you know. Maybe they swim to Tahiti. Maybe a cancer starts or leukemia. There's no shot for cancer or leukemia.'

Pepe and her family listen intently now.

'How did Marie Mariterangi, the famous singer of the Tuamotus, die? Cancer, right? There's lots more. They go to hospitals in Paris and they never come back.'

'People always die. Maybe they die of cancer before the bomb and nobody knew. Maybe it was always here. There are many bad things in the world these days, but Mel, the French bread is so nice and we don't work so hard. We have television! If we no got bomb, we got *nothing*! No money! No cars! *Nothing*!' She pauses. Her vehement words hang suspended in the hot humid tropical air. 'Television! I almost forgot. My *tifaifai* going to be on television.'

Stumbling over each other, the family breaks into excited Tahitian and pokes at the television set, almost overturning it in their eagerness to turn it on. The timing is perfect. As the picture clears, a newscaster is speaking about the upcoming show in French. Behind him, on display, is Pepe's *tifaifai*. It photographs exquisitely. The camera pans in for a close-up of her orchids. Then it moves to her poinsettia *tifaifai*, dwelling on it lovingly. The president of the Federation is interviewed. Finally, the show closes with close-ups again of Pepe's embroidered orchids.

The next night, the show is hung. Maeva and Luisa have jobs at a nearby resort and can't get the night off. This time, my offer of assistance is accepted.

The Woman's Federation building is one of the few surviving old French colonial-style buildings on rue Paul Gauguin. We wrestle a big mattress upstairs and into the ballroom-size gallery, which takes up the entire second floor. Colorful *tifaifais* are being tacked to walls and screens by small groups of women. Handmade goods are piled in gaudy disarray.

Frederick climbs a ladder, hauling the first of Pepe's masterpieces after him, and I pass thumbtacks. Our display area is officially staked out. We prop up the mattress with carved wooden stools and cover it with cloth of rich turquoise, over which goes the lacy white crocheted bedspread. Next come two hunter green pouf pillows with white crocheted fronts. We step back to admire.

'No. That's wrong!' Pepe says, arms akimbo. The bed is in the wrong place and so is the orchid hanging. Everything must be taken apart and moved.

We dismantle the display and set everything up again in a new arrangement. The artist doesn't like that either. Again, we take the exhibit apart. A younger woman walks in carrying an iron bedstead with her daughter. They pause to eye our half-completed display: mounds of poufs, crocheted fancywork, mats, hats and perfumed soap sachets in baskets of curly ribbons. The two look slightly contemptuous and mince off, noses in air. 'I no say nothing', vows Pepe grimly, fists clenched.

The silent critics put their bed down nearby and pull *tifaifai* after *tifaifai* from a huge bundle. They must have a dozen or more, an astonishing output. The appliqués are childlike vivid posies, crude next to Pepe's meticulous workmanship. The color combinations explode: orange flowers on burgundy, yellow on scarlet, purple on green. They're certainly original and there's a lot of them. I feel a tug of worry.

As more women arrive and set up displays, the room literally glows. They work mostly in silence. Everyone looks exhausted. Finally, mats are piled into a raised dais in the middle of the room and the workers drop gratefully to rest, unconsciously adopting classic Gauguin poses. Like cats, Tahitian women of all ages and builds seem to make their every move and non-move an art. I watch them spellbound, still lifes themselves, more beautiful than all the work they had produced that year.

I had moved to a hotel downtown to take the hostess burden off Pepe's overworked shoulders. Her exhibit hung, I stroll through the dark streets of Papeete, now alone. Cutting down a side street, I come upon a plump woman in a shabby blue and black print dress leaning on the hood of a parked car. A child of about three sprawls on the sidewalk at her feet. They watch a movie on a television set in a shop window. Even though no sound comes through the plate glass, they're so mesmerized, they don't seem to know I'm there.

I pass great mounds of women and children sleeping on mats on the sidewalk, surrounded by bags of flowers and ferns for the morning's *hei* making. A fat old man I passed at 7:30 that morning making *heis* is still making then as I pass at 10 p.m. I wonder if these people are homeless. Men lurk in doorways. There's a menacing air about Papeete I've never felt before. I quicken my pace.

Strolling down the Quai where it's lighter, I buy a skewer of barbecued beef heart from a Tahitian vendor along with a chunk of bread and mustard. At least, I sigh, some of the finer things in life can still be found in poor old upscaled Papeete. He's surrounded by fast food French crepe vendors.

I leave for Rarotonga the next day. I can't wait for the judging because I'm on a business trip now with a schedule to meet. My vacation is over. We pile into the pickup truck: suitcases, cameras, Luisa and Maeva in back; Juliette at the wheel; me in the middle and Pepe beside me in the front seat. Pepe has heaped me with beautiful hats and bags as farewell gifts, then hands me a Johnnie Walker whiskey bottle filled with a cloudy fluid. 'Coconut oil', she says. 'I don't know why I no think of this when I see you scratch and scratch. Put this on you and the mosquito they no can hang on. You take when you go to Rarotonga and Samoa. Lots of mosquito this time of year.'

Curious, I open it and sniff. It has a sweet herbal smell verging on rancid. 'What's in this, Pepe?'

'You grate the coconut meat and put it on the tin roof in the sun. Then you mix it with a little oil from the crab. You leave in the sun and the oil rises. She come out all nice. Then you mix in flowers.'

'God, suppose it breaks on the plane? I'd better hand-carry it', I growl ungratefully. We approach the turn-off to a popular resort hotel. Soldiers with rifles roar by us, swerving down the drive. I glimpse troops on the lawn. 'What's that all about?'

Juliette replies shortly. 'Trouble. Old landowners make demonstration. Want their land back. Too late. Now hotel. Some climb in windows, steal things from tourists. Soldiers there to protect tourists.'

'Some of those soldiers look like Tahitians. Would they shoot their own people?'

She shrugs. 'Tourism is important to us. Gives us jobs. Those radicals, they spoil things for everybody.'

'But was their land stolen from them for the hotel?'

'No', Pepe says. 'They get plenty monies. Now money all finish. They want land back.'

Distracted suddenly by something on the road, Pepe leans out the window. 'You see that?' she shouts. 'That man, hitchhiking? That's against the law!'

'What? Last time I was here, people stopped their cars, their motorcycles, even their bicycles and asked if you wanted a ride if they saw you walking.'

'No more', she said. 'New law. Last month, a tourist got beat up on Moorea and his rental car got stolen by a man he pick up on the road. Government say, "That's it! No more hitchhike. You pick somebody up, he hurt you, it you own fault. You broke the law!"'

I always cry when I leave islands and people I love. My tears this time are for more than the pain of separation. A solicitous flight attendant from New Zealand offers me a pack of tissues, 'You all right?' I blow my nose and nod. He looks amused. 'Once you see Rarotonga, you'll never cry for Tahiti again. It's a real South Seas paradise! Everyone is laid back, always smiling, happy. It's like the whole island is on marijuana!'

I try to call Pepe from Rarotonga the next day but can't get through. I write but there's no answer. I write again from California weeks later. Nothing. A year later, I finally learn the outcome of the Woman's Federation competition. I get a postcard from Pepe. It's from Paris, from the Woman of the Year – Pepe, the Queen of Tahiti.

## 11

# LIFE OF AN ARIKI

Thousands attended state funeral services for Pa Tepaeru-a-Tupe Ariki Lady Davis on 9 February 1990 on Rarotonga in the Cook Islands. Business and government offices closed for the day as the country went into mourning. It was the first time in history a state funeral of such magnitude had been held. Although Pa did not rule an entire country but only the district of Takitumu on Rarotonga, she was one of the most extraordinary hereditary queens of the South Pacific.

She was a woman of paradox, courageous, headstrong and humble. Her first years were spent at the lowest village subsistence level. She bore nine children and worked as a private secretary before assuming her royal duties, divorced, and scandalized the island's gossips with her dancing til all hours in the local night spots. She was threatened with exile for her religious beliefs, married a prime minister, led her people in an unprecedented rebellion against an invasive tourist resort plan perpetrated by her husband, suffered physical abuse for her convictions and died with the secret of how the prime minister (now a Knight of the British Empire) came to be slashed so grievously about the ear, chest and groin that it took numerous stitches and ten days for him to recover. Between crises, she also managed to have a glamorous life, calling on royal and political leaders worldwide with her husband, who like leaders of most Third World countries, spent an inordinate amount of time seeking funding and loans for all the twentieth-century frills that island ministates can't buy with coconuts and fish.

I first met her in 1979. I was on Rarotonga hoping to make connections with a boat to Pukapuka for some research on the late author Robert Dean Frisbie. It's easier to meet a queen than it is to get to Pukapuka.

On the island of Rarotonga, it's almost impossible to keep a secret. The place is only some nineteen miles around with about 9,000 people, of whom less than half are adults, who watch each other when they aren't watching the children. This is pretty easy since everyone has been settled in coastal villages since the missionaries rounded them up from the mountains and valleys and placed them there to keep an eye on them in the nineteenth century. There wasn't much to watch in the 1970s except each other, anyway, since there was neither TV nor video and only a modest trickle of strangely dressed tourists.

People of power are adept at secret coups. Thus it came to pass that the country's controversial new premiere, Dr Tom Davis, managed a secret wedding right under everyone's noses. What made this even more incredible was that the bride was a hereditary queen, one of the most powerful chiefs in the Cook Islands. She was the forty-seventh person to hold the title of Pa Ariki and the first one since the nineteenth century to be a non-Christian. Pa was a Baha'i and the pair had actually been married in a Baha'i ceremony. It was a second marriage for both.

This was a stunning bundle of news to dump on the grateful people of Rarotonga, who hadn't had anything this juicy for years.

The ramifications of such a union were fascinating. A queen, a real Queen Elizabeth kind of Royal Highness Queen and a man who was his country's equivalent of the British Prime Minister. This premier was rather exotic in his own right. A medical doctor, born on Rarotonga and educated in New Zealand, he spent twenty years of his career in research in the US working for NASA in the space program and for Arthur B. Little in the US Food and Drug Administration. This did not exactly make him a hero in a country with an acute shortage of local doctors, plus, he had forgotten more of his Cook Islands Maori language than he ever knew. He was not Premiere by election, but by default: as the runner-up, he had unseated the winner on a legal technicality.

I asked my landlady, a half-Mangaian, New Zealand–bred woman I'll call Miri, for suggestions as to how I could arrange an audience with her majesty for an interview.

'Why, just ring her up and ask her', Miri said.

'Just like that? Ring up a queen?'

'Of course. She won't mind.'

'Do you have her phone number?'

'You don't need phone numbers here. Just ring up the operator and say you want to talk to Pa Ariki out at Takitumu.'

She showed me to the public telephone in the courtyard gardens of her little motel, set in the jungle at the base of an imposing weathered volcanic cliff face. The phone was about the size of a small satchel.

'Where's the dial?' I asked in puzzlement.

'You just turn that handle there', she said.

I did. Nothing happened.

'Here, turn it hard and fast like this several times.'

I cranked and cranked, sweating in the hot sun. Finally, a Rarotongan operator, sounding as if she had better things to do than answer the silly phone, came on the line. Apologizing for disturbing her, I asked if she'd be so good as to ring up Pa Ariki.

'Pa Ariki', she said. 'Pa, out Takitumu way?'

'Yes. The queen.'

Dead silence followed.

'What's the matter?' asked Miri. 'No answer?'

'I guess that's what's happening', I said.

'Oh well, not to worry. Try later.'

After the third try, the operator showed mild interest. 'Oh, I remember now. They're off the island visiting Aitutaki, I think. They should be back about six.'

Hot and tired from a day of hiking about, I finally reached her about 6:15 p.m. It was Friday, 4 May 1979. It was unreal, standing barefoot in a jungly garden in a *pareu* and an old sweaty shirt, cranking an unmarked phone, hoping to reach a secretary or an aide to a queen to request an interview. She answered the phone herself. Stunned, I almost forgot why I'd called. Then, hoping I sounded more professional than I seemed, I told her I would like to interview her.

'Yes', she said thoughtfully. 'I would be glad to talk to you, but tomorrow is not possible. I must do the family shopping. What is it you want to interview me about?'

I did a double take. This powerful *ariki* who had just wed her nation's leader was going to do the marketing? Stifling my incredulity, I plunged ahead: 'I would like your views on the status of women in the Cook Islands from your perspective both as queen and – now that you've married the premiere – as first lady.'

There was a roaring silence. It dragged on until finally the operator broke in with: 'Working?'

'Yes', said Pa from her end. 'We're still using the line.' She was silent a while longer, then finally responded: 'I do not mind being addressed as "queen" but I do object to the "first lady". I did not have to marry a politician to become a first lady. I was *born* a first lady!'

Barbara Walters, I said to myself. You will never have competition from me, ever! I will get a job in the tuna cannery in Samoa, hosing entrails off the floor. She seemed unperturbed by the silence on my end. 'How do you propose to get out to Takitumu if we meet on Monday?' she asked.

'Taxi, I guess', I mumbled.

'Taxi? Oh no!' she said. 'I'll pick you up. You're at the Hibiscus Court, are you? I must go to Avarua Monday morning anyway. Taxis are very expensive.'

I had just been reprimanded by a queen for grossly improper address. Now the lady didn't want me to have to pay for a cab. I decided this was either going to be the greatest interview of my life or I was about to be deported, since beheading was not in fashion.

Pa arrived promptly Monday morning in the premier's chauffeur-driven Cadillac Coupe de Ville, the only Cadillac on the island. She was tall, slim, vital: dark hair swept back off her strong Polynesian face, a large yellow and white *frangipani* over one ear. Her brown eyes sparkled with amusement as they met mine. She glowed with the serenity of one who knows exactly who she is, a shimmer of amusement in her eyes, probably in acknowledgement of the havoc she could wreak with her candor. Despite a humble and kindly façade, she impressed me as one who could be dangerous if crossed. History-making events soon to come would validate this impression. I was immediately drawn to her.

On this first interview, she wore American western clothes, a blue denim jacket over a long-sleeved, faded blue shirt with a denim skirt. Her only jewelry was a handsome blister pearl ring and a pendant, a starburst of gold and small baroque pearls suspended from a chain. I admired it. She made a small grimace. 'I'm not the first woman Tom's given this to.'

Before I could encourage more on this provocative subject, she changed it to one that really disturbed her. 'What gave you the impression I had to marry somebody to *be* somebody?' she asked sternly as the incongruous luxury car picked its way along the semi-paved road around coconuts and potholes the size of bomb craters. 'There is only one role in my life: that of *ariki*. I was born an *ariki*. I have always considered "first lady" as a political title, and I stand neutral as far as politics are concerned. That is not to say that I close my eyes to what is happening. As for the people as a whole, I have the greatest interest in their welfare, but being a first lady because of politics, I consider that an insult! I have always considered being an *ariki* as being a first lady. That is traditional. I am born to it.'

We drove nearly halfway around Rarotonga before we turned inland. Though that represents only about nine miles, with a thirty-five mile-an-hour speed limit on a fifteen to twenty mile-an-hour road, it was a leisurely trip of some thirty minutes. Finally, we turned inland onto a well-maintained track through fields, lush with food crops, bordered with trees. The ever-changing, mist-trailing volcanic peaks made a brooding, mysterious backdrop.

An anachronism reared up in a clearing before us, a large, A-frame chalet, modern, airy with lots of glass.

'Is this your palace?'

'No. This is Dr Davis's house. His private home.'

'Ah, then it's the premiere's official residence?'

'No', she said patiently. 'This is not the premiere's residence. That's in Avarua. This is his private house.'

Inside, the house itself was so unobtrusive, the windows so large, one couldn't be sure where it left off and the lush tropical gardens began. The living room flowed into a dining area separated by a counter from a modern open kitchen. Bedroom lofts over the living room were connected by a catwalk. Pa pushed buttons on the stereo system and traditional Cook Islands music flowed softly, adding life to the almost spartan room with its collection of island arti-facts, fine mats, baskets, dance skirts and shell necklaces.

She stepped out back and shouted a name. 'I don't know where that girl has gone', she said, returning to the kitchen. 'Would you like some coffee?' She scooped instant Nestlé's from a tin. 'Do you like it strong?'

'May I?' I asked, belatedly rushing to help. I felt decidedly strange about a queen making coffee for the likes of me, but the job was finished in an instant and she had cups, cream and sugar already on a tray. We settled down then in the living room and I set up my tape recorder for an interview with a real South Seas queen as never played by Dorothy Lamour.

My faux pax loomed like a cockroach on an operating table. She smacked it again. 'My people have *always* considered me not only their *ariki* but their first lady, too.' She tucked her long legs under her skirt on the soft, overstuffed chair. 'They consider it an *insult* that I should be called the first lady because Lady Henry, the wife of the first premiere, was one because of [her husband's posi-tion] and they couldn't understand why I, as an *ariki*, should become one be-cause of politics! I wasn't flattered at all. I felt it was an insult to the things that I believe and the things my people believe. *They* felt insulted to think that I should be called a first lady because of politics.

'He [her husband] understands. He said to me, "Please, don't tell the lady that you are insulted being my wife." He was so concerned. He said, "Look. I *am* the premier and it is only a natural thing that people will think that you are the first lady because of me."'

'Do you work with your husband?' I tried to distract her and dispose of the carcass of my overkilled gaffe.

'We both work together', she said, accepting the offering of a new subject. 'If I have a problem concerning my people ... I must go to the government to get satisfaction for my people. We will talk about it, but I have never, at any time, interfered in the governing of the people.

'My husband is there to govern ... the best way he can to the best of his ability. ... As I said, I can only play one role, being an *ariki* – being queen.'

The couple's roles were on a collision course, however, and a day would come when they'd clash with bloody results.

'You make official appearances with him, don't you?'

'Yes, as president of the House of *Ariki* [similar to the House of Lords in England]. I make official calls on the people ... as Pa Ariki, not as his wife.'

'What do you call him?'

'I address him as the premiere of the Cook Islands in front of people. I do not call him Dr Davis or Tom.'

'And how does he address you?'

'By my title, as Pa Ariki.'

'Was his rank below yours before your marriage? I read that your *kopu ariki* or royal family has now bestowed a special title on him.'

'It's protocol to do so, the same as that of Queen Elizabeth. When she married Prince Phillip, she made him the Duke of Edinburgh. We do the same thing.' She explained that her people of Takitumu bestowed the title of Pa Tu-te-Rangi Ariki on him in accepting him as part of the family. 'We are equals.'

'Is your role as an *ariki* very hectic?'

'Yes, it is. I am expected to do such a lot for my people. We have a council in Takitumu. This is a traditional thing composed of the thirty-five chiefs of the district. They may want me to hear what they have to say and make comments. I attend the meetings. It could be once a month, twice a month, three times a month, depending on what it is. It could be something to do with agriculture. It could be something to do with education. It could be the general welfare of the people. It could be child welfare ... personal matters.'

'What do you do besides listen?'

'Well, depending on what the problem is ... if it's educationwise, then we put it in the hands of the minister of education. This is the government's business. We could talk about land that could be cultivated ... We ask people that they plant their earth for their own good ... We are agriculturists here... this is where we get our money. Not everybody ... has a job ... these people who have no jobs ... till the land. They work very hard ... Certainly, we have those people who are just lazy, and they are poor because they don't do anything about it. It's impossible for you to show any kind of sympathy because they are well-built people that can do these things. You have this kind of people in your country?'

I nodded.

'So you encourage them', she continued with spirit. 'You have to do it in such a way that you do not offend them. You talk to them, you tell them reasons why these things have to be done.'

'Can your council override your decisions?'

She flicked assent with her eyebrows and said, '[They] can override my decisions if they put it to a vote. We are democratic. But, if I find that I am right, then my decision is final. I always give them the right to say what they want to say and maybe my ideas are too modern ... too far ahead for the Cook Islands. I'm always willing to come down and meet them all the way, so I let their decision override mine because it makes them happy.'

'Have you ever had to override their decision?'

'Yes.'

'What was the issue? Can you think of one?'

'There's so many, I really can't. So many. Yes. And they know that I am right.'

I managed, with great effort, not to call her on her contradiction. 'Are most of the chiefs men?'

'Men and women. There is always equality.'

'Do you have many Cook Islands women in professions?'

'Oh yes, men and women do whatever they want to.'

'How does a professional woman work it out with her home life? Is her husband the traditional breadwinner and does she traditionally take care of the children? Or do they share roles?'

'They share. They would have family help – the grandmother. The grandparents play a very important part in our lives. We cannot think of putting our grandparents into a home. That's an insult, to us, to think that we cannot look after our own people. So they are at home. They love their grandchildren. It doesn't matter where we go, we take our grandparents with us.

'If I was the premiere's wife and a doctor and if Dr Davis is a doctor, I will be the doctor and he will be the premiere. It does not interfere with our home. Both of us are interested in our own profession. I don't mean to say the lady is not interested in her family. It doesn't matter how professional she is, she still has so much time for her family.'

'And this is because the grandparents take care of the children and do all the housework?'

'No', she said patiently. 'We [women] do all our housework before we go to work.'

'Even you, a queen?'

'Oh yes.'

'But you do have a staff?'

'Oh yes, but I like doing these kinds of things. Mind you, I've never done them before. But I'm learning and I like it. I'm a lousy cook. I have other people cooking. They're not my servants, they are my people and, okay, I'm learning. And it's interesting. I don't know how my husband could survive on my cooking. He's a beautiful cook himself. He would never starve if I'm not here.'

'Tell me about the House of *Ariki*. You said you are the president?'

'Yes. The House of *Ariki* is composed of all the high chiefs of all the Cook Islands. We are based on the House of Lords of England and we elect a president every year. We are, by law, part of the Constitution of the Cook Islands. This is the only country where the royal family is included in the Constitution, Pacificwise. We do not make law, but we can question the government if they've said [something] in the Assembly that we did not like. And the Assembly can submit to us for our consideration, any subject they think that we should know before they make it law. This has been in operation since we became a self-determined government.

'We have to hold a meeting within a year. We can have a meeting every week, literally. So you get the views of the Outer Island *Arikis*, they come together and present to the meeting all of the problems of their islands. And we accordingly submit them to the government for their consideration and recommendation.

'We try to get our business over within two or three months when we get all the *arikis* together because they have to return home. We have a meeting every other day, giving time for the clerk and typist to get our minutes together ... all typed up and sent back to us.

'We each pay homage to the other as *ariki* and we stand on equal status, not one of us above the other. Each island has its own subchiefs, too, and they're all royal family. Each one of us has a duty to perform and we do it according to our best ability.

'Most certainly we make mistakes. Even kings and queens make mistakes. But, by doing so, we learn. It's always your people that are your first concern. My [Takitumu] people are my first concern. I honestly believe that they are God's trust in my hands. They come first. I deprive myself of practically everything so my people can be happy. I really do. ... To be an *ariki*, you do have to humble yourself. I do. I'm not talking about the rest of the *arikis*, ma'am, just myself. I come down to other people's level to be able to learn how my people live. I am a queen and I know this, but a queen without her people is nothing.

'Some of my people live in an appalling state. But they are so happy. They're not poor because they're lazy. No. If my people can live like that and smile right through their life, I call that noble. I pay a tribute to my people – to their nobility – to be able to live like that. They don't grumble. They don't say anything. They're happy.

'My people are sophisticated enough, ma'am, to be able to accept what they have. They live a very simple life, knowing full well they have to work to be able to survive. And they have accepted what God has given them for free: their land, what they can get out of the sea, the trees, the air they breathe in, the beauty of

their country, their district, the beauty of their flowers, the beauty of everything. My people are taught always to look for the beauty in everything. This
alone makes them happy that they can see the beauty and disregard the sordid-
ness of things ... The unpleasant things of life will always happen. You can never
solve them. The only way I can solve that kind of thing is to be happy with my
people and to come down to their level and to be able to live like them.

'I will give you a story about myself. My grandfather had ... beautiful plans.
He brought me up in the most primitive ways, where you only have an iron bar
on a stone to boil a billy can of water, and we just ate out of coconut shells, off
of leaves, you know. We have an earth oven where we cook everything. We
would just sit around it. I enjoyed it. I was brought up this way. There was a
reason for it, ma'am. If I did not know how my people lived, as young as I was,
I would never know how to live in a palace. My first lesson was: Learn to live
like my people.

'They lived in thatched houses; we slept on mats on the dirt floor. I never
had any toys, ma'am. My grandfather couldn't afford it, so we made do with
what we can. We used to make our own tops. You know the empty tins of bully
beef? We just nailed them on a thin stick and we'd run and use them as a train
or car. We used to use the very young coconut for a ball and we had seeds like
marbles and we played marbles.

'Rice and flour used to come in a calico sack and my underclothes were
made of those. That's the way my people lived. The simplicity of it! They were
not unhappy.'

'Where were your parents during this period?'

'My father died when I was four months old. Then my mother remarried.
My mother never brought me up, my grandparents did.'

'Was that because you were an *ariki*?

'Yes, and I am an only child from my father. My father was an only child.'

'Then it was his parents who raised you?'

'I'm referring to my father's uncle. He was an *ariki*. His name was
Makea'nui Tinirau Ariki of Avarua. He brought me up when my father died,
and I have always referred to him as my grandfather (and his wife as my grandmother). They are the only grandparents I know, and ma'am, he was king, and
at the same time, he was also a human being, understanding what it was like,
the lifestyle of his people.'

'Why was he so poor if he was king?'

'He was not poor, but this is the way he lived. We were not poor in the
sense that we starved. My grandfather was an agriculturist. He was also a great
fisherman. As I said, we all worked, even though we were royal. We had to. My
grandfather ... was the greatest planter in Rarotonga and the greatest fisher-

man. Of course, he enjoyed the work. He was not just sitting in council all the time. He couldn't stand it. He was a hard-working man. He loved the soil.

'I was not spoiled. I was, and yet, was not. He didn't give me toys to play with like grandparents normally do, but he gave me enough food to eat. That meant more to him than giving me royal toys. I never had toys. I never had birthdays. My grandfather thought it was just a waste of time. I had to be taught the simplicity of life, so when I came back home here, nobody had to teach me. I already knew.'

'Were you educated here or in New Zealand?'

'Locally. I had my finishing school in New Zealand.'

'Have you ever had a job?'

'Yes ... about thirty, thirty-five years ago, I worked for the Government as a secretary and then I worked for a firm as a private secretary. I enjoyed that work.'

'That was when you came back to the Cook Islands to assume your role of Pa Ariki?'

'Yes. I was right about twenty-two. The people in Takitumu, they were my uncles, my aunties, my grand-uncles, my grand-aunties, they waited to see what I was going to do because I was just fresh from New Zealand. And they said, "We'll just let her make all the mistakes." They weren't about to help me. They were going to let me stew in my own juice until I learned the right way, ma'am. They just let me go on and finally, they made the roll. [She clapped sharply.] "Young lady, sit there and you'd better listen!" They were people in their late sixties, seventies, eighties, nineties. They waited for me.

'These were the wise people of my land. They were not educated like you and I, but they were educated in their own culture. They believed if you did not know your culture, it's no use your coming here and telling them about some-body else's. They were not ready to accept it. They wanted to see what a fresh one from New Zealand [would do] ... they let me make all the mistakes.'

'Did you make many?'

'I certainly did, ma'am, I certainly did.'

'What was the worst thing you ever did?'

'The worst thing that I did was to tell them that I was queen, that I did not want to be disobeyed, that what I said was law. So they [snaps her fingers sharply] brought me down to their level. "Young lady, you do not give orders like that!' So I sat, ma'am."

She stared into space for awhile in silence. 'I didn't let my education from New Zealand fly out the window. I kept it. Education never stops, ma'am. It goes forward. So what do you do? I accepted what they had to give me because it meant so much. This is the foundation of everything that they had.

'At the same time, they forgot they have young people who are educated. They're not going to think the same way they did. ... You try to point out to them that they have to think of children who are going to grow up someday to be the leaders of this country and those yet to be born. The destiny of these people lay in their hand.

'They cannot always ask us to live on tradition or on custom. Tradition yes, custom no. 'They have to change to suit the time and the education of the people themselves because, as you know, the education today has gone so far ahead, we are inclined sometimes to forget who we are. You have to know who you are, what you're doing and where you are going. This is the Polynesian way.

'When you put tradition and custom aside, ma'am, you must be prepared to replace it with something better, not only for the people around you, but for the benefit and the welfare of the Cook Islands people. We have children who have gone overseas for their education and come home and they are trying to work for their own people.

'They say, "Oh, you're old-fashioned!" That's rude, as you know. It's not your money or your clothes that maketh a man, it's your manners. There's nothing worse than for us to be rude to our people, especially when they know what they're talking about.

'Most certainly we have to make changes, but we're not going to make them that fast that we don't know where we're going. We cannot afford to rush into it ... and make a lot of mistakes and be sorry afterwards. We can't. You think about it, talk about it ... you ask the advice of people who are aware of agriculture or fishing ... You get these people to advise.'

'I was interested to read in the press that your faith is Baha'i. My paternal grandmother was a Baha'i.'

'Oh, how beautiful! Yes, I've been a Baha'i for ten years. I didn't go blindly into it, ma'am, I really didn't. It took me six years to study this. It went against the grain of my family, but they're all right now. They've accepted it. Yes, ma'am, I stood my ground. It has given me insight into so many things. ... If I was to choose between being a Baha'i and being an *ariki*, I'd give up the title, because it is immaterial. It's just for a day.'

'How did you ever hear about this exotic religion?'

'Two pioneers came down here, a Mrs Dyer from New Zealand and a Mrs Danielson from America. They invited all the *arikis* to an afternoon tea and I was the only one who attended. They asked me to become their translator and interpreter. In those days, there was no [government religious] restriction at all. Everybody was so happy about this, but unfortunately, politics crept into everything, even religion, so we were banned by law.

'Only four denominations were recognized by the Cook Islands government: Seventh Day Adventist, Mormon, Cook Islands Christian Church and Catholic. This government has removed the restrictions.'

'Well, what in the world could they do to you?'

'They could make quite an issue to remove me from this island!'

'Exile you, an *ariki?*'

'Yes, ma'am. They could have, but it would have caused an upheaval ... One of the ministers said to me: "Pa Ariki, you really have to do something about being a Baha'i. Your people are very angry with you." I said, "If my people ask me to give up being a Baha'i or leave the country, I'll leave the country", and he looked at me, and I said, "I mean it!"'

'My people [held] a meeting [and said]: "Young lady, your ancestors accepted the Gospel" and all this kind of thing and I said "Yes, they had their reasons and I've got mine. What are you asking me? Give it up? I would rather give you up. If you ask me to give the title up and leave the country or give up being a Baha'i, I'd leave the country." And they looked at me, because ma'am, they knew I meant it.

'My auntie, she sticks to protocol and etiquette. This is the other queen, Makea. She was very angry. You see, we pay her the greatest respect because she is old. We never go above her. No, I come down. She was given the K.B.E. by the queen of England for services rendered to her country. She said to me, "I don't like you being Baha'i, it's against our family tradition."

'I said, "You don't know what it is, how can you judge? Until such time as you are willing to let me tell you, then you can judge."'

'As I understand it', I said, 'it's a relatively new faith, founded in Persia, made up of elements of all major religions. Isn't its basic message unity – one people, one world?'

She nodded emphatically. 'It's no threat to anybody. It doesn't conflict with anybody else's religion or try to make converts.'

'As an *ariki* and now, wife of the premier, aren't you expected to make sort of a public show of attending Christian church on Sunday? How do you handle that?'

'I told my people, "Very well, I will attend the churches",' she smiled conspiratorially. 'What I do, ma'am, I say: "Lord Jesus Christ, this is *your* house. Please open the eyes of your people to see the truth." What else can I say as a Baha'i?' she laughed. 'Then I sit through [services] and I don't hear a thing. Every church I attend, Catholic, you name them, that's the only way I can take it.

'You know why I became a Baha'i? ... I was always the elite. I was a fashion center. One day, I opened a Baha'i book and one line spoke aloud: "Powers of kings and ecclesiastics will be removed." Well, I looked through the book and I'm told that all of the other kings and queens of the world have been removed because they did not believe and the only one that survived was Queen Victoria ... she lived the longest, sixty years as queen.

'Look around the world. How many kings and queens have you got living, ma'am? Even in the Cook Islands. These people have been removed because they misused, abused their beautiful word that God gave them. They want more power. My grandfather said to me when he was about eighty, "Come here. Another lesson! You listen to me. You go that far and no more."

'I thought and I thought and so one day, I said, okay, you win, you tell me.

'He said "Everything you have, my dear, as queen, God put it here. If you want to know what's there, step over there. You'll find there's nothing. When you come back again, you'll find you've lost everything. Everything that God made for you as an *ariki*, you've got it here. There's so many *arikis* who are power crazy. So they step over the line. When they turn around to come back, what they had was taken away. They were not satisfied with what they were supposed to have. Can you see the lesson in that? Don't you *ever* overstep the line!"

'As a Baha'i, I started thinking about it and it was true. Look around the world today. You see so many of these rulers. Their people are starving. There's food to share. An uncle said to me, "You're supposed to share what you have because God gave it to you to share. He didn't give it to you for yourself."'

'Your husband is a Christian like most Cook Islanders. Didn't he resist having a Baha'i wedding?'

'I *insisted* on a Baha'i ceremony. If the premiere of the Cook Islands and his ministers and the people concerned were not going to allow me to have a Baha'i ceremony, ma'am, I would *never* marry the premiere. But he knows about my being a Baha'i and he said, "I think that's beautiful", and I said: "(A Baha'i ceremony) *before* the other one!"' She laughs, 'So we had a Baha'i ceremony.'

'This was a second marriage for you both, but I read somewhere that you were betrothed as children?'

'Yes, but he went his way and I went mine. But we have always been the greatest of friends. We've always been very close, very close indeed. And we have always gone flying to each other if we have trouble of any kind – especially, I do.'

Looking at her watch, Pa gasps. She has a luncheon appointment in town with the premiere and visitors. I offer to call a cab but she says no, orders the car and we continue the interview en route.

'Who will your title go to?' I ask curiously.

'It depends. I have nine children by my previous marriage. Being an *ariki* has so many demands. My children are educated in New Zealand and they've become accustomed to the New Zealand way of life. I'm not quite sure which of them would be able to take the title. It's time-consuming and it's challenging.'

She switched to small talk. 'What are your plans while you're here?'

I told her of my frustration in learning there would be no interisland boat to Pukapuka for two months. 'I've booked deck passage on the *Mataora* for its five-day cargo run of the Southern Cooks beginning with Aitutaki as a sort of a compromise', I said.

On impulse, I asked her advice on appropriate swimming attire for female visitors. She confirmed what I'd heard about the Outer Islands.

'We go into the sea fully clothed.'

'In a *pareu*?'

'*Pareu* or dress. I go swimming in a dress.'

'Isn't that hard to swim in?'

'Oh, we don't swim. We just paddle around. When we go into the water, we go for food and to cool off.'

'What's the reason for going into the water fully clothed? Missionary laws from the old days?'

'Yes, I suppose so. Our old people would never have accepted the swimsuit. It is not a thing that you parade around to be stared at.'

'In other words, it might be a problem if tourists in the Outer Islands wore bathing suits.'

'It's okay in Aitutaki because they have a hotel there. In Mitiaro, though, they wear dresses when they go in the sea. That's a beautiful island. Beautiful people. You must visit Mitiaro', she said.

We parted at the restaurant, but a relationship had begun that would continue intermittently until her sudden death, eleven years later.

## 12

# DAMN YOU, ROBERT DEAN FRISBIE

Shuddering, protesting, the old cargo ship plunged through the pass in the reef to grapple once again with the turbulent southern ocean beyond. I leaned against the rail and gazed ahead with the eyes of the veteran romantic. Somewhere out there, strewn over hundreds of miles of lonely, moody Pacific, lay the fouteen Outer Islands of the Cook group like bits of litter carelessly dropped millions of years ago by picnicking tikis. I whispered their names like an incantation: Aitutaki, Manuae, Mangaia, Atiu, Mauke, Mitiaro, Takutea, Manihiki, Pukapuka, Penrhyn, Palmerston, Rakahanga, Nassau, Suwarrow. Oh God, to see them all, especially Pukapuka, some 700 miles distant.

Did its lagoon still mirror the stars as it did when Robert Dean Frisbie courted young Ngatokorua-a-Mataa, then drank and wrote his life away? Did the memories of their children, Whiskey Johnny, Hardpan Jake, Alkalai Ike and little Nga, still live on in these isles for which their father gave up America, the land of his birth? Had they ever returned?

Salt spray misted my 'intrepid-explorer' sunglasses as Rarotonga's volcanic spires shrank in our wake. The ship pitched and reared. Seas foamed by, now swollen and troubled. I could still taste the bitterness of the seasick pill I'd gulped ten minutes earlier without water. Suddenly, I felt feverish. My face was sweating, breathing, shallow. Then I knew.

'Oh *shit!*' I screamed in disbelief against the wind. Dizzy, unable to stand, I sank to the deck, snatched the glasses from my streaming face and thrust my head between the rails. Too late the seasick pill, too old the dream. Weeping, furious, wretched and retching, I cursed my inadequate body.

I was alone among strangers (nine passengers, four pigs and a crew), reduced from an omnipotent 'Frisbie' to a middle-aged lady on a storm-crazed sea.

I curled up miserably on the filthy deck of the interisland freighter *Mataora*. Cheek on the lower rail, I stared at the driving rain that now hid the mountains of Rarotonga.

Someone poked my shoulder. I swiveled my eyes, afraid to move my queasy body. Knees. I saw bony knees, bulging from a pair of sunburnt legs covered with heavy fuzz.

'You oughta be on the other side of the ship, luv', said a voice above the knees. The twang was Cockney; the tone, bossy. 'You stay on this side, the diesel fumes'll make you sick.'

'Well, what the hell do you think I am now?'

'Aw, you're not sick, luv. You just need to get away from the diesel fumes.' The legs moved away. 'Go on, now', the words nagged on the wind, 'get yourself over on the other side.'

Weakly, I hauled myself to a standing position and fumbled with my glasses. The sun was already setting somewhere in the steamy gray sky. Flung here and there, grabbing at railings, lurching through open space, I struggled to the port side. He was right. The air was better. I inhaled deeply. A pair of Islanders stood nearby, leaning against the bulkhead, laughing.

'There we are, luv', chirped that damned voice behind me again. 'I see you took me advice.'

I barely had time to glimpse my tormentor's face before another spasm brought me to the deck and I was hanging over the bottom rail again. I had caught just a flash of a whimsical mug – thirtyish, rosy-cheeked, topped by dark curly hair. He was repugnantly cheerful and healthy.

'You really shouldn't sit on the deck. It's filthy, you know', he said, hunkering down near me. 'Where are you headed?'

'I can't stand up', I moaned and stuck my head overboard again.

'You didn't mention where you're going', he persisted as soon as my head was back inside the railing again.

'Just around', I said, wiping my face with a melting tissue, not looking at him. I wondered why on earth he was trying to talk to me at a time like that. Couldn't he see?

'Oh, you mean you're on for the whole five-day circuit, are you? Aitutaki, Atiu, Mitiaro, then back to Raro?' He made them sound like the next three stations on the London tube.

'Yes', I panted, 'but I don't think I'm going to make it. Not in this storm.'

'Oh, you'll make it, all right. You ever read any of those books about the South Seas by Frisbie?'

Shocked, I really looked at him for the first time. This jerk read Frisbie?

'Are you kidding? How do you know about him?' I was incredulous, a tad condescending.

'Oh', he crowed, 'I'm a regular expert on Frisbie, I am.'

'Me too', I said, stunned. 'There aren't many of us around! I may be writing a book about him soon.'

'Oh, so you're a writer, are you? You look like a schoolteacher.'

Before I could debate the typecasting, I left him for another close look at the waves.

'You ever read that one, *Island of Desire*?' he rattled on as if I were a normal person with a clean face sitting on a bench in London's Hyde Park.

'Why are you talking to me?' I asked. 'I can't talk now. I can hardly sit up. I'd like to discuss Frisbie with you, but I am dying!'

'You ought to read that one', he went on as if he hadn't heard me. 'You think *this* is a bad storm – he tells about this *hurricane* on one of those islands ...'

'Suwarrow', I filled in weakly.

'Oh, so you know it. Suwarrow. Right. And he had his little children with him and he tied them up in the trees ...'

'*Tamanu* trees', I whispered, faintly.

'Well, I don't know what kind of trees, luv, but the storm was so bad, it blew down everything but those trees. Wiped out the whole bloody island, it did.'

The power of true fanaticism can run the mouth, even though the body is nine-tenths dead, especially if there's a chance of scoring. 'Yes', I half-whispered. 'That was his masterpiece, as far as I'm concerned. Nobody on earth ever wrote a scarier hurricane sequence in the history of literature. No one!'

'Oh, then you did read that one, did you?'

'Read it? I've read and *own* all his books and his daughter Johnnie's. It's taken me years to find them all.' I looked at him triumphantly out of the corner of my eye.

He almost sat back on the dirty deck. It was very satisfying, even to a dying South Seas adventuress. 'All of them? You even have *Puka-Puka*?'

'*The Book of Puka-Puka*? Of course I have it', I said grandly.

'I wonder, luv, can you try to locate any for me if I give you a list?' he asked, but I was throwing up again. He waited, a little impatient now, fingers drumming the rail.

'How can you stand to be around someone who's throwing up all the time?' I asked. 'It's indecent!'

'Oh, I'm used to it', he shrugged. 'Most of me chums do it when they first go to sea. Not me, though. I've never been seasick in me life!'

'What do you do, anyway?' Obviously, he was no ordinary tourist.

'This', he replied, gesturing expansively. 'Just what I'm doing now.'

'What do you mean, "this"? Entertain seasick ladies?'

'Oh, too right', he chuckled, 'I'm a regular cruise director, I am. No, luv. I go to sea for an honest living. I'm a sailor. That's me trade if you must be so nosy.'

'Oh, then you're part of the crew.'

'Not this one. I'm on holiday. I work on big ships, luv, not grubby little cargo tubs like this one.'

He stuck out his hand. 'My name's Michael, by the way. What's yours?'

I told him, wiped my hand and we shook, squatting there on the foul deck in the storm. 'British', he said, pointing to his chest.

'I figured as much', I replied.

'You Canadian?'

'No, American.'

'A Yank!' he crowed. 'I should have known that the minute I heard you speak.' He slapped his forehead with his palm. Then, abruptly, he stood up. 'I'd better check on my kids', he said enigmatically.

'Ciao.' I muttered, bewildered, feeling unaccountably abandoned as he walked sure-footedly toward the hatchway.

The storm worsened. Night closed in. A crewman called to me to go below to one of the cabins. I shouted back that I simply couldn't. I had to have fresh air.

'All the deck passengers are in the cabins!' He yelled. 'Captain says nobody sleeps on deck tonight!'

'No, please!' With all the strength I could muster, I shouted over the wind: 'I must stay out here!'

'Can't stay out there. You have to go below.' He disappeared around the corner. With no interest in what was going to happen next, I dozed off. A tap on my arm brought me awake with a jolt. It was Michael.

'Kids okay?' I mumbled bad-humoredly.

'Fat and happy', his voice beamed in the dark.

'Where's your wife? Does she know you're out here carrying on with a dying woman?'

'Oh, don't worry about her. She's back on Raro. Hates these interisland boats. Won't go home if she can't fly, she says.'

'Ummm', I muttered, 'she may have a point.' Then, 'Home? Where's she from?'

'She's an Atiu girl', he volunteered. 'Born there. Grew up in New Zealand. We live in New Zealand, now. I thought she was going to take the kids home to meet the relatives, but she backs out at the last minute. So, here I am with a boatload of brats while she lives it up with her sister on Raro.'

'How many brats?' I mumbled with difficulty.

'Three.'

It was all too complicated. I started to doze off again.

'Tell me more about old Frisbie', he said insistently, shaking my arm. 'I'm on this boat today because of old Frisbie. If it wasn't for *Island of Desire*, I'd never have come out to these islands and married myself a Polynesian girl. She's a good sort, too, like Frisbie's woman, not like some of these tarts you can't turn your back on.' He stared out into the darkness. 'She's like you, in one way. Gets sick every time she goes to sea. Can't understand it with her people being the great navigators they were and all.'

The boat groaned and pitched. Somewhere, something tore loose and started slamming back and forth with rhythmic metallic crashes. 'Hey there, Yank', his voice broke through my stupor, 'you ever read any of his magazine stories?'

With enormous effort, I roused myself and tried to think. 'No. Not yet.' My tongue was so thick I could hardly speak. My thoughts were blurred. I wanted to pull myself together, desperately. Except for a few people I'd met on Rarotonga, I'd never known anyone I could talk Frisbie with.

'When I get back to the States', I said, 'I'm going to find a library with a file of *Atlantic Monthly*s and *American Mercury*s going back to the twenties, and I'm going to photocopy all his stories.'

'If I give you my address, will you make some copies for me, too?' he asked.

'Sure', I murmured benevolently. No longer was he a jerk. He was a soul brother. Was I not here in these islands because of Frisbie, too?

'What ever happened to all his kids?' Michael asked.

'I'm not sure. I heard some went to New Zealand, some to the States. I don't know where. God, how I wish I'd had a father like that.'

He thought for a few minutes. 'Oh, it wasn't all that rosy a life, Yank. I don't want to disillusion you, but on Raro, you don't even want to mention his name. My wife's friends say old Frisbie was crazy when he drank. Half-killed that little Pukapukan wife of his. Hit her so hard, she went deaf. That's the truth. He burned himself out with his drinking and brawling. If it hadn't been for that, he would have done a lot more writing.'

'He probably wrote at least twenty books.' I was now wide awake and defending. 'That's not exactly copping out! Only six got published. He probably wrote a hundred magazine articles too that didn't make it. They're all gone, now, thanks to the hurricane. He broke his damned heart out there on his miserable atoll. Every time he finished a new work, he'd ship it off when the boat came, which was about every six months. He always believed each new one was the finest thing he'd ever written. New York publishers just kept sending them back, all but a handful.' I paused for breath.

'Listen, Michael', I said. 'When you get home, wherever that is, try to get a copy of *The Forgotten One* by James Norman Hall and read his story, "Frisbie of Danger Island." He was Frisbie's closest friend, and mentor. Part of it's got a lot of Frisbie's letters to him. I'll send you all the Frisbie I can, but if you really want to know what it was like for him out here, read his letters in Hall's story.'

My eyes were teary, nausea was crawling up my esophagus again and I wished Michael would just go away. He, however, was totally unmoved by my piteous 'leave me alone' gesture at him. Fishing a pen and a scrap of paper from his pocket, he wrote his name and address in a loopy, extravagant hand and tucked it in a corner of my tote bag. 'Don't forget, now. You're going to send me copies of those magazine stories.' He rose to his feet. 'And now, Yank, you're going to have to go below. That's the captain's orders.'

'No way', I said through clenched teeth. 'The diesel fumes down there will kill me for sure.' To myself, I added, 'And no Frisbie would ever sleep below.'

He shrugged and told me I'd better climb up to the top deck by the wheel-house or I'd get myself washed overboard and he'd never get those magazine articles. Then he walked off. I fell asleep like a sick animal, covered with filth, curled up in a fetal position, oblivious of the storm and danger.

It must have been much later when he came back. He was forceful this time. 'You have to go up or down, Yank!' he hollered above the storm, shaking me. 'You cannot stay out here. Come on. I'll help you. What's it to be, up or down? It's going to get worse before it gets better.' He was drenched. So was I, but I was beyond caring.

'Up', I said indifferently.

We struggled down the heaving deck. Somehow, with him pushing and me inching upward with all my strength, I made it up the ladder. He helped me to a spot in the middle of the ship against the bulkhead under an awning. I slumped to the deck immediately. 'You'll be all right here', he said, 'but you've got to stay put. Don't change your mind and try to get below.'

'Okay', I agreed. 'Thank you. But there's one more thing. Would you mind bringing me my mat and blanket? I think the crew put them below with my typewriter.'

He stared down at me, a look of incredulity on his face. 'Oh, I have to wait on you now, do I, Yank?'

Before I could tell him to forget it, he was gone. I stared across the deck in the dimness, wondering why he'd sounded so aggravated. Then I noticed something strange. Hadn't we climbed to the top deck just a few minutes ago? How come the waves were sometimes even with the rail? 'Oh my God!' I gasped, feeling the first tinges of fear as I made a mental calculation of the height of the freighter. I wondered if Michael had made it. Had I sent him to his death with my silly request? He reappeared abruptly, handed me my mat and blanket and stalked off across the bucking deck to disappear down the companionway, sure-footed, indifferent, silent.

I unrolled my mat. It wasn't a proper Cook Islands one, of course, just a *tatami* beach mat that I'd bought in Honolulu – the kind with a little plastic inflatable pillow attached. It seemed absurd in that wild environment.

I dropped off to sleep again. A rending crash shocked me back to consciousness. The ship was now pitching more horribly than ever. Occasionally, a wave would slop over the top deck. One of the big galvanized vent hoods had torn loose. Like a crazed monster-barrel, it came clattering toward me when the ship reared, then veered away, just in time, when she plunged. I knew I could not stay there any longer. There wasn't a soul on deck. The agonized groaning of the old ship as it climbed the monstrous waves; the sickening boom as it plunged down to the depths of the valleys between; the scream of the wind and the thunder from the waves left me without a scream of my own that anyone could hear. I would have to rescue myself.

It took every ounce of cunning and strength I'd stored in my brains and body since birth to make that perilous trip across wet slippery decks and down ladders with waves washing over me. Unable to stand against the wind, I crawled part of the way.

Somehow, I made it down to the galley and half fell into the foul-smelling hold below. The bunks were full except for one lower berth that was missing a mattress. I collapsed on the bare slats. 'Damn you, Robert Dean Frisbie!' I cursed. 'Damn you for luring an old fool like me into a mess like this!' Too weary to get out of my wet clothes, I fell into a thick black sleep.

Dawn's light revealed that everyone on the ship including the pigs had been sick. Everyone, that is, except the crew and Michael, who was having his morning beer.

The ship was strangely still. I staggered out on deck and filled my lungs with fresh air. Aitutaki lay nearby, sprawled on the rain-swept gray ocean like some dead animal. The sea was calm, the sky overcast. The long night was over. I had arrived by copra boat at my first Outer Island. I had had my first encounter with a genuine South Seas sailor. A touching romance. Two strangers in the night in love with the same author. Deceased.

An unmistakable land-smell reached my searching nostrils. There was an olfactory tickle of earth and copra, flower and smoke that set my heart beating with excitement. A motor launch carved a triangular wake in bas relief on the vast gray slate of the lagoon before me. Islanders on board waved and shouted to their friends on the *Mataora*. The little boat pulled alongside. Behind, the island beckoned. My knees were trembling. I was weak as a wet paper towel but very much alive and glad of it.

I was, after all, only a flawed human being, made by God for the earth and not created by Frisbie for a novel. I forgave them both for their oversights as the sun broke through, turquoise streaked the lagoon and the tradewind ruffled my hair.

'I made it, Ropati', I said, using the Cook Islands version of Frisbie's first name. 'Look. No books. I have both hands on the rail. My eyes are open and they're looking straight ahead, not inward. Your South Seas is a tricky, dangerous lady, but this time, she has one of her own kind to contend with!'

I pondered for a few minutes. Here was this beautiful, remote island, Aitutaki. Was I just going to see it from the dock while cargo was loaded on the *Mataora*? Terrible! Think what I'd miss! Somehow, the prospect of four more days at sea throwing up paled in comparison to the possibility of sampling life on Aitutaki, a mass that appeared to be quite stationary. I made two trips back down to the hold for my bags. Struggling under the load, I set off across the deck toward the lighter.

'Where you going, luv?' Michael called. 'You don't need your bags to go ashore. Nobody's going to pinch them here.'

'I'm jumping ship, Michael', I yelled back.

'Yank! I'm ashamed of you! You've got no guts. There's no more storm.' He looked at me indignantly, beer bottle clutched to chest.

'Bye', I called as I climbed down into the launch. One pig and four other passengers were already aboard. 'Maybe I'll see you ashore later.'

'Aw, you're yellow, Yank', he hollered. 'You'd better not forget to send me the Frisbie papers. Then I would *never* forgive you!'

I looked back at him over the widening gulf of water and waved again. 'Come ashore on the next launch and I'll buy you a beer, you silly limey.' For some reason, there were tears in my eyes.

## 13

# GHOST WOMAN DREAMING

# ON AITUTAKI

I stood alone on the wharf at Aitutaki. The lighter that had landed me was offloading one sullen pig and three relieved Islanders, still queasy from our stormy night on the high seas between Rarotonga and Aitutaki.

I overcame the urge to look back in farewell at the rusty old interisland freighter anchored beyond the reef. I knew my British sailor shipmate was watching from the rail. I was a deserter. I'd jumped ship. The *Mataora* could go on without me to the rest of the isles of the Southern Cooks on its circuit that I'd dreamed of for years.

Eighteen hours of the worst storm I'd ever been in at sea; eighteen hours of throwing up and trying to find a clean sanctuary on the filthy reeking old tub were quite enough. Too frail the body, too old the run-away-to-sea dream.

Aitutaki was a perfectly suitable choice of remote, undeveloped South Sea Island. I would miss seeing Atiu, Mauke, Mitiaro and Mangaia by jumping ship, true, but did not Aitutaki have a tiny mountain plus a huge lagoon, bound to turn blue as soon as the storm clouds cleared? Were there not pristine jungle-clad reef islets to explore? Real Polynesians to meet that I knew only as characters in the romantic fiction of the likes of Frisbie, Nordhoff and Hall? What were real people of the 1980s like?

I set off toward a lone building across the road. It looked important. It was. It was the post office. Inside, I asked the clerk if there was a public phone. No. No public phone. A telephone directory with addresses, perhaps? No, only five or six telephones on Aitutaki. What about a taxi stand? Was there one nearby? What is a taxi stand? The clerk looked at me in astonishment. Who was I?

Where had I come from that I was now standing in the fine Aitutaki Post Office asking for things that didn't exist? Her dark eyes stared at me curiously as she adjusted the big red hibiscus blazing in her thick, waist-length black hair.

I told her: Here I am just off the *Mataora*, survivor of a night of hurricane-force storm, in need of lodging that doesn't rock and a bath – a long, hot, soapy bath.

'You don't want stamps, then?' she asked musingly.

'No', I said. 'I need someplace to stay.'

She sat lost in thought for awhile. Finally, she rose slowly, shuffled to a telephone, cranked it several times, then chatted and joked endlessly in Cook Islands Maori. Irritated, I was about to leave when she hung up, shuffled back and sat down with the grateful slump of someone who's worked hard and has just found a chair for a well-deserved rest.

'Not to worry', she said, shrugging her eyebrows. 'There is room for you at Tiporo Guesthouse. Mrs Cameron will send her girl for you.'

'That's awfully nice of you', I said, embarrassed. 'I thought you'd just gone off to chat with a friend for awhile on the phone. I didn't realize you were trying to find me a place to stay.'

I went back to the wharf, collected my bags and had them up by the road in two fast round trips, then stood craning my neck, first one way, then another, watching for – what? A van, perhaps, with 'Arani' on the side? About half an hour passed. That's all that did. There wasn't a sign of life in the nearby village; not even a vehicle in sight.

Suddenly, with the roar of an amplified mosquito, a little Honda 50 motor-cycle buzzed out of nowhere, made a U-turn and stopped in front of me. The driver, a brooding-faced, slim, dark girl in her late teens looked at me intently. 'Are you for the guesthouse?'

Relieved, I broke into a torrent of explanations and questions. She stared at me, expressionless. Finally I stopped babbling and stared back, quizzical. 'I do not speak much English', she said, pronouncing each word carefully. 'Please to speak slow.' Her name was Rau and I soon learned she smiled only when she was drinking. The few teeth she had were broken and yellow. She talked as little as possible, even in Maori to others, when I was around and in the week that followed, melted into shadows like a beautiful, sulky ghost every time we made eye contact.

Speaking slowly now, I asked her if there was a car she could get because I had luggage. I gestured at the heap.

'No. No car. I take you on this.'

I looked the little bike over in disbelief. 'But the luggage?'

Rau seemed to notice the odd assortment of suitcases and parcels for the first time. Her face remained impassive. 'It will go', she said flatly, and clearly if it didn't, it could just sit there in the road for all she cared.

She stuffed the two canvas suitcases up front behind her legs. I took my briefcase-sized purse, travel typewriter and big plastic bag stuffed with mat, blanket, pillow, ship's biscuit and tinned bully beef I'd packed anticipating a long deck voyage. Somehow, I managed to straddle the back of her seat with all this stuffed between our bodies. We wobbled down the dusty coral road going about five miles an hour.

Tiporo Guesthouse was an old colonial mansion set back in a park – green lawn shaded by huge mango trees. An elaborate grave topped with a white marble box and tombstone reared up in the center, the grave of Mr Cameron, whose widow now ran the guesthouse alone. She met us: a tall, thin, taciturn woman with the angles of a *tiki*, staring at me from heavy-lidded eyes. Her long gray hair was twisted into an untidy bun and she looked as if her face had never smiled in her sixty years or so of life. Here was one Polynesian woman who could have modelled for Grant Wood but never for Paul Gauguin.

Nervously, I tried to explain my presence at her guesthouse without prior reservations. She listened stolidly, without response.

'Do you have a room?' I asked finally, wondering if I was unwelcome after all. Rau stood off to one side offering no help whatsoever.

'Tupu!' the widow called out sharply.

A girl who appeared to be about fourteen or fifteen ambled in from the rear of the house. She sized up the situation with a mocking expression. A few words of Maori passed between them.

'Please excuse Mrs Cameron', the girl called Tupu said. 'She fears her English is not good and that you will not understand her.'

'Oh, gee! I'm sure her English is 100 percent better than my Maori.' No one smiled.

I soon learned that I was the only guest that day in the huge, airy old frame house. There was an unaccountable feeling of *déjà vu* when I looked around. I knew this place. I had been there before. Impossible!

The front parlor overlooked the garden through a broad screened verandah. Next was a huge room, straight-backed chairs lined up on either side, a number of doors leading off and a great dining table down the center covered in hand-crocheted lace. Family photographs, their frames festooned with shell leis, covered the walls. Farther back was a big kitchen: inside it, another huge table. Voluptuous pillows padded every chair and settee, each a baroque masterpiece trimmed with lace, appliquéd and embroidered with vivid flowers, the work executed with impressive skill.

Then I knew. I had first seen such a South Seas house in the word pictures of Somerset Maugham, Robert Louis Stevenson and other novelists from the British Colonial period of the South Seas. All that was missing was the ceiling fan, but electricity was scarcely a year old on Aitutaki and such refinements were yet to come.

Later, alone in the small room to which I had been assigned, I started to unpack. There was a gentle knock. Before I could respond, the door opened and Tupu sidled in. She smiled, showing fine white teeth. She wore a tight cotton skirt and an unbuttoned blouse tied together below her high, jutting breasts. Conscious of every glance in their direction, she would respond with slight, almost imperceptible squirmings, nipples rubbing against thin cotton. She was obviously a healthy young thing, ready to mate and reminded of it by every glance, change of posture, contact with her clothing or passing breeze.

'Can I help you unpack?'

'No thank you, Tupu.'

She didn't leave. She stayed where she was, eyes sorting and analyzing everything I took out. She coveted my eyebrow tweezers from the moment she spied them. Her desire was so sharp it dulled her hearing.

'How old are you?' I repeated for the third time, trying to break her focus. She started.

'Fif... eighteen', she lied, her eyes still one with the tweezers. I reached over, picked them up casually and tucked them back out of sight in my toiletries bag. She sighed, an ancient Polynesian expulsion of breath laden with all the light, hope and life left in her body. Then she slumped down on a corner of the bed and went into what seemed to be a coma: slightly uptilted brown eyes dull; flat, pretty child-face turned to stone. The silence was awful, but they were the only tweezers I had with me and it would be a month or more before I boarded a plane back to the States.

'Are you really eighteen?' I challenged. No answer. 'Were you born here on Aitutaki?' No answer. She had abandoned her body there on the bed.

'Look, would you like to see yesterday's edition of the *Cook Islands News*?' No response. 'You don't get it here until it's a week or two old, do you?' It was published daily on Rarotonga, 140 miles beyond the reef to the south.

I put it on the bed beside her and proceeded with my unpacking. Suddenly, a palpable shock of returning life rocked the room. 'Where did you get this paper?'

'Rarotonga. Yesterday.'

'Do you know him?'

'Who?'

'Him! High Chief Tavana?'

Her hand was trembling as she pointed to the front page headline story:

'High Chief Tavana in Rarotonga.'

'Um, well, I was introduced to him in Hawaii but I can't say that I *know* him.'

'Did you see him on Rarotonga? Did you speak to him?'

'Yes, as a matter of fact, I did. He came into the premiere's office as I was leaving and we chatted for a moment.'

'Did he ask about me?'

I stared at her. 'No. Of course not! I didn't even know you yesterday!'

'Well', she said, a bit huffily, coming off the bed with a thump, hands on her hips, 'you don't know much! The reason he's in Rarotonga is that he is coming for me. He will fly to Aitutaki this afternoon on the plane.'

'How do you know?' I reread the story. 'It only says he's here exploring some sort of a trade deal. It doesn't say anything about you or Aitutaki.'

But she was halfway out the door before I finished. Soon, I heard a shower running. I'd read about the legendary coconut wireless of the Islands. Was this an example of that mysterious telepathy?

She was back in the sun-flecked room in the old boarding house within ten minutes. Her long black hair, now wet, turbanned in a white towel, skirt and blouse abandoned for a red and white pareu, butterscotch skin shiny with coconut oil. It was almost possible to believe she really was eighteen.

'Excuse me', she said loftily, 'but you should know some things if you are going to stay here on Aitutaki. I am just like you. I have traveled overseas. Do you know why? I am a dancer, that's why, and I have danced in Honolulu. You didn't know that, did you?'

I stared at the Aitutaki teenager with the requisite amazement: 'I had no idea!' Honolulu is to Pacific Islanders what Hollywood is to the rest of the world that doesn't live there – a vortex of glamor. Paradise!

A bit mollified, she unwound the towel and began rubbing her hair. 'I was discovered by the famous High Chief Tavana. It was for him that I danced in Hawaii.'

Tavana, not really a high chief, was at that time one of Hawaii's foremost impresarios with one of the most effective Polynesian floor shows at Waikiki. He and his scouts would comb the islands and atolls of the Pacific for fresh young talent. They'd bring the youngsters to Hawaii, closely chaperoned, and quarter them with local families. Then, the often shy children, who had never seen the outside world before, would be show-trained to please Waikiki audiences.

The exuberance on stage of these masses of young people singing their hearts out together, dancing skills polished by expert choreographers, dressed in exquisite versions of authentic Island costumes, brought a poignancy to Tavana's spectaculars that sent tears cascading down the cheeks of thousands of boozy tourists. After a few months, the kids would be shipped home to make room for a fresh batch of star-eyed recruits.

'Honey', I said patiently, 'I don't really think he's on his way to Aitutaki. If you read the whole story, you'll see he's going to Auckland and then Japan. Why, if he were coming here, everybody would be getting ready to welcome him.'

'He is coming here, but only for me.'

'When? How can he manage it?'

'He will come this afternoon on the Air Rarotonga flight. Mrs Cameron will have to get one of the other girls to take care of you.'

She hurried out of the room, stopped short as though struck by an after-thought, ran back in and cried out: 'Oh! I almost forgot. You loan me your eyebrow tweezers, okay?' She held out a broad hand, chin tilted, eyes challenging.

I never saw them again, of course.

She preened and practiced all morning, enlisting two young boys next door to drum and play guitars for her. Lunch came and went and so did the afternoon plane. We could hear it like an angry insect, a little Cessna mixmaster. But no one came from the airport and Aitutaki slumbered on into afternoon. It woke finally and busied itself playing netball in the clearing among the palms, cleaning fish on the beach or hustling up food for dinner from the trees or small shops. Tupu brought the afternoon tea, still looking beautiful and older than her years but now rather pensive. 'He didn't come, did he?' I asked sympathetically.

She shrugged. 'He will. He could not come today but he will come for me soon. He will not forget me.'

If she grieved, she didn't show it. She put the teapot in the kitchen, changed her skirt for a pair of blue jeans and invited me to come with her and her girlfriends to pick breadfruit for supper, or tea, as it's called in the Cook Islands. I loped along eagerly, a middle-aged teenager among peers, ready for action. We giggled and teased one another as we ambled along. Young men lounging at the local general store hollered abusive endearments to our group in Maori as we passed, repartee that is apparently the same in all languages at that age.

A slightly built little girl joined us, carrying a fat baby. This was Kati, who looked to be no more than eleven or twelve. She had just been nursing and her dress was half-open, revealing a small breast, swollen with milk. Her face was streaked with dirt and one knee was skinned. Except for the baby and the care-less breast, she could have been taken for a wild young tomboy. She carried the child absently on one hip, giggling and gossiping with the older girls.

Finally, we came to a tree laden with ripe breadfruit. Large as soccer balls, they hung high up over the road about thirty feet, just visible among the big-leafed foliage. Two of the girls scattered on various errands. Kati stayed behind to help, parking her baby in the grass. Tupu shed her sandals and started up the tree like a young ape in blue jeans.

High overhead, she called down and started pitching the huge fruits at Kati, faster than the frail child could catch them in her out-held skirt. The two would shriek with laughter when the breadfruit missed and split on the stones. 'Enough?' Tupu screamed in English. Kati called back to her in Maori. The two looked at me, then burst into fits of giggling. Then Tupu disappeared momentarily, the tree shivered and she reappeared higher up. Crawling out onto a thin pliant branch she began to swing back and forth upside down, arms free.

'My child must liiiiive!' she screamed suddenly from the treetops. 'My child must liiiive!'

Kati was laughing so hard she was crying. When Tupu finally stopped clowning and came down, I asked her what that scene had been all about.

'You mean you don't know?' she asked in her haughty voice, arms akimbo. 'You're an American lady and you don't know about *Ghost Woman*?'

I confessed to total ignorance.

'It's a movie!' she said impatiently. 'It's not real. Haven't you ever seen *Ghost Woman*?'

'No, Tupu', I said. 'Never. Honestly. Did you see it in Hawaii?'

'No! Not Hawaii. Right here in Aitutaki. We have movies here on this island. Everybody saw *Ghost Woman*!'

'Well, maybe it was a British film and we didn't get it in America', I said by way of a lame excuse.

She looked at me the way women look at each other when one has scored. 'If it ever *does* come to your country', she said commandingly, 'you go see it!'

We started back down the road to the guesthouse, arms filled with breadfruit. A small motorcycle buzzed by in the afternoon heat. 'Helloooo, Yank!' a familiar voice trailed back.

Excitedly, I tried to wave, nearly dropping my breadfruit. 'Michael!' I called after the retreating bike. 'Where are you going?'

Lazily, he made a U-turn and started back toward us. 'You know him?' asked Tupu. 'Is that your husband?'

'No, he's not my husband, just a British sailor I met on the boat. His wife's Atiuan.'

He drew up beside us and stopped. 'Want a lift?'

'No, thanks. We're just going back to the guesthouse.'

'You really are staying, then?'

'You better believe it. I don't even want to look at another boat for a while.'

He shot a look of undisguised contempt at me. 'Who's your friend?' he asked and then, without waiting for a reply, grinned down at Tupu: 'Hello, you pretty thing, are you married? What's your name?'

Tupu immediately went into a bout of giggles. 'Of *course* I'm not married!' she said. 'Do I look like I'm married?' The breadfruit had slipped to the grass and she now had her hands on her hips, manipulating the cloth of her tied shirt with some creative deep breathing.

Leaning forward, Michael tried to look down her shirt. 'My, aren't they lovely!' he exclaimed.

'What?' cried Tupu. 'What you mean?' and grabbed the edges of her blouse, pulling them together above the knot with a shocked look.

Michael laughed, delighted with the game. 'What's your name, pretty?'

'Tupu', she replied, casually loosening her hold on her blouse front, which spread open again, assisted slightly by a mighty inhalation.

Another motorcycle pulled up bearing two teenaged girls, one about Tupu's age, the other younger.

'Dad!' cried the girl driving. 'You said you were going straight to the wharf!' She looked Tupu up and down as if she might spring from her motorcycle any minute and tear her apart. Tupu glared back at the half-Atiuan teenager.

'I'll be along in a few minutes', Michael said in annoyance, 'get on with you both. I said I'd meet you at the wharf and I will. Later!' Leaning toward Tupu again, he said softly, 'Tell me about yourself.' His eyes were riveted on the knot of her blouse.

With a small roar, the other motorcycle flounced off. 'If you're not there in ten minutes, Mum is going to hear about this!' the older girl called back.

Laughing, I said to him: 'You're absolutely impossible. Your daughters are going to kill you and I don't blame them.'

'Come see us off, then, Yank, and bring your lovely friend', he said. 'That's the least you can do.'

Tupu agreed, handed the breadfruit to a group of passing children with instructions to take them to the guesthouse, and we set off on foot, Michael wobbling along beside us at low speed, bantering with Tupu.

The last I saw of Michael, he was waving from the deck of the launch, heading across the big lagoon toward the *Mataora*. He had spoken but little to me. I was a failed sailor. With mixed feelings, I watched the old cargo ship until it blended with the horizon. Tupu never brought Tavana up again. I mentioned him a few days later. 'He didn't come after all', I said.

'No', she shrugged. 'He will. Pretty soon.'

'How do you know that?'

'Because he came to Rarotonga. Your friend won't come back for you', she said, 'but High Chief Tavana, he will come for me.'

## 14

# THE YOUNG UNMARRIED

*At night there are shadows in the coconut groves of Puka-Puka – lacelike shadows of fronds, shadows of stiff-limbed pandanus trees, of ground bush, and of the fleecy trade-wind clouds skimming low overhead. And there are the shadows of the young unmarried, wide awake now and slipping from tree to tree on their way to the love fests on the sea side of the islet.*

Robert Dean Frisbie
*The Book of Puka-Puka*, 1930

It's been raining all day again. Tupu squats on the floor beside my bed in the Tiporo Guesthouse, drawing a quarter-section of the design for a small *tivaevae* (appliqué) on the folded paper in which the red trade-store cotton was wrapped. Painstakingly she cuts out the shape, unfolds it to full size, then traces around it with my ballpoint pen.

Kati joins us, lugging fat three-month-old Manea in her thin arms. Her younger sister, Marama, about ten, follows. Except for their heights, the two could be twins, bony thin, big-eyed with a hint of freckles sprinkled across *café au lait* noses.

More girls drift wetly on to the verandah outside, call out to others in the rain and join Rau, the senior housegirl, to peer in through my bedroom door from the parlor. The bolder youngsters squeeze inside my small room to lean against the wall or squat on the mat. Tupu shoos a couple off the bed. It's a subdued group as the rain clobbers the tin roof overhead.

With hardly enough room in the crowd to move her elbows, Kati starts to baste the red cloth leaf shapes to white fabric for a pillow cover while Marama holds baby Manea between her legs. She pauses, wrinkles her small nose, then turns to Tupu with an excited flood of Cook Islands Maori words.

'What did she say?' I ask. 'What's wrong? Doesn't she want to do it?'

'No. She say this pattern, *Kuru* [breadfruit] is no good.'

'Why?'

'Because *Kuru* is a green pattern.'

I ponder her objection. Kati watches my face intently, needle poised in air, motionless. Our audience mutters.

'Well', I say slowly, 'all we have is red and I like red better than green anyway. Besides, it's just for me to practice sewing on. It's not real.'

The 'committee' argues about the situation with much animation. Finally, Tupu cuts off the babble with a sharp sentence after which all look at me gravely, in silence. With a shrug, Kati goes back to her basting. We are violating a tradition. Our *kuru* leaves and fruit are going to be red – a terrible thing, but then, such an abomination will never grace a good Aitutaki household. *Papaas* are notorious for bad eyesight and appalling taste.

'You could buy one already finished from Mrs Cameron or from my grandmother', says Tupu hopefully for the third time.

'No', I tell her. 'I want to learn how to make a *tivaevae* myself.'

Changing the subject, I ask little Marama, kiddingly: 'You got a boyfriend yet?'

'No!' she cries indignantly, widespread eyes enormous. The *papaa* has made another gaffe. 'I am not a woman yet! When I am woman, then I get boyfriend!' She is outraged that I could not see this for myself, and is not flattered that I thought her older. About boyfriends and sex, she is a realist.

We talk about families. One girl says she is one of twelve children, only three still living in the Cook Islands, the rest in New Zealand. Another is one of nine kids but only two living on Aitutaki. Tupu says her mother left her, her small brother and their father and went off to Australia, where she now has five more children with someone else. Her own father lives on Rarotonga with his new family. She speaks of them indifferently, as one speaks of strangers. She is now Mrs Cameron's feeding daughter. Have I got any children? Only one? They look at me and confer in hushed tones.

'You got boyfriend?' Marama asks impudently.

'No, I've got a husband.'

'Where you husband?'

'He left on the *Mataora*', says Tupu.

'No, Tupu, I told you, he's not my husband, just a friend. I hardly know him.'

'You get only one childrens from husband, you not get one baby with friend. You find Aitutaki man. You get many childrens', Marama promises me seriously.

'How come you know so much, eh? Do you talk to your mother like that, you little hardcase?'

'I hate my mother!' Kati suddenly joins in. 'She won't take care of my baby!' There's a moment of embarrassed silence from the young ladies. The roar of rain now dominates. A moon-faced, plump teenager speaks quietly to Kati in Maori, they get up and leave, Kati lugging her fat infant along like a bag of groceries through the pouring rain. The group disperses, Kati's shocking statement lingering on behind them in their wake. Tupu finishes the basting in silence on the mat.

The next day, it does not rain. It's the kind of hot, humid day you get sometimes in the tropics when just breathing seems the most strenuous exercise one can bear. It passes finally into warm, sultry night. I go to bed early but can't sleep. As I lay there listening to the strange night sounds, I hear the shuffle of someone creeping by outside in the grass. I tense. Then I hear it again, but from another direction.

A feminine voice says 'shhhh' somewhere near my window outside. Someone giggles. Then I hear a murmur which is most certainly Rau's throaty voice. More laughter. Soon, the earth drums with running feet. More whispering voices, male and female, rustle like leaves in a breeze. I peer through my lace curtains into the yard. The shadows are rich and dense. Clouds obscure the stars. Mr Cameron's grave looms like a white bunker in the dimness. There is no moon, no sign of life in that ghostly still garden.

The whispering, giggling and shuffling go on for hours. I lay back and stare at the ceiling, thoughts not of the supernatural, but of Frisbie's tales of the game he dubbed *tango tango*, where nubile teenagers would stalk each other and do secret things on certain moonless nights in faraway Pukapuka.

At such times, when the madness was on the island's young, no one of the age of reason stirred from their houses or interfered in any way. Many, though, were the old gray heads who, listening from their sleeping mats, remembered a deliciously wild youth of long ago. I thought with sadness of my own staid youth and all the wildness I had missed.

The next morning, a hungover Rau and Tupu could be seen sneaking around the lawn picking up beer bottles.

'*Tango tango*? That just means dark night', says Tupu. 'No game. I no hear anything last night. I sleep at my grandmother's. No Aitutaki people go outside last night. Maybe these bottles left by *tupapakus*.'

*15*

# ILLUSIONS OF PARADISE

*A man needs something to live for but nothing to do.*
Tom Neale,
*An Island to Myself*

Heavy tropical rains lash Aitutaki for days, massaging lush banana groves, flinging *tipani* blossoms to the mud below with gusto. Finally, a day dawns fine, morning sun vaporizing jewelled drops of water on the scarlet ginger outside my window. The old rooster in the yard bellows and mounts clucking chicken after chicken.

I pull on my bikini, wrap a *pareu* around me so I'm chastely covered from armpit to midcalf and slip out of the guesthouse early to explore the beach ringing my volcanic atoll and its 'towering' 400-foot mountain.

Crossing the road, I cut through the tropical brush down to the lagoon. I stroll along the water's edge until I reach the deserted beach by the shabby Government Hotel. This is the 'tourist-designated zone' where I can drop my *pareu* and tan or swim wearing only a bathing suit without offending local sensibilities.

I share my beach with a heron. He paces the lonely shore, shoulders hunched, looking like a no-neck pirate captain calculating his booty. Suddenly, his body tenses. His head shoots up on a long thin neck. He studies the ripples. No, nothing. He retracts his head, hunches his shoulders again and broods, a black lonely figure.

Far away, across the turquoise lagoon, white surf foams almost silently on the fringing coral reef. The sea beyond looks like a low cobalt wall. Nothing moves quickly here but clouds, speeding by on the trade winds.

Nearby is a handsome outcropping of black lava rocks of the sort used in ancient times for *marae*. I wonder if it was used as a sacrificial altar. A few *toa* trees, the feather-branched, smoked-green ironwood trees, look out to sea, weary-looking creatures. Palms chatter and whisper as vagrant breezes first tickle them, then rake their fronds with invisible fingers. The first person I've seen all morning passes, a man in an outrigger way out near the reef. Without my glasses, he's a small black smudge.

Mynah birds gossip, squeal and meow like lost kittens in the underbrush. The sand is fine white stuff, littered with bleached-white and rust-colored coral and the rippled shells of *pa'ua* (*Tridacna*) clams. There are a few old coconuts lying about, some sprouting, but no signs that humans have come this way since the dawn of time.

Spreading my *pareu* on the sand, I settle down, grease myself well with *monoi* and open my book. It's a paperback edition of *An Island to Myself* by Tom Neale. To make the scene complete, I must reread it in the kind of setting where it was written.

I turn to the part where Neale, a New Zealander already in his fifties, has finally landed on Suwarrow, the island Robert Dean Frisbie immortalized in *Island of Desire*. It is 1952. Neale has yearned for this moment for years, when he can start life over as Adam, without Eve and the kids. Suwarrow is as familiar to him as the inside of his eyelids. He's studied *Island of Desire*, discussed every aspect of Suwarrow with Frisbie before his death, and devoured every scrap of information available about this lonely ring of reef islets and its vast, shark-filled lagoon.

He arrives on a trading vessel, *Mahurangi*, and lands on the beach with his assorted crates, Gladstone bag and a mother cat and her kitten. The only signs of civilization are an old shack, ruined pier and water tanks left by coastwatchers after World War II. How does he spend his first night? 'When the cats had settled down, I lit the glass table lamp, carried it to the bedside table, and soon I was tucked in reading *The Island of Desire*', he wrote.

Neale lived alone with his cats as master of this lonely universe, growing and hunting his food, surviving with competence and a rather fitful, curmudgeonly joy for the next twenty years. Medical emergencies were the only things that periodically drove him back to the civilization he rejected. His death in 1977 was no closer to the poetic passing of the beachcomber Frisbie conjured up in his *Book of Puka-Puka* than was Frisbie's own death, twenty-nine years earlier:

> A beachcomber's death! Well, that sort of death is often the most peaceful known to man. Many a beachcomber has eaten of the lotus, forgotten the world, loved native women, lived without malice, labor, or pain, and has died in the hope that Paradise will be like the isle he is leaving behind. The storybooks often make it different, but what do the storybooks know about it ...

Neale lost a long, agonizing battle with stomach cancer in the Rarotonga Hospital at age seventy-four. He was buried in an indifferent grave in what Rarotongans refer to as the 'new people's cemetery' and, sometimes, the 'Brych (pronounced brick) Yard' in the weeds across from the Rarotonga International Airport on the sea side.

His companions are mostly other expatriate cancer victims who flew to the Cook Islands from all over the world seeking the costly 'miracle cancer cure' offered by self-styled doctor Milan Brych. Brych, a Czech immigrant, lived on Rarotonga at the invitation of then premiere Sir Albert Henry, who was also said to have been a patient of the charlatan. He fled to California in 1978 after the fall of the Henry government.

Stories in these islands have tentacles reaching out all over the globe. Neale's links Czechoslovakia, New Zealand, Rarotonga, Suwarrow, the United States and beyond. His book draws yachties worldwide on pilgrimages to the lonely outpost of Suwarrow. No island is an island, if anybody knows it's there.

But back to my beach on Aitutaki and the illusions of paradise I'm trying to free from the pages of a book before the black mynah birds of reality scavenge them like overripe fruit.

Men such as Frisbie and Neale died for and of their dreams. I know their longings. Dreams have no gender. I wonder if Neale, Frisbie and I had lived together on Suwarrow in the same time frame, would we have been as close as I feel to them through their writing? Probably not. I put the book down and stare off toward the reef. Our compulsions, character flaws and lifestyles would have stirred nothing in us but mutual loathing and possibly would have reduced us to rock throwing! Frisbie would have lived on one motu, Neale on another and I on a third, wishing each other far away across the sea.

I suspect most of us white misfits who flee to South Sea Islands like homing pigeons would probably shun one another's company, at least while we're sober. Our restless, treacherous minds are burdened with absolutes and useless knowledge. We yearn for the company of the heirs to these islands. Surely they must be wiser, finer sorts than the likes of us. We lay on the clear skin of their world, bobbing on their currents, watching through masks of which we can never be free. We imagine ourselves darting along with them in the depths.

No wonder whites drink so much in the tropics. I wonder if I will, if I hang around long enough.

'Damn you, Robert Dean Frisbie', I say aloud, 'and all the rest of you motley crew of misfit dream spinners, including you, James Norman Hall and Charles Nordhoff; you, Beatrice Grimshaw and Frederick O'Brien; damn you Robert Louis Stevenson and W. Somerset Maugham – I wish I loved you less.'

The heron seemed to hunch his head even closer into his body, probably out of embarrassment at my outburst.

'Damn you for making such a glory out of unrequited love. Damn your loneliness, damn your pain. Damn your longing, damn your books, your words, your sirens' words – which can be the only mates of people like us who yearn to belong to an image of the South Seas ...' I wonder if all whites addicted to these South Sea Islands have periods of ranting and raving as I do?

Who is that heron? Is he real or is he a *tupapaku*? Captain Bligh pacing the deck or the great navigator Ru straining for signs of land in the lonely southern seas? Or is he a writer, yet to be born?

## 16

# WHAT YOU CALL DAT T'ING?

The fuzzy fisherman is still out there. I put my prescription sunglasses back on and peer at him. He seems to be just sitting there. I wonder why.

Pulling off my now-greasy glasses, I drop them in the island hat Pepe gave me, rise and leap into the warm, jade-green, still water, so clear you can see every detail of the white coral-sand bottom. My plunge ends abruptly with a shriek. The mynah birds respond with a hiccup of silence. I've landed on my kneecaps. Hard! The water's as deep as it looks – about two feet.

Groaning, I try to stand. So far, so good. I examine my knees. No apparent damage. I try to walk. Nothing seems to be broken. Determinedly, I decide to work off the pain in the water. I wade out toward the reef, stepping gingerly around fat black slugs the size of Italian sausages, but the water doesn't seem to get much deeper. Finally, I lie down on it, floating and finger-propelling myself back to shore, stretch out on the pristine coral sand and promptly fall asleep.

I come to, burning. The gentle early morning sun has matured to an equatorial clinker. Covering as much of me as possible with my *pareu*, I unbraid my hair and spread it over my shoulders and back for protection, too lazy to go back to the guesthouse to fetch a shirt.

The fisherman has raised anchor and disappeared. I amble alongside the vast turquoise lagoon for about two hours, sometimes under fiery sun, sometimes under cool trade-wind clouds, picking up shells. My world seems lost in a time before human history, where the only sound is the chuckle of the trade-winds in the palm fronds and the scratching of the crabs in the coconut grove debris.

Suddenly, a white wraith rises in the templelike grove of coconut palms ahead. Startled, I stop. Is it a *tupapaku*, a ghost? It seems alive but insubstantial as smoke. My heart pounding, I venture closer. My apparition is only a fisherman engulfed in a huge nylon fishing net he's bundling. I wonder vaguely if he's the one I saw out by the reef.

'Where you go?' he calls out, as though waiting for me.

'Nowhere. Just walking.'

He motions me to follow: 'Come. I get you coconut to drink.' He leads me inland to a clearing in the grove. In the center is an old-fashioned, thatched-roof bungalow woven of leaf strips, a true *kikau* house. It's very beautiful compared to the motley assortment of coral limestone, tin-roofed bungalows and New Zealand prefabs that now make up Aitutaki's villages.

Picking up a long pole with an iron hook on the end, he knocks a nut down and husks it on a sharpened iron bar wedged in the ground at a slight angle. Whacking the top off with his bush knife, he hands it to me. The whole operation takes less than a minute. Just then a stocky woman approaches dressed in ragged tee shirt and *pareu*, her face quizzical. 'Your wife?'

'Yes', he replies and motions her to join us. She advances shyly and he walks off down the beach to continue working on his net. We watch him for awhile, a man of about sixty wearing an old baseball cap, torn tee shirt and ragged shorts, face furrowed with the look of one who's worked hard and known many troubles.

'My husband, he is *ariki* of this district. You know *ariki*?' There's pride in her soft voice. She tilts her head and looks at me quizzically.

'Yes, I know the word. *Ariki* is a high chief.'

'Is right. *Ariki* is chief. You say king. My husband has much land on Aitutaki. His family kings, all the way back to the great navigator, Ru, maybe farther.'

We watch him now in respectful silence. Sensing our stares, he straightens up and looks our way. Suddenly, he calls something to us that I can't make out. 'He say do you want to go out to the reef?'

'Oh, yes, I'd love to. I've never been out there.'

'He will show you. It is his pleasure and pride.'

Barefoot, I start back down the beach toward him. She runs after me waving a pair of new-looking tennis shoes. 'You must wear these. The coral is very sharp.'

The *ariki* shoves the outrigger canoe into the water, makes 'get in' motions and tells me to remove my *pareu*. 'You get him wet', he warns. This seems strange advice coming from a chief whose people go into the water in *pareus*, dresses, shorts or whatever they happen to be wearing.

Embarrassed, I demur. 'I am wearing nothing but a bathing suit underneath, sir. I have not seen any Aitutaki women in bathing suits, only *pareus* and dresses.' If this was the same man I saw earlier in a canoe, was he fishing or watching me? I study the *ariki*'s detached expression. Paranoia, I conclude.

'You are a visitor!' he says shortly. 'You no have to dress like our women!'

'I feel fine the way I am.' Pa Ariki had warned me about local standards of decency. I'd also read in the *Cook Islands News* that the movie *Blue Lagoon* had been banned from the packing-shed movie house by local censors. It was 'too blue for Aitutaki', an island that visually could have served as the movie set.

He glares an imperial *ariki* glare. A minute ticks by, then another. It's obvious we'll go nowhere unless the *ariki* is obeyed. Reluctantly, I remove the offending *pareu*, fold it up and sit down self-consciously in the outrigger, *pareu* in my lap. I feel absolutely naked. Is the old king trying to show me how worldly he is?

He poles the canoe across the vast shallow lagoon. It's pleasant to drift on the glassy turquoise waters, hearing only the gentle growl of the surf breaking ahead on the barrier reef. Finally, we reach the first coral outcroppings. At first, I can see nothing but seas swirling in and out among boulders of fantastic convoluted shapes. The *ariki* starts to point things out: sea urchins with spines as thick as pencils; *pa'ua* like white ruffles clamped to the rocks; schools of darting fish.

The reef itself is like a stony beach with the waves breaking on the shore. The sea is calm and mellow. He ties the canoe to a coral outcrop and we slog through the water. It's hard going. You can't see where you're putting your feet. Fine coral sand swirls up with every step, turning the crystalline water opaque. It would be easy to step into a crevice and snap an ankle.

Suddenly, he reaches down and brings up some small shells. Grinning at me wickedly, he cracks them like eggs on a piece of coral. He hands me one, then proceeds to eat the contents of the other. Shocked, I meet his eyes and steel myself. This hospitable king is sharing his world with me, a total stranger. I can't be rude. Trying not to wince visibly, I bite into the still-living creature. It isn't bad. The texture's leathery like cooked squid. He shows me which is the best part to eat. We stand there knee-deep in the sea, from different worlds, gnawing gravely on the poor little devils.

He picks seaweed for me covered with grapelike clusters of beads the size of caviar eggs. It doesn't taste the way I expected. It's neither salty, fishy nor redolent of iodine. It's more like a crisp salad vegetable. Delighted, I snack on my fat bunch as we go. He picks up live cowry shells as big as my fist that look as if their brown and tan backs have been varnished. He doesn't expect me to eat them, too, thank God.

Something catches his eye in the distance. We return to the canoe and pole over to what turns out to be a large fragment of fish net with about a dozen fish trapped in its folds. He takes out his knife and cuts away the tattered strands. I join him, working struggling fish free and tossing them into the boat. Side by side, we toil like good buddies, joking about our catch and conspiring to fool his wife about it.

'What you call dat t'ing?' he asks suddenly and starts to describe something in what he thinks is English but sounds more like Maori to me. I shake my head, mystified.

'You know. Dat t'ing! How you say in English?' His eyes search my face urgently, a little sly for some reason.

'Tell me again. I don't understand what you're saying.' He tries, words tumbling, hands flailing pictures in the air. His every attempt ends with: '... dat t'ing! What you call in English?' He's growing agitated.

'Let's ask your wife when we get back. Maybe she can translate it.'

He hoots a sharp, snorting laugh and shakes his head violently. 'No! She not know dat t'ing. You no tell her!'

When we return with our 'catch', we find her in the shade, straddling a low wooden stool, half a coconut in her hands, meat down, grating it over a lethal-looking sawtoothed blade lashed to a projection on the end of the stool. A snowy mound grows higher and higher in the big dishpan at her feet. Around her is a heap of dark brown half-shells, scraped clean. She looks up, aging face radiant, and insists, 'You stay for tea!'

'Thank you, but I can't. Mrs Cameron is expecting me back for tea at the guesthouse', I explain.

If that's the case then, I must eat immediately. Serenely, she scoops up a handful of grated coconut meat, folds it in a clean, faded scrap of *pareu* cloth and squeezes the cream through it into an empty half shell. I have to taste the fish we caught. I have never tasted these Aitutaki fish, now, have I? No, of course not. 'I fix. You like. You see.'

The *ariki* returns from the beach and hands the cleaned fish to her, then with the flourish of a lord of the manor, he ushers me into the elegant *kikau* house. I gaze up into the intricate lashings of the rafters and woven roof high overhead with a low whistle. 'This is gorgeous! Your house is truly a palace!'

'This not my house. I make this house for New Zealand man. Very rich. Come here every year. I work for him. Make house and garden nice. My wife, he cook.'

'You're an *ariki* and you work as caretaker for some Kiwi? Where do you live, then, and when do you take care of the affairs of your people?'

'My English, he not good. You talk to wife.' The silence grows uncomfortable. I pretend to study the weaving of the floor mats. He seems to be studying me. His wife returns with a plate of steaming fish poached in coconut cream. With it are tempting chunks of taro and breadfruit. 'No more talk. Now, you eat.'

My hosts serve me and hover on the sidelines, watching every bite attentively. I eat alone, self-conscious and embarrassed. According to local custom,
men don't eat with women, even if they're guests. The women and children of
a household eat only after men and guests are finished. They get the leftovers.
It's very quiet. Talking to the guest during a meal is limited to relevant phrases
such as: 'More fish?'

I manage to swallow enough food to comply with the laws of hospitality
but not enough to make a serious dent in what I'm sure is my hosts' dinner. 'I
mustn't eat too much. Mrs Cameron is preparing my tea and she'll think I don't
like her cooking.'

As I rise to leave, the *ariki* speaks at length to his wife in Maori. She translates: 'My husband says you come tomorrow. He will take you on his Honda and
show you the island.'

'You're wonderful! *Meitaki maata*. Thank you, thank you.' I hug and kiss
them both shyly – another local custom still awkward for me.

The next day, I wend my way through the palm grove and find the *ariki*
hard at work, clearing brush. As I approach, he straightens up, face impassive.
'You no got bikini?' he asks by way of a greeting.

'No. I thought you were going to show me the island. Are we going to
swim, then? I can go change.'

'No. No swim. I show you island. Come.'

I straddle the little Honda 50 behind him and we putt slowly down the lane
to the main road. His wife, working in the garden, waves. 'I take you inland', he
speaks over his shoulder. 'I no take you on main road. People, dey will talk.'

'What?' I ask, leaning closer. 'Talk about what?'

He laughs a strange laugh. 'You don't know people on dis island. Dey see us
together, dey say bad t'ing.'

I shrug. The motorcycle crosses the main road and we wobble down a rut-
ted trail winding through palm groves. It doesn't look as if any vehicles have
come this way in a long time. 'Sit closer', the *ariki* instructs. 'You fall off.'

I'm sitting as close as I think I can, but I try to wriggle closer. The bike is
moving almost at walking speed while he dodges crab holes and fallen coconuts.
'Closer!' he commands. I squirm again, but there simply is no more space between us.

'That's about as close as I can get', I call out as we bump along.

'Dat's good!' Howling with laughter, he wriggles his royal behind against
me lewdly. 'I like dat. You sit close.'

Why the old devil's not as regal as I thought, I say to myself, amused at his
attempt at a joke. We inch through a few deserted villages, dilapidated huts of
wood and limestone. We pass a group of men splitting coconuts for copra with

their bush knives. Somehow, it's a relief just to see people. Finally, we stop on the shore of a mangrove swamp. He's taken the little motorcycle where I couldn't imagine any bike going, through sand and puddles, potholes and mud, over a trail which hardly exists.

The spot where we now stand was one which American GIs used as a base during World War II. He shows me rusting relics of that distant occupation and talks to me of servicemen who were there, which accounts for freckles and occasional black frizzy hair on some of the locals.

'How old were you then?' I ask. 'That was back in nineteen forty-two or forty-three. You must have been a kid.'

He thinks about it, puzzled. 'Youth', he says. 'I was youth.' He keeps returning to the subject of GIs and of the children they had made with the Aitutaki women. Then he commences what seems to be a tall tale about a black GI he'd seen. He gestures excitedly and rambles on and on, not realizing he's no longer speaking English and I can't understand. Abruptly, he fixes me with soft brown eyes and asks me as he had in the lagoon: 'What you call dat t'ing?'

'What thing?'

'Dat t'ing. I jus' told you. Dat black GI, he had t'ing dat big!' He holds his hands about a foot apart.

'A weapon?' I ask. 'Some kind of gun?'

'No, *no!*' he cries. Exasperated, he grabs my hand, pulls me over to a clear spot of beach, releases me, kneels and begins to smooth the sand flat as a slate. Picking up a stick, he draws with great concentration.

First, comes a device which looks vaguely heart-shaped. Then, as he continues, I see it's on a long stalk growing out of something – a sea creature rising up from seaweed on a lump of coral? Suddenly, realization of what it is breaks through my weed-entangled mind. The *ariki* has drawn a precise picture of the male genitals. My God! I catch my breath sharply. It's the last thing I thought 'dat t'ing' would be and, looking at this sour-visaged old monarch, the last thing I would have thought was on his mind. I back away, embarrassed, angry, thoughts racing. We're in a very isolated swamp. How am I going to get out of this one? You dumb, dumb broad! I say to myself. You *fool!*

'*Dat* t'ing', he says, pointing to his drawing with pride. 'What you call dat t'ing in English?'

'I don't really know', I reply, something inside cautioning me to go extremely carefully. Mentally, I compare us. I'm bigger, heavier and younger, but he's undoubtedly stronger and faster. Running is futile. I don't know where the nearest settlement is. We're in deep jungle with the lagoon on one side, Aitutaki's one mountain on the other. I must keep my wits about me and be very alert, very tactful. This is no ordinary man, after all, he's a king and culturally,

I'm out of my depth. I fence. 'I don't know!'

'You see dat t'ing, now?'

'Yes', I say. 'I see. But I don't know what the word for dat t'ing is in English.'

Incredulous, he looks at me, then grabs the stick and starts another drawing. This one grows into a graphic representation of that portion of the female anatomy into which 'dat t'ing' fits.

'What you call dat t'ing?' he asks. 'Dat woman t'ing? How you say *dat* one in English?'

Both drawings are fine, executed with great skill. I consider complimenting him on his artistic talent, but figure I'd better not push my luck. 'I have no idea', I say seriously, putting on my most scholarly face, which is easy when you wear glasses. 'I'll try to find out when we get back, if you like. I have a dictionary in my bag at the guesthouse.'

'What dat?'

'Dictionary? It's a book. A book that tells what words mean.'

He stares at me in disbelief. Obviously, I must be retarded. 'You see dat t'ing?' he asks, ready to start another drawing if these aren't clear enough.

'Yes', I respond. 'I see that thing. I just can't remember the English word. We don't say it much.'

To my relief, he suddenly wants to get on the motorcycle again, but, no sooner are we seated than he reaches back and grabs my crotch hard through my denim skirt. '*Dat* t'ing!' he hollers, gives it a squeeze, laughs uproariously and starts the machine on its wavery way out of the swamp. I see two men coming with bush knives. I wave gaily, realizing with gratitude they're the reason we're leaving so abruptly. I ignore his assault.

'I told you', I say formally. 'I do not know the English word, but I will find out and I will tell you later. I really do not know it!' I put a knife-sharp warning edge on my voice.

We ride in silence for a while. Then he asks me to sit closer, ready to start the first game all over again. This time, I don't fall for it and don't laugh. Finally, he gives it up.

'Have you met many American girls here?' I ask, hoping to distract him.

'I see one girl. She very nice. Very nice.' He chuckles. Evidently, he's not going to sulk over the denseness of his under-sexed companion. 'I take her to the reef in my boat, same as you, one time. She got bikini on.' He veers suddenly to avoid a hole.

'I see her lean over to pick up shell and I look close. Her bathing suit very small dere. Dis wide.' He holds his thumb and forefinger up about an inch apart. 'I can see it, you know? I tell her, "Oh, dat's so nice!" She stand up and look at me. "You want it?" she ask, but I say, "No, I too ashamed. All the peoples on beach dey see us close together, dey know what we do. I too ashamed." I tell her dat. When we get to hotel beach, she show me dis book she has. "Here", she say. "Look at dat. You ever see anyt'ing like dat?" and I look at dat book for long time. I never see anyt'ing like dat. White womans in dat book and you could see dere t'ing. Very plain. I never see dat before.'

'White women are no different from Aitutaki women', I say. 'We're all the same down there.'

'No!' he booms, an imperial *ariki* tone in his voice again. 'White womans *not* the same down dere.'

'That just isn't true', I protest. 'What was the name of that book, anyway. Do you remember?'

'I don't know. I no look at the words when I see all dose lovely t'ings.'

'Was it an American book?'

'Yes, I t'ink so.'

'Was it like a magazine?'

He's quiet. Then, finally, 'I don't know dat word.'

'Okay. Was the cover soft or hard? Did you notice that?'

'Dis t'ing *hard* when I see dat book', he roars, reaching down and patting his genitals.

'No, no!' I said. 'The book. Did the *book* have a hard cover? Do you remember?'

'I don't know dat cover.'

Inspired, I ask, 'Did the book have a big page in the middle that folded out with a large picture of a girl on it?'

'Yes!' he shouts, laughing in remembrance. 'You know dat book? Can you get me dat book?'

'Sure, I can. That's easy. I think your book is a magazine called *Playboy*.'

'Yes, yes, *yes*!' he says, almost singing. 'Dat what she call dat book. *Playboy*. You get me dat book?'

'No problem. I'll mail one to you when I get back to the States.'

When we pull into the grounds around the big *kikau* house, his wife meets us, eyes searching my face suspiciously. I grin at her in relief. 'I'm *so* glad to see you!' I cry, giving her an extravagant hug.

'*You* take her home', he mutters to his wife.

Nodding, she beckons me and we get on the motorcycle. Just before we roar off, he comes close and whispers: 'You not forget dat book?'

'No, I won't forget. I want you to study that book and see how silly you are. We are all the same.'

He ignores my whispered lecture. 'You not tell her', he hisses, jerking his chin toward his wife. 'She not know dis book. She not know dat t'ing.'

'I promise. I won't say anything to her.'

'You will send dat book from the States?'

'Of course. I promised, didn't I?'

I kept my promise. Girlie magazines showing 'dose t'ings' were banned in the Cook Islands then. Even for *arikis*, they were *tapu*. I sent him one anyway with a foldout of a blonde Swede displaying her t'ing in full color. I mailed it in a heavy manilla envelope on which I printed in big black letters: 'Educational Material'.

## 17

# BOARDINGHOUSE, ISLAND STYLE

Rain, which roared like some mad torrent from a giant ruptured valve, has finally died away. There is no sound now but the drip, drip, drip of the leaves. A wind revs up once in awhile causing a new flurry of water. My curtains writhe, then lie still.

It is warm. I keep thinking it's cold, but it isn't. I associate windy, rainy nights with winter. It is winter, but winter in the South Seas.

This big, airy, colonial relic of a house is silent tonight, lonely again with nothing of last night's gaiety but echoes. The widow has shut herself up in her room. Ill at ease with Europeans, she keeps to herself even when we're alone together. She looks every inch the old matriarch: part white, part Maori, tall, lean with hooded eyes that have seen some sixty or more hard years.

Yet, late last night, I came home to find her perched drunkenly on a kitchen chair, one bare bony knee under her chin, dress carelessly off one shoulder, flowers in her gray hair. She was laughing and flirting, stern aristocratic face crumpled into girlishness. Her drinking companions were a retired Aitutaki policeman, rumored to be her lover, and the rather strait-laced young Maori father from next door – he who trains the village children to drum and dance in his coral cement barn-sized house, which is simply one vast rectangular room: two beds, a line of mattresses on the floor, an ancient wooden bench against the far wall, photos draped with shell *leis*, clothing strung indoors to dry, and a lone light bulb, too frail to push away the shadows. Patient. He's always so patient with his wild child dancers, even Tupu, who's a handful happy or sad. Pious too: he starts and ends each class with prayer. Yet there he sits drinking beer just like any Joe, with the *grande dame* who seems to have misplaced her dignity and the ex-cop who never seems to lose his. Somehow, they make an incongruous trio.

The widow was almost giddy this morning, a *pareu* tied over her white brassiere, waist-length gray hair hanging loose. Her mood gradually changed to thoughtful productivity as she sat crosslegged on the floor mat, skinny brown legs bared, surrounded by a pile of partially completed appliquéd, embroidered pillow covers, sewing strongly and masterfully, a bit on this one, now some on that: thirty-six grandchildren, three great-grandchildren, all needing *tivaevae* pillow covers to make islands of color in their drab New Zealand homes.

'Sure, he's her lover', says the gossip (who runs the small trade store down the road) of the ex-cop. 'You gotta have a little tickle once in a while, especially when you're old, eh?'

Today, the rain was incessant. About noon, the widow retreated to one of her rooms to snore away the afternoon, satisfied with love, work and life.

Tupu prances over to my chair and demands immediate attention: 'What would you like for lunch today?'

'Something left over from last night', I reply.

Last night's dinner was memorable, all of it from the yard: fried breadfruit chips, sweet potato, taro in coconut cream, fried bananas, *poke*, the rubbery pudding I love so much, chicken and pork.

Tupu rustles about, then hands me a plate of banana sandwiches. Her face is impassive. If she's joking, she doesn't show it. I grimace but try one. Terrible idea. It wasn't at all what I had in mind. I pass on to the fruit salad.

Last night had been good here, really good. We were seven at the big table in the kitchen. Two of the guests even spent the night in this loneliest of guest-houses. There were two young men from the United Nations Development Program; two Cook Islanders from the Wharf Commission in Rarotonga and a pair of tourists who'd strayed in from the rundown, inhospitable Government Hotel down the road.

The conversation was lively. At the core of it, bright, witty, as at home at that tropical table as though written there by Somerset Maugham, was the couple from the Hotel: she, Danish-born with charming accent; he, British, a retired civil servant who'd served in Burma, 'Injah' and Africa. He looked it, too: tall, lean, tan and fit; khaki shirt, matching creased shorts and knee socks. He was a man who could say 'jolly good' and get away with it. Though the pith helmet was no longer part of the tropical uniform, its essence was implied.

Intuitively, I had set the mood for the evening, though never had I dreamed I would have dinner companions straight out of a Maugham novel. I had donned a long white dress with red embroidery at the throat, shoulder and cuff, piled my dark hair on top of my head and added a couple of ivory and yellow *tipani* blossoms from the tree out back. Then, I'd settled down in the parlor with my appliqué work on my lap to await their arrival. Radio Cook Islands played a medley of hit songs popular on the capital Island of Rarotonga, 140 miles away – songs that hadn't been heard in the outside world for at least twenty-five years like 'My Echo, My Shadow and Me', 'Mona Lisa' and 'Que Sera'.

Our guests trooped in on this tropical colonial parlor scene and recognized me instantly as a lady of the past. 'Charming!' the Danish woman cried. I bowed my head modestly, a ghost woman dreaming.

It was a far cry from the dinners I endured nightly in this farm-sized kitchen, alone at a table for twelve. Cook Island protocol demands that the guest eat first and alone. The family eats what is left over, first the men, then women and lastly, children. If the guest is a man and the host is male, the host might sit down with the guest, but apparently, a lone woman guest is an anachronism.

Every bite was performed under the piercing scrutiny of Tupu and Rau, who served me. The Widow Cameron supervised from across the kitchen. Conversation was discouraged. My table manners disintegrated alarmingly under the intense watchfulness of the women. Half of everything ended in my lap. Reading at the table only made matters worse and from the expressions on the faces of my audience, I gathered it was a breach of etiquette.

One night, I unwittingly broke so many dining rules that my reputation as a barbarian was sealed forever. I was led astray by the plight of a hungry hippie. A small band of itinerant Europeans somehow found Aitutaki and set up a commune intending to live off the land. A lanky woman in her early twenties, thin sliver of a face peering from a frizzy shower of white-blond hair, drifted into the house one evening. She was wearing a trailing, not particularly clean, ankle-length creation, handsewn from floral-printed flour sacks. Beside her, one arm wrapped possessively around her waist, was a local Maori girl of about sixteen, as dark as the newcomer was pale. White shark with pilot fish sprang uncharitably to mind.

The hippie wanted to buy some taro. The Widow Cameron held a couple of brown-skinned tubers the size of grapefruit out to her, taking in dirty bare feet and gown disapprovingly. 'Oh, is that what it looks like raw', she said. 'I've only seen it cooked.' Fumbling in a grimy shoulder bag, the girl produced a few coins. The widow waved the money away. Tupu and Rau began serving my dinner. I sat there alone at the head of that long table with a dozen dishes before me, heaped with the best Aitutaki had to offer, acutely embarrassed in the presence of such obvious want. 'Why don't you join me?' I asked her daringly. 'There's plenty!'

'Oh, no, that's all right', she said. 'The others are waiting for me, you know. It's just that nobody went out to pick taro today.'

'Pick it? I thought you dug it like a potato.' I mulled the mysteries of taro over in my mind. '*Do* you pick it?' I asked, no longer sure.

'I really don't know', she replied. 'That's one of the problems we have, you see. We don't know what some of this stuff looks like. The natives say, "Just go pick what you need. The growing food is for everyone", but we don't know where to find it and then, if we do find it and recognize it, sometimes we don't know how to get at it. Like the papayas, you know? And breadfruit and coconuts. They all grow up so high. I'm getting awfully sick of bananas.'

She edged over to the table to inspect my dinner. 'Please, sit down', I urged her.

'No. I don't want to spoil your dinner, but I just want to ask you – what's that?' She pointed to a bowlful of thin crisp chips. 'Fried breadfruit chips. Here, try them.' I passed her the bowl. She gobbled one like a starving dog, whereupon I insisted she sit down and eat. She glanced over at Mrs Cameron, who promptly turned her back and busied herself chopping something. Nervously, she sat. Tupu brought her a knife, fork and plate. She ate fast and silently, putting something of every dish aside for her chums.

'Are there many of you here?' I asked. Chewing, she shook her head and held up five fingers. 'What are you doing, setting up a commune?' She nodded and reached for the bread. 'Do you have permission to stay here on the land? Camping's illegal, as far as I've heard.'

'One of the boys went to school with a native guy from here in Auckland. It's his family land we're on. They said it was okay. They don't speak much English.'

'How long have you been here?'

'Me, I came over on the *Mataora*. I saw you, but I was so sick, I stayed below in my bunk the whole time', she said. 'I was with my boyfriend. The other three have been here two weeks.'

'You sound like you're from the States?'

'Yeah, I am, and so's Mark. The rest are Kiwis.'

I was fascinated. 'What are you going to do here, just farm or something?'

'Oh', she paused in her chewing, blue eyes darting about the room, 'we're just going to live off the land and in exchange, try to help the poor people here. We've all got skills. I'm a midwife. Mark's a potter. One of the guys makes jewelry, the other one is a cabinetmaker and Sheila's a secretary, or she was.'

'What poor people?' I said in a low screech. 'On Aitutaki? Nobody's starving. They grow all the food they need and the sea is teeming with food. Everyone has shelter. It's not fancy, but it's there. No one's ever frozen to death on Aitutaki.'

She smiled beatifically. 'Isn't it lovely? They never have winter.'

'Right.' I said, 'and they also have midwives who apparently do okay, judging by the sizes and look of these families. I think you're going to have to come up with other ways to pay for what you're using. Your potter friend might have a problem finding clay here and there's not much call for jewelers or cabinet-makers. The secretary could teach the young girls office work, I suppose, but I doubt there's more than a couple of typewriters on the island. You guys are nuts! It's the people here who could teach you a few things.'

She rose, wounded, and tucked the extra food into her bag. 'Maybe they don't need our help now, but when more people join us and they see what a beautiful model for communal living we've created from nothing, they'll come around.' She plucked at herself nervously. 'Thank you for the meal and the taro', she said. 'I've got to get back to my family.'

Her Aitutaki girl shadow disengaged herself from whispered conversation with Tupu and Rau and flitted quickly to her side. She reached out and stroked the platinum blonde bushy mane of her hippie girlfriend, flexing her eyebrows at Tupu and Rau with pride of ownership written all over her.

'Let's go, shall we?' said the fair one and the two glided out into the night, the island girl in her clean little shift, her ethereal companion in her grubby flour-sack dress, arms around each other's waists.

'Wasn't she beautiful?' sighed Tupu. 'Oh, I wish I looked like that.'

'Who? The blonde?' She jerked her chin up, eyebrows flexing agreement. 'Oh for heaven's sake, Tupu', I said in annoyance, 'you're a hundred times more beautiful!'

The Widow Cameron, too, was unimpressed, not just with our exotic visitor, but with her tenant. She spoke rapidly to Tupu in Maori. 'Excuse me, but Mrs Cameron says you must pay extra for your guest's meal', she translated with an embarrassed shuffle.

'No problem. I expected to. She can just add it to my bill', I said, rising. 'I think I'll go down to the Manuae and see if there's anyone about.'

I was halfway down the verandah steps when Tupu called out to me. 'Mrs Cameron says you pay her now for your guest.'

The hippies were deported by a Cook Islands Immigration Officer a month after I left Aitutaki. There was a brief item in the press. They were found to be in desperate straits, suffering from malnutrition, unable to find food in the midst of plenty, stealing from their neighbors. Their only contribution was to agriculture, but it turned out to be cannabis, or so it was thought by Tupu, who'd heard of it in Hawaii.

The day of the beachcomber in paradise had passed on into history along with the pith helmet.

# 18

## MANUAE TAKEAWAY; OR,
## THE GREAT RU LANDED WHERE?

It's midweek in Aitutaki. The rain has finally stopped, stars blaze overhead and the Manuae Takeaway is open at last. It's the only spot on the island where you can buy a drink besides the Government Hotel, which is dead anyway, except on Friday nights when locals get falling down drunk as fast as possible in an exercise advertised to tourists as 'Island Night'.

The Manuae is an informal scattering of picnic tables in someone's front yard. Here you can buy a sandwich, chips and a bottle of beer most nights except Sunday, and always find someone to debate or flirt with.

On this brilliant evening of luminous trade-wind clouds and rustling palm fronds, an important group has gathered. Two cabinet ministers from Rarotonga are on Aitutaki for a conference and here they are, at Manuae instead of the fine Government Hotel. I recognize the Minister of Public Works (I'll call him Moko) and the Minister of Education (Teariki seems a good name to use here) among the drinkers. With them are two teachers from the local college: one, an Australian with an aid program and his writer-wife; the other, Aitutaki-born, plus a couple from a nearby banana plantation. Hailing me and my companion, they call out to us to join them.

The topic, as we plunked our bottles down on the table, was the fall from grace of the founding father of the self-governing Cook Islands, its first premiere, the former Sir Albert Henry. It was an emotionally charged subject everywhere in the country in 1979, but on Aitutaki, Henry's birthplace, it was volatile.

'They should not have taken the premiere's seat from him!' said one local thickly. 'Queen Elizabeth should not have been so quick to take away his knighthood, either! He did what any man would do.'

'But look here, mate, don't you think what he did was stealing?' asked the Australian teacher.

His Aitutaki colleague tilted his beer bottle, drank deeply, slapped it on the table and jumped into the fray. 'Our ways are different from yours. What was wrong was taking his seat away!'

'Papa won the election! The people voted for *him*, not Tom Davis!' a local called out from the next table. 'You can't just take a man's seat away when he's stood for office and won!'

'Hack off, mate', argued the Aussie, an edge in his voice now, 'Sir Albert won by fraud. He dipped into next year's postage stamp revenues to fly voters home from New Zealand free to vote for him. That wasn't his money to give away. That was *your* money, the public's money. Don't you think that's wrong?'

'No! You don't take a man's seat away after he's won it! You don't take away his title after you give it to him for service to his people. That's not our way. We don't need outsiders telling us how to run our elections.' The other teacher, usually so diffident in the presence of visitors, was growing belligerent. 'Papa trusted the wrong people.'

'Then what you're saying, mate, is that the only thing Sir Albert did wrong here was to get caught.' The Australian's normally red face was growing purple. 'Is that what you Aitutaki people want me to teach your little ones about your history?'

The Manuae's owner appeared with a tray of fresh beers and started distributing them noisily.

'Excuse me, but I don't think you have much of a chance of winning an argument about that election on Sir Albert's home island', I cautioned the young Aussie with a grin. He smiled back.

'Too right. Must be the beer.'

Up to this point, the two politicians in the group had been silent, taking it all in with bloodshot eyes from behind a veritable forest of empty beer bottles. The momentary silence roused them from their stupors.

'History! No white man will *ever* write or teach the true history of my people. Never!' Moko shouts suddenly.

'How about a white woman?' Jean, the Australian teacher's wife, parries.

'White woman? Well, maybe. I think about that one. See, woman is boss here.' He slams the table with his hand, making the beer bottles jump and tumble. Dropping his voice a few decibels, he explains how it is in the world of Aitutaki: 'I never leave the Cook Islands. I was born right here on Aitutaki and I never leave the Cook Islands, not until I am sixty. I promise my wife. Man, you know, has an animal nature. All the time he go after young woman. He can't help himself.'

WHITE SAVAGES IN THE SOUTH SEAS

He gave a seductive wag of his bushy black eyebrows at Jean. 'After sixty, man no good for woman anymore. That's why I promise my wife I wait until I am sixty to go to New Zealand. Woman is boss here. I wait and I form new government. Put all women in my cabinet some day.' He rises, weaves over to the bar and returns with eight bottles clutched in his big, work-worn hands. He distributes them around the table, sinks to the bench with a deep beery exhalation and appears to nod off.

'Hey, Teariki', says the Australian teacher to the Minister of Education. 'I hear there's a new book about to come out on the history of the Cook Islands. Remember the Kiwi from Auckland University who was here last year doing research? That's the chap who wrote it.'

'No one', Teariki growls, 'has *ever* told the truth in *any* book about these islands. It is not possible for any man to tell the truth if he did not learn it from his parents.'

'How about a woman?' Jean asks. We all laugh.

'Well, maybe woman. No. No woman either. No man is going to lie to his son!' Teariki springs up and pounds on the table, making the beer bottles dance. 'No woman is going to lie to her daughter. That's why our history is told to us by our parents. Nobody can tell you our history until their hair is gray!' He glares around the table to be sure we three white faces understand. Moko and the local Maori schoolteacher nod in solemn agreement. 'The only true history of the Cook Islands is what is passed on by word of mouth from father to son, from mother to daughter!'

To make his point, Teariki drains his beer and raises the bottle aloft, commanding attention.

'Where did the Great Navigator Ru land when he came to Aitutaki? Show these *papaa*s how we know our true history as we learned it from our fathers who learned it from their fathers all the way back to Ru!'

Instantly, local Maoris at our table (several with gray hair) rose to their feet, beer spilling, index fingers pointing, unfalteringly, no two in quite the same direction.

Locals at adjoining tables joined in, shouting. Historical facts were proclaimed, bandied about and debated. Ancient canoe names were hurled back and forth, ancestral names of crew members from the ancient time of Ru were quoted as irrefutable proof. The argument lapsed into Maori. All interest in educating the foreign listeners had evaporated. How could *papaa*s like us drunks possibly understand, anyway, since we didn't even understand local politics?

We three from the outside world excused ourselves and walked off down the moonlit road. 'God help any poor bastard of a serious scholar on this island!' muttered the Australian schoolteacher.

# 19

## SOME ENCHANTED EVENING ...

Polynesian nights are sensual with a thousand voluptuous fragrances. Great seas spend themselves on reef and shore, pounding out primal rhythms of creation and destruction. Colors, blazing by day under a hot sun, smolder in the moonlight. The great phalluses of coconut palms dwarf all life, immense fronds lashing back and forth eighty feet overhead in the tradewinds, fat coconuts bobbing. Now and then, one wrenches loose and hurls itself to earth in the endless orgies of Rangi and Papa. The great Polynesian creation story is always a palpitating presence.

In the beginning, the sky, Rangi, lay on the earth, Papa, in an endless, copulating embrace. Nothing existed but their offspring, born and living in the dark, hidden between their bodies.

As these young gods grew, they yearned for light and space. Each, in turn, strove to push the parents apart. It was Tane who finally succeeded, thrusting his father, Rangi, so high that never again could he lay on Papa, leaving her and their issue in perpetual darkness.

In the upheaval, many of the Sky Father's penises were left behind, impaled deep in the Earth Mother to become coconut palms. These would remind her ever of Rangi when his winds made them vibrate and dance. The rains are said to be Rangi's tears as he yearns to be in the arms of his beloved mate once again.

Just breathing such engorged air is enough to drive even a vacationing accountant to flights of purple prose! Unfortunately, romantic fantasies manufactured to western specifications by poets, novelists and filmmakers tend to pop like bubbles when they hit a real South Sea Island beach. Polynesian heirs of these Edenlike bits of geography have an unsettlingly pragmatic attitude when it comes to romance, more related to survival of the tribe than to finding 'true love.' The myths survive anyway, their perpetual flames sheltered by the rather large egos developed by sexually satisfied western male visitors who don't speak or understand Polynesian languages and haven't a clue when they've been 'had'.

The pink, beery, middle-aged man regales shipmates with his tales of a shore conquest as his cruise ship leaves Tahiti: 'I don't know what happened last night, but it must have been something. I passed out finally, but this morning, I found out I had myself a Tahitian name. Ask anybody in Papeete who Big Mahu is and they'll tell you, "Aloma's boyfriend. He was the greatest lover she ever had and her heart will break if he doesn't return to her someday."' Aloma and her waterfront sisters wave from shore, shrieking with laughter, trading explicit descriptions of the sexual performances of their departing tourist visitors, the word *mahu*, or effeminate, cropping up most frequently.

A tourist boards his plane after an idyll in a small hotel on one of the outer Cook Islands with a twinkle in his eye and a smug smile. Wait until he tells the guys this one! Is he a big stud or what? The girls were so crazy for him, they climbed through his windows at night and into his bed. They couldn't get enough of him! There was one in particular – nearly broke her heart when he left. He would never forget her.

Commercial fishermen, forbidden to land on isolated atolls, fish offshore and return to their homelands boasting of their amazing sexual magnetism. South Seas sirens swam or paddled canoes right out to the ship for a few secret giggling moments in their embrace in the lifeboats.

Nine months later, fat, sassy babies are often the result, their fathers remembered gratefully for their donation to the gene pool. It's hard to find anyone to whom one isn't related to father children on isolated Outer Islands with few visitors. Even if the brief liaison didn't result in a new villager, it was still a welcome break in the monotony of island life.

On islands such as Rarotonga with international airports, the sport of mating still tops rugby in popularity, but nowadays, it's more for novelty and adventure than for the grand prize of a genetic contribution. Male visitors can take care of themselves, but God help the occasional lone woman traveler who comes ashore humming 'Some enchanted evening …' who isn't at least armed with Mace!

Live electronic music in the Banana Court on Rarotonga's waterfront is so loud Friday and Saturday nights, the vocalists have to scream just to stay even. The famous dance hall is body-to-body with locals dedicated to getting enough beer and copulation to hold them over the long, dry Sunday ahead.

I barged into this urgently merry scene alone one Friday night when I was new to the island and still abloom with delusions of the Romantic South Seas.

Before I'd even found a table, I was grabbed by a lurching, red-eyed, disheveled, beer-belching Rarotongan male and asked to dance – at least, I assumed that was the question.

I declined, peeling him off arm by arm, and headed for a space at the bar. Immediately, another grabbed me, this one so far gone I had to hold him up while he breathed alcoholic endearments in my face in broken English. After about ten minutes of rebuffing similar encounters, I gave up and let myself be groped onto the dance floor. It was packed. The music was deafening. My partner sagged against me. I put my arms around him to hold him up. Gratefully, he wrapped himself about me and proceeded to make motions with his pelvis not usually done on a public dance floor.

Indignantly, I shoved him off into his fellows and dry swam back toward the bar. I was grabbed by another local with an erection, this time by the hips, and fuck-danced to the pounding drums and electronic excesses of the guitars.

'Goddammit, quit that', I hissed, trying to free myself. He held on tight, face against my face, pelvis thrusting at mine. Risking a fall, I brought one knee up hard. He grunted, hands flying from my hips to his crotch, bloodshot eyes filled with tears of betrayal and pain.

Angrily, I forced my way through the whooping crowd of oblivious dancers and whatevers, gained the door and half ran the quarter of a mile up the dark coral road inland to my room at the Hibiscus Court. No one followed this cruel bitch of a visitor.

The next day I told Miri, my half-Maori landlady, 'See why I wouldn't go with you?' she laughed. 'Don't get so upset. That's just the way Cook Islands men are. They're harmless. They're so shy, they think they have to be drunk to talk to a girl they like. They must like you, that's all. You should be flattered! Just hardcases, all of them.' (She called everyone hardcase, from naughty children to wife beaters.)

'How can they expect any woman to be attracted to them when they're so drunk they can't even walk, much less dance? Do they think a woman gets turned on by a man who talks like his mouth is full of pudding, whose eyes are bright red and who stinks like a brewery?'

'Well, the local girls don't seem to mind, but then, they're used to it. Just stay away from them when they're drinking. Stick to the floor shows in the hotels. I'll go with you to those, but not to the Banana Court.'

'Yeah, but I want to see something of real Island life, not just tourist stuff.'

'My friends and I go to the hotels and we're locals. Come along tonight. You'll see a real Island-style floor show and hear some dreamy music.'

That night, Saturday, we climbed into her little Holden and drove to the Rarotongan Hotel. The floor show was pure Cook Islands dancing, more athletic than sensual, young ladies moving their hips at great speed, but chastely, side to side, never forward or revolving rapidly as their Tahitian counterparts do. The boys did a fast, rhythmic, bent knee–rocking, elbow-jabbing calisthenic-like routine that looked like great fun. The dancers were obviously joyous island teenagers just having a good time after school. The effect was endearing.

Then the dance band took the floor, which was what Miri had come to hear. The tourists filed out to a waiting bus for a taste of 'Real Island Life' and locals streamed in late, half of them New Zealanders with Rarotongan or half-Rarotongan wives and girlfriends, ready for action. The music now was in the Guy Lombardo–style of the 1940s and 1950s. A half-caste crooner in an island shirt and white trousers took the microphone and Miri moaned with pleasure as he sang 'Vaya con Dios'.

The dance floor quickly filled with Rarotonga's elite: shuffling, bobbing half-castes and white New Zealanders. The women's frocks were reminiscent of the 'housedresses' my career-girl mother sniggered at thirty years ago when 'Vaya con Dios' was a hit song we sang together on car trips. Flower crowns or single blooms behind one ear relieved the frumpiness only slightly. Their fair-skinned escorts were more dashing in crisply ironed Island-print shirts and white long trousers. No one asked me to dance, here. 'Maybe it's because they're all sober', I whispered in some amusement to Miri.

'No, hardcase. They're all couples or people who've known each other for years. If you want to dance, I'll ask someone for you.'

'Forget it', I said, embarrassed. 'I'm having a lovely time just watching.' I buried my muzzle in my Meyers and Miri danced off with an old friend. Romance in the South Seas, bah humbug! I commented to no one in particular.

As we drove along by the lagoon toward Avarua, Miri chattered on and on. 'One nice thing about our little island is that a woman is safe here, anywhere! I hear it's dangerous in the States for women to even walk alone on the road after dark.'

'Well, I don't know if it's that way everywhere in the States but it sure is in California. But how do you *know* it's safe to go walking alone here at night? You never do it.'

'Really. You don't have a thing to worry about. Our men are very shy with strangers.'

Miri, as I soon learned the hard way, was quite out of touch with reality.

One Friday night, I went to bed early, but the moon was so bright I couldn't sleep. I gave up, pulled a long, sacklike Mexican dress over my head and meandered down to the waterfront.

Faint sounds above the surf crashing on the reef proclaimed that the Banana Court was going full tilt. I strolled in the direction of the music and laughter. Couples were sitting on the low wall or weaving drunkenly down the empty road, laughing and greeting each other. A tangle of motorcycles and cars sprawled under the trees. Feeling invisible and pleased, I watched the happy scene, the music muted by the old coral walls of the Banana Court. I sang along with a familiar melody softly, glad I'd come out into the moonlight.

Finally, I drifted back the way I'd come, took one last lingering look at the sea and the breakers far out on the reef, foam gleaming like snow in the moonlight, then headed back toward the Hibiscus Court.

The lane was dark with arching trees overhead, but it was a familiar stroll and I felt no fear, even though clouds started moving across the moon.

As I passed the open stretch by the grassy expanse of the athletic field, I heard someone walking behind me. I turned. It was a young man I'd never seen before. Something about his gait made me nervous and I decided to speed up, not slow down and greet him with a polite *kia orana*. He speeded up too.

I slowed then, and moved toward the edge of the road to let him pass if he was in such a hurry. He drew abreast and grabbed me, roughly. Shocked, I backed into the shrubbery bordering the road while trying to free myself. 'Are you crazy? Leave me alone!' Up close, I could see he was nothing but a kid in his teens.

Hissing obscenities, he grabbed my neckline and ripped my dress half off, shoving me to the ground in one violent motion. My immediate response was outrage, not fear. I started screaming so loudly, I thought my vocal chords would tear loose.

Somewhere down near the seaward end of the dark lane a female voice called out: 'Do you need help?'

'Yes! Helllllp!' was my shrieking reply. 'Raaaaape!'

My young assailant rolled off me, jumped up and ran across the field with the speed of an athlete. I struggled to my feet, gathering the torn pieces of my dress together over my chest, panting. A large, wild-looking woman in her early twenties came rushing up out of the darkness.

'Are you all right? Do you know him?'

Suddenly, I got the shakes. 'I've never seen him before. He went across the playing field, that way!' I pointed one quivering arm. 'Call the police, quick!'

'Did he do anything to you?' she asked, one arm encircling me, the other hand stroking my hair soothingly, just a big, warm Polynesian woman comforting a wounded stranger – or so I thought.

'No', I said, tears now streaming. 'He didn't have time to do anything, but he tore my dress. He would have raped me if you hadn't answered. Just get the police. He's not far. I feel it. They can catch him if we hurry.'

'Well, you don't have to call the police if he didn't do anything to you', she rationalized soothingly.

My tears dried up. 'What *are* you talking about? That man tried to rape me. He's crazy to try to do that to someone. Maybe you'll be the next one, or some child! A guy like that should be locked up!'

She kept patting and stroking me, begging me not to fret, telling me it was okay and I wasn't hurt. 'I know who that boy was', she confided. 'You don't have to call the police. I'll just tell his father.'

But every cell in my body was thoroughly charged by then with feminist outrage. 'I'm staying at the Hibiscus up ahead. Come! I want you to be my witness. I'm going to call the police immediately from Miri's phone. Nobody has the right to push people around like that!'

She walked with me, arm around my shoulders, but when we reached Miri's big house, she hung back, refusing to come farther. 'Okay. Stay, then. But don't leave. Wait for me!' I commanded. 'Wait.'

Miri had little sympathy to waste when my knocking and shouting woke her. With obvious reluctance, she invited me in and motioned me to one of the big rattan chairs in her parlor. I told my story quickly with only occasional tears. She listened in silence.

'Well, then, he's gone now and you don't appear to be hurt other than a few scrapes. Pity about your dress. Maybe it can be mended. Cuppa tea?'

I nodded. 'Tea would help. Yes, please. But I must make that call immediately. Do I just ring up the operator and ask for the police?'

She called out from the kitchen as she plugged in the electric kettle: 'Don't be so upset. It's all over. It's silly to call the police if you can't even identify him. What's the use?'

'I think the girl outside can identify him.'

'Who? I didn't see anyone with you.'

Miri rushed outside to see who was lurking about. She called out in Maori. My rescuer's voice replied. The two spoke briefly, then Miri returned. 'You're quite right. She does seem to know him and his family. I know his father, of course. If you really want to call the police, I'll do it for you.' She cranked vigorously, then spoke rapidly in Maori to the operator.

We waited for about thirty minutes after her call before two constables arrived looking smart and official in their khaki shorts and shirts. They studied me for a moment, taking in the torn dress, the bloody elbow, the matted hair threaded with grass and asked me, in some embarrassment, if anything had happened beyond a bit of rough stuff. 'No, he didn't succeed in raping me', I said, since it seemed difficult for them to ask the question. 'He would have if the girl outside hadn't called out. He's a dangerous young man. Next time he might really hurt someone!'

Both policemen now seemed amazed at being called at all. 'Our boys don't tend to be dangerous. The bloke probably had a bit too much to drink, that's all. He'll be right in the morning', said the young Maori officer.

'I didn't smell any alcohol on his breath', I said. 'He wasn't drunk. He knew exactly what he was doing.'

With a heavy sigh, the older of the two officers, a Kiwi, scribbled some notes as I described the incident. Then he closed his book and prepared to leave.

'Does this sort of thing happen around here often?'

'Yes, I rather think it does, but the local girls sort of expect it. They can take care of themselves. They don't need to call the police.'

The other agreed. 'Anyone try that on one of my sisters, if she didn't want him, she'd break his head', he said simply. 'Our girls are strong. They know what the boys are like.'

The New Zealander nodded. 'But sometimes, girls do end up in hospital. You're lucky he didn't use a rock on you.'

They beckoned to Miri and the three strolled outside to question my shrinking rescuer, who refused to come in out of the dark. They talked to her at some length in Maori. Finally, Miri returned alone. 'They've gone now to talk to his father and pick up the boy if they can find him. It's all right. He won't bother you again. Come. I'll walk you to your bungalow.'

I unlocked my door, turned on the light and hesitated. 'Suppose he got in and he's hiding in here? All you have to do is pull a few louvers out.'

'There's no one inside. Look, I'll show you', she said, walking briskly through the main room, past the kitchen and into the bathroom. 'You'll be all right.' Her voice dropped to almost a whisper. 'You must not let that one who helped you in. Lock your door tight after me when I leave and do not open it again until morning. The police told me to tell you that.'

'The police said not to let that girl in? Why not? She probably saved my life. She wouldn't hurt anyone!'

'Your life?' She laughed. 'That boy wouldn't have killed you and he's not going to come back tonight anyway. That business is over. It's the other one you have to watch out for. I didn't know he was back on the island. Neither did the police. They told me to tell you not to let him in and lock your door', she repeated.

'What do you mean, him? That was a girl who helped me.'

Miri looked rather embarrassed now. 'No, that one is a real hardcase. It's part boy, part girl. That's the way he was born. His real name is Trevor.'

'You mean he's a hermaphrodite? The poor thing.'

'Yes. That's the word. I can never remember it. Thanks. Well, he/she, Trevor, was supposed to get an operation in New Zealand, but I don't think he really did. He got in trouble there for stealing. Instead of sentencing him to jail, they just shipped him back here. We don't want him either, and if I were you, I'd do what the policeman said: lock your door, get some sleep and just forget the whole thing!' She left as I protested that he'd been kind to me, whatever he was.

Outside the wind freshened until the night was filled with rustling leaves and the occasional hard thunk of a coconut hitting the ground. I tried to sleep, but I was too jittery. Suddenly, I realized one of the night sounds was human. Someone was scratching the wall near the window. As I watched in the dimness, two dark hands closed around a louver, pulled it out and a wistful familiar feminine face appeared in the space.

'I thought you might be scared alone so I thought I'd stay with you', the 'girl' I now must think of as 'Trevor' said gently.

'I'm okay, thanks', I whispered.

'Can I come in?'

My heart pounding, I said, 'No. I can't let you in. The police said I must keep the door locked.'

'I can come in through the louvers. Then you wouldn't have to unlock the door.'

'No, that's fine. I really need to be alone.'

'We could talk through the window. You could tell me about the States.'

I tried to analyze the situation. Was it threatening? I had no room phone and Miri's house was too far away for shouts to reach in the wind. The motel was empty, except for me. 'The police don't want me to let you in or even to talk to you because of your trouble in New Zealand', I parried. 'I wish there was some way I could thank you for your kindness to me. I know you don't mean me any harm and I want to let you in, but I'm a foreigner here and I mustn't get mixed up with anything the police ask me to avoid. Can you understand that? I'm a cowardly foreigner.'

Trevor watched me with pleading dark eyes. Finally, he flexed his eyebrows. 'Do you have any cigarettes?'

'No. I quit two years ago.'

'Do you have anything to drink?'

'Just a little rum. Here, you can have it', and I passed a half-full bottle of Meyers through the louvers.

About two hours later, I was finally dozing off when I heard the scratching again. 'Go away, Trevor!' I called rudely this time. I listened for footsteps. Did I hear them or was it the wind? There was no point in kidding myself. I wasn't going to sleep tonight. For the first time in ages, I wished I had a cigarette.

Months later, back in the US, I got a letter from the Rarotonga police. My assailant, who was only seventeen and a member of a prominent family, had been found guilty of assault and fined NZ$20 for tearing my dress. The police said they hoped the money would replace it. I wrote back and suggested they donate it to the library. When I asked Miri a year later how things had turned out for Trevor, she pretended she'd never heard of him.

How does that romantic song from 'South Pacific' go? 'Some enchanted evening, you may see a stranger ...'

## 20

# DEFECTION TO MITIARO

Even if I waited for the next boat to Pukapuka, the sailing date couldn't be confirmed. I turned away from Silk and Boyd's shipping office on Rarotonga with mixed feelings. To be so close and not be able to get there after all those years of anguishing to see the atoll Robert Dean Frisbie called home – that hurt.

On the other hand, if I could extend my stay in the Cook Islands until the next boat day, did I really want to spend two weeks throwing up? It was a 715-mile voyage by interisland cargo boat. That's at least a week out and a week back. Maybe if I waited a year, medical technology would come up with something that would bring my stomach into harmony with the sailor in my soul. Better yet, maybe the government would build airstrips in the Northern Cooks, including Pukapuka.

In the meantime, one could fly to any island in the Southern Cooks, even if they didn't have tourist accommodations. This didn't mean strangers couldn't stay on these islands. They could, but there was a catch. They must get permission and arrange for housing with a chief administration officer (CAO). This could be difficult without connections. Air Rarotonga's manager agreed to make a few inquiries for me. A week passed. Finally, he called. 'Have you ever heard of Mitiaro?' he asked.

'Mitiaro? Yes! Pa Ariki mentioned it when I interviewed her. She said it's beautiful with beautiful people. It's very special to her.'

'It's a nice little island all right, and only about an hour's flight. Good thing you're so enthusiastic because it's the *only* one with a CAO who'll take you.'

'Well, I'm glad you found *one*, anyway.'

'Right. Old Papa Raui had some reservations about it, seeing you're a woman traveling alone. He asked me if you had any friends on Raro who could vouch for your character. I told him you were staying with one of his daughter's old friends. He must have called Miri because now he says you're welcome to come.'

My feminist sensibilities rumbled. 'Would he have checked on me so closely if I were a man?'

'Now, now. This is the Cook Islands', he said. 'They look at things a little differently.'

'I'm going to talk to Miri and find out what he asked her. How long do I have to make up my mind?'

'Two days', he said, 'but space is limited. Don't take too long about it.'

I ran into Miri at the post office and immediately started a tirade. She laughed at me, which she does quite a lot, and said Papa Raui just wanted to know if I was out to steal Mitiaro husbands, seduce the teenaged boys, run around drunk and naked and sneak booze to the menfolk. 'Mitiaro is a dry island', she said. 'No alcohol allowed.'

'What did you tell him?'

'Oh, I said your idea of a good time is a morning in the churchyard weeding Frisbie's grave, followed by an afternoon at the library, topped off by an evening alone with your typewriter. I told him if you didn't like the way the local boys said hello, you just called the police!'

'Thanks a lot', I said, annoyed. 'If a local boy said hello to you by knocking you down and half tearing your dress off, you'd call the cops, too!'

'No, I wouldn't', she said, 'because it wouldn't happen to me. I know everybody *and* their parents!'

'Right', I said. 'What about this CAO on Mitiaro. Does he check up on strange men who ask to visit his island like he did me?'

'Oh, you know, hardcase, it's different with men, but it's not a question of equality here so don't start on one of your lectures. Our men and women have different but equal roles. Women don't travel alone and they seldom sleep alone. If they aren't with their men, they'll sleep with female relatives, children or girlfriends. We don't even go into the bush alone. If we do, the boys accept it as an invitation.'

'Okay, fine, I've read about that, but I'm almost fifty. I'm hardly a girl.'

'Oh, your kind is the worst!' she laughed. 'Your man isn't here, which means you aren't being taken care of and probably need a bit of action in the worst way!'

'Oh for Pete's sake, you know I'm not here looking for a man! I just like traveling alone. If I'm with someone, I'm worried about are they having a good time and do they want to do this or would they mind if I went off on my own? My observations are all cockeyed because someone else's are in the way and I end up spending too much time talking to someone I know. I can't write!

'I'm intensely curious, for instance, to experience life on a remote island in the middle of the ocean. All I know is what I've read from a male viewpoint.

'What do women like me do all day on a little island? What's important to them? Are they really nothing but mindless sex objects in grass skirts living only for pleasure? I don't believe it. What do they dream of? I'll bet my life on it that we have a lot in common.'

She looked at me strangely.

'Well, what's it feel like to wake up on a speck of land surrounded by a universe of water. Alone! That's the kind of thing I'm interested in. I'm no Sadie Thompson!'

'Well, that's all very well to say', she replied, 'but suppose you get pregnant?'

'Miri! You aren't listening to me.'

'Yes, I am. But you want to know about us from locals, not books, and I'm trying to help you. This is the way we look at visitors. We are very realistic. If a *papaa* man goes to an Outer Island and gets a girl pregnant, that can be a good thing. The baby grows up on the island and helps with the fishing and planting and takes care of the old people when that time comes.

'It isn't very romantic, as you *papaas* like to imagine, but if the baby's father is intelligent, and he must be if he's got enough education and money to travel this far, then the baby inherits that as well as all the brains and skills of his Cook Islands ancestors.'

'What about the Church? I thought missionaries frowned on such fooling around.'

She spread her hands, palms up. 'On Outer Islands, it's hard to find anybody you aren't related to to father your children. If you go with a *papaa*, maybe the child's skin will be fair. We think that's beautiful. If the child is sent to Cook Islands relatives in New Zealand or Australia, it gets a chance at a good education and a job and he can send remittances home every month to help the family back on the island.

'Now if a woman visitor, like yourself, gets pregnant from a local man, she goes away and has the baby overseas and it's lost forever to the Islands. It never helps the family at home, it never sends money to help when it grows up. If the man who got the woman pregnant goes with her, he's lost to the family too, because a European wife would not let her husband send part of their money home to his family. She would want to keep everything: baby, man and money. That's not our way.'

For once, I had no smart retort.

She laughed merrily. 'You'll be all right, hardcase. You'll have a wonderful time on Mitiaro. It's paradise!'

'Paradise? You still haven't told me one thing about the place.'

'I can't. I've never been there.'

'Then how do you know it's paradise?'

'Because', she paused and cocked her head, 'I haven't been there and if I never go, it always will be.'

'You Cook Islanders are so full of contradictions, you give me a stomach ache!'

I returned to my flat and cranked up Air Rarotonga on the telephone. 'Okay', I said, 'if you still have a seat on the Mitiaro flight, I'll take it. But don't ask me why. Can *you* tell me anything about the place? What's the name mean, for starters?'

'There isn't much to tell, actually', the manager replied. 'Mitiaro means face on the ocean, I understand. Used to be called Nukuroa in the old days. That just means "big land". It's a makatea island with no lagoon so you won't have much swimming, I fear. There's a lake on it, or rather, a swamp. Quite a rare eel lives in it. It's a great delicacy to some people, though I don't care much for it.'

'Eels', I said. 'I can't wait.'

'Let me see here', he paused. I could hear the rustle of papers as he found what he was looking for. 'Ah yes, it's the fourth largest of the Cook Islands and it's 142 nautical miles northeast by east of Rarotonga. You'll be staying with Papa Raui Pokoati and his wife, Taimata or Mama Tai. They have a lovely large home. You'll have your own private bedroom. Mama's a beautiful cook. The house is quite modern. In fact, it's the only one on the island with electricity and a flush toilet!'

'What exactly is makatea?'

'Well, that's your coral island that's been thrust up from the sea by volcanic action long ago. We have several in the Cooks: Mangaia and Atiu, for instance. It's very sharp going and you must wear tennis shoes walking around, but it's worth it. These islands are fascinating. They're all hollow, more or less, with great caverns. Sometimes they make an eerie booming sound. This one, Mitiaro, is pretty flat. No hills. It's only a few feet above sea level.'

'Is it heavily populated?'

'Oh my, no! Less than three hundred people are left.'

'Fascinating. Could I fly over, spend the night and return the next day?'

'Afraid not. If you go at all, it has to be for five days because that's how frequently we fly there.'

'Five days or nothing?'

'Afraid so.'

'God, suppose I break my leg or my neck out there? Oh, go ahead and book me', I said. 'When do we go?'

'We fly out on Thursday. We'll return you to Rarotonga Tuesday morning, and you're really in luck because you'll be there when the *Waikato* arrives. That's the big New Zealand naval ship that was on the front page of the *Cook Islands News* this morning. They've never seen a navy ship there.'

I failed to see what was so wonderful about a visit from a military vessel. It ranked somewhere below eels in my wish book. I mentioned it to Miri with a wrinkled nose.

'The *Waikato* calls while you're there? Oh, then you're really in for a treat. The New Zealand Navy has never made a call on Mitiaro, official or unofficial. It will be the biggest, most modern ship the Islanders have ever seen and the most outsiders since the missionaries put a stop to cannibal raids from Atiu. Why, when the Kiwi sailors land, it will probably double the population! Mitiaro will have the biggest *umukai* (feast) they've ever had or ever will again!'

'I wasn't looking to share great moments in history', I grumbled. 'I wanted to experience the small moments.'

'You're in for a treat! You'll see, hardcase!'

I went into Avarua to find something to read about Mitiaro. There was very little. The Government Survey Department had a booklet of maps, distances between islands and terse descriptions. The following did nothing to lift my spirits: '*Mitiaro*. One of the poorest islands in the group today. Its three hundred inhabitants have practically no cash income.

'The majority of its young people migrate to Rarotonga for the final stages of their education and to obtain work. Many have later gone from there to New Zealand.'

The words conjured up newsreel pictures of people in rags, children with distended bellies and pitiful stick-thin arms, living lives of desolation and hardship in the meanest of hovels, scrambling to escape on the next plane or boat. How would they react to a stranger in their midst? Would they swarm all over me begging for coins as they had in Ethiopia?

I got two more bits of information from another government office. There were 123 registered voters, which was probably the entire adult population since it's illegal not to vote in the Cook Islands if you're eligible. That meant most of the population were children. I also learned that there would be a language problem with people in my age group since there hadn't been a school on Mitiaro prior to 1950. Adults not educated on Rarotonga would know no English whatsoever and my Maori, so far, was limited to *kia orana* ('hello, may you live') and *meitaki maata* ('thank you').

Though my pulse wasn't exactly pounding with excitement at that stage, it never occurred to me to cancel the trip. I was hungry to learn about Islanders.

Much of what I'd experienced since arriving in the Cook Islands could hardly be called fun; lonely, humbling, sometimes scary, physically uncomfortable at times, but damn, it was interesting!

So, the next morning, I flew off into the unknown with my travel type-writer, camera, tape recorder, a couple of cotton dresses, a modest one-piece bathing suit (just in case), *pareus* to cover it up with and tee shirts so I could wear the *pareus* as wraparound skirts. 'No shorts, hardcase', said Miri. 'They're very backward. The women don't wear shorts yet. Better leave them with me. Can I borrow your white ones for lawn bowling, by the way?'

The mosquito-like aircraft perched on the runway of Rarotonga Interna-tional Airport looked made to order for alighting on a microcosm of 5,500 acres of makatea and swamp of which less than 100 acres was fertile soil. It was a little Cessna 337 'mixmaster' which looked to me like a toy model of what I recalled of the World War II P-38 with its twin tails.

It sported three engines, one on each wing and one behind the cockpit, which gave it its nickname. It held five passengers and a bit of cargo. Visibility was superb. It was a dandy little plane with a young Kiwi pilot full of jokes and local lore. He liked the Mitiaro run. My spirits began to rise.

'They have the *best* airport in the South Pacific!' he swore. 'That may be a poor little island as far as ready cash, but for hospitality, it's the richest. Wait until you see their terminal!'

The empty ocean stretched away endlessly below, wrinkled like rich gray-blue leather. Far away on the horizon, mounds of lavender-shaded trade-wind clouds jostled each other as they hurried about their business.

'Keep your eyes open when we come in to land', he advised. 'Take a good look at their airstrip. Those people cleared and leveled every inch of it with garden tools and their bare hands, that's how much they wanted that airstrip.'

'Didn't the government help?'

'No, not one bit', he said. 'Not until the very end. Then they sent someone over to survey it and found out that the people had done such a good job, it was almost perfect the way it was without machinery. It's kind of a classic story of local politics. Ask Papa Raui to tell you about it sometime.

'You know, he was a cabinet minister under Sir Albert. He's a very straight chap. He thinks like a reverend. After a while, he decided he didn't like what was going on in government, so he resigned and started the Unity Movement. It was supposed to do away with all political parties in the Cook Islands, eventually. He's shrewd. Don't ever underestimate old Papa Raui. He figures the main prob-lem with the Cook Islands since self-government is political parties. I think he has a point, myself. Place is just too small for them, especially with everyone related. Causes some real splits in families around election time.

'There were other reasons too that the premiere was a bit upset with Raui. I'd best not say, but maybe, when he gets to know you, he'll tell you. Bit of a sex scandal, it was. Anyway, when Papa asked Sir Albert to send over the bulldozer for the airport, government just kept putting him off, even though it was promised to Mitiaro before the big blowout.

'Papa Raui is a stubborn man. He called a meeting and told his people if they wanted an airport, they'd have to make it themselves and they'd better get busy. There were a lot of ironwood trees to pull out and only the one old tractor to do the job with.

'Every able-bodied man on Mitiaro Island (which is maybe thirty men, all told) pulled out those trees, chopped the brush with bush knifes, filled and leveled that rough makatea surface with every tool they could get their hands on – even teaspoons! The women kept them fed and looked after the little ones. They finished that airstrip in twenty-nine days. There it is right ahead of us.'

'Sounds like my kind of people!' I grinned and strained to make the island out in that vast empty sea. Little did I dream that my pompous Sadie Thompson disclaimer would be false by local standards. That fictional scarlet woman visitor to Pago Pago created by novelist Somerset Maugham was about to be reincarnated – at least, that's the spirit in which I'd be remembered for my unwitting 'wickedness' that was to rock Mitiaro.

# 21

# FACE ON THE OCEAN

Mitiaro emerged from the low clouds like a bruise on the sea. Small, flat, of indefinite shape, it lay there looking as if it would be engulfed at any moment. 'I don't see the face', I said.

'You have to be quite close to see it', the pilot said. 'Some people never do.'

The landing was smooth as coconut cream. Outside, a smart breeze was slapping the palm fronds, blowing, as winds always seem to wherever there's an airstrip. The field was bordered with low scrub and brush. There were no buildings in sight, but Mitiaro Airport, indeed, had a terminal.

At the edge of the clearing was a shelter consisting of a thatched roof about twenty feet long, supported by pillars made from coconut palm trunks. Inside, a reception committee of stout Mitiaro mamas beamed a welcome beside a table covered with white linen trimmed with hand-crocheted lace. On this, prettily arranged, was a large thermos of coffee with plenty of milk and sugar, teaspoons and a stack of gleaming china teacups and saucers, laid out to refresh the pilot (it was a turnaround flight) and to welcome his three passengers: two locals, one tourist.

Judging from the size of the crowd, most of Mitiaro's population was there to celebrate the weekly arrival of the airplane. Despite this, there were no parking problems. I counted the vehicles: one tractor, five small motorcycles and a yellow Honda Civic, identical to the one I'd left behind in California. This car, however, was hitched to a flatbed trailer longer than it was. I learned later that I had just seen all the island's vehicles. A slightly built man, near seventy, huge smile lighting up his somber features, greeted me. It was the owner of the Honda trailer rig, the famous Papa Raui Pokoati himself.

All the luggage and cargo for the island were piled on the trailer along with the Welcome Mamas, thermos, teacups, tablecloth and table, followed by as many villagers who could hang on without falling off. From behind, you couldn't even see the trailer. Papa and I rode in the front seat. Carton boxes filled the backseat. The tiny auto had been substituted for the tractor, so Mitiaro's only tourist could ride in style.

We bumped along a track through settlements of tidy, brightly painted houses, all with fresh-looking print curtains fluttering from screenless windows. The people I saw were neatly dressed in clothes that had been painstakingly patched and ironed. Most were barefoot. They looked plump, well-nourished and scrubbed – the matrons *very* amply nourished. A well-rounded wife, I was to learn, is a symbol to the community of a husband who is a good provider. I saw no poverty cases except myself mirrored in their eyes as they evaluated their tourist: one undernourished mama, no man to fish and plant taro for her, no food gifts visible for her hosts amongst her luggage.

'Why on earth do they describe Mitiaro as the poorest island in the Cooks?' I asked Papa Raui before we'd even reached his house. 'This is a beautiful island! Your people look healthy and prosperous.'

'Who said we are the poorest?' he asked, shocked.

'That's what I read in a handbook put out by the Cook Islands Government Survey Department.'

'I am surprised! We aren't a poor island. We're self-sufficient here. We grow all our food or catch it in the sea. We earn a little money by selling copra and dried bananas, and when the plantations begin to bear, we will do even better. We cannot grow everything here. We still need coffee and tea, sugar and flour and clothing, but you see for yourself, we are not a poor people.'

Papa Raui's house, as could be expected, was the showplace of Mitiaro. He even had electricity. He showed me the generator out back with pride. It had been installed the previous year, in 1978. Housed in a neat outbuilding, its most important task was to run two large deep freezers in which the CAO could store excess fish caught and provide the island with the greatest luxury in the South Seas, ice cream.

Spacious enclosed verandahs ran the full length of the house on both the inland and sea sides. Sheer curtains of a smoky yellow-orange filtered out the brightest of the sun's rays through the glass louvers, bathing the rooms with golden light. There were two single beds at either end of the inland verandah, each covered in a bright patchwork, done Cook Islands style, without quilting.

Beyond the verandah was a large vibrant parlor with shell 'ei-festooned family group photos on walls and tables. Handmade lace and crocheted doilies decorated every surface not already brightened with patchwork, appliqué and embroideries, a room almost singing of its industrious creators and of their love of color, texture and gracious living.

Formal tea was served to welcome me: china cups, elegant little sand-wiches, some cucumber, some banana, and imported biscuits. Mama Tai, hand-some, face radiating peace and intelligence, smiled a shy welcome but would not even attempt to speak. 'She understands a little English, but she's very shy', Papa Raui explained.

A little girl of about seven sat beside me, making an admirable effort to look prim and unafraid. Her great brown eyes gave her away. She was terrified. Sitting beside me was, in itself, a feat of courage. As is customary, I had my tea alone. Like all well-bred Cook Islands children, she would not touch so much as one biscuit set out for a guest. Even when invited by the guest, no amount of urging could tempt her.

My room was a gleaming chamber, soft double bed covered in more beau-tiful patchwork appliqué next to curtained louvered glass windows overlooking the verandah.

There is little or no fresh underground water on makatea islands and atolls. Rainwater is collected and stored, mainly by channeling runoff from corrugated iron roofs into steel drums. This does not necessarily lead to an efficient indoor running water system. The Pokoatis demonstrated how to operate the beautiful modern flush toilet. All one had to do was slip out the back door, fill a bucket from a tap, haul it inside and pour it into the tank. It took two bucketsful. The first full one was set hospitably beside the toilet for the guest's convenience.

The family preferred the wooden outhouse in the backyard. I soon followed suit, pointing to my feet and going through a pantomime about not tracking sand all over the house when Mama Tai caught me heading that way and ob-jected with a graceful assortment of gestures.

The bathroom adjacent to the toilet was pretty as an illustration in an inte-rior design magazine with its stainless steel shower and elegant little pedestal wash basin. Either the shower was not yet hooked up to the water supply or the water level was low because there hadn't been much rain lately. Papa Raui ex-plained that this magnificent appliance worked quite well if one followed a sim-ple routine: first, put stopper in sink firmly; turn on tap (oh yes, the tap was connected and water trickled out); fill sink almost to top; step into dazzling steel shower, dip water from basin with coffee mug provided and pour it over your-self. This was how I was to wash myself and my almost waist-length hair. There was no hot water, but the water was naturally tepid from the heat of the sun. The family evidently had a more humble bathing arrangement somewhere that, even if more efficient, was not deemed modern enough to offer to female for-eign guests.

As he showed me through the house, Papa Raui told me he had once had eight guests here, all at the same time – all Americans, too, he grinned. He was no stranger to tourism and its quirky expectations. He soon excused himself to drive inland to pick up the men working on the plantations.

'May I come and see what you're growing?' I asked.

'The women are all busy today preparing for the *umukai*', he said. 'Mama Tai would accompany you, herself, but she, too, is very busy.'

'Well, that's okay. I wouldn't want to bother Mama Tai or the others when they have so much to do. Couldn't I just go along for the ride?'

Avoiding my eyes, he tried to explain the situation. 'There are no women working on the plantations, just men. Better you wait until one or two of our women can come with you – maybe Monday.'

'Well, perhaps I could just walk to the lake then. I've heard so much about it.'

'Ah, you know of our lakes', he beamed. 'There are two, you know, Te Rotonui and Te Rotoiti, but they are too brackish and shallow for swimming. They grow fine eels, though. You will soon taste them.'

'What do their names mean?'

He pondered a moment. 'Te Rotonui means Big Lake and Te Rotoiti means Small Lake', he said finally. 'They are very far away and difficult to get to. Next week, maybe some of the women will take you there.'

The enormity of the restrictions on unaccompanied women finally hit home. My tourist status exempted me from nothing except participating in household chores. I was a prisoner of missionary laws. I milled about the house. All was silent, lacy and Victorian genteel. I felt like tiptoeing on the beautiful handwoven pandanus mats that covered the cement floors. I'd make a lousy princess, I said to myself.

As he'd driven me home from the airport, Papa Raui had told me there were four villages on Mitiaro: Takaue, Atai, Auta and Mangerei, all clumped together on the west coast. His house was in Takaue.

I strolled through the scattering of homes, not sure where one village left off and another began, staying in the middle of the track in plain sight. I was probably taking liberties with protocol, even doing that much. Torn between curiosity and courtesy, a wave of shyness threatened to catapult me right back to my guestroom and a book, any book. Curiosity was stronger.

It was late afternoon. Spying a broad coral road, obviously much used, I turned down it instead and found myself on the shore. The sun was low on the horizon. The sea stretched away empty as far as the eye could see. The only opening in the barrier reef lay a few feet ahead of me. There was no blue lagoon between that maelstrom and the shore which was little more than a boulder-strewn shelf of coral, partially submerged. Tidepools, some running like miniature rivers in shallow crevices, fed into broad, shallow ponds. The reef and the shore were one.

A crowd of mostly naked brown children laughed and shrieked, paddling about fearlessly in the huge waves surging through the break in the reef into the vortex that passed as a swimming hole. Nearby, a group of young men lounged, too old to join the children, too young, apparently, to join the men out fishing. They spoke little to each other, staring out to sea, faces impassive. Emaciated-looking dogs lay in a group, listless, hungry, waiting. Would there be handouts this time?

Canoes, carved of a local wood the color of ivory, rested on the sand like pale birds. They were elegantly smooth, of exquisite proportions with graceful, high, upcurving prows.

The lonely sea was unbroken by any sign of life or land though Mitiaro is not a great distance from other islands. It is one of three islands in a triangle known as Ngaputoru or The Three Roots. The others were Atiu, twenty-seven miles in one direction, and Mauke, thirty-two miles in the other. Atiu, once home to some of the fiercest warriors in the South Seas, had sovereignty over both Mauke and Mitiaro when the missionaries arrived in the early 1800s (1823 on Mitiaro). Atiuans once told me their ancestors had succeeded in killing off everyone on Mitiaro except for the beautiful women, whom they kidnapped. Therefore, they claim, the people of Mitiaro today are really descendants of Atiuans who settled on Mitiaro.

Some Mitiaro people remember it a little differently and insist that their island's name, Mitiaro, is really from Miti Vai Aro, slang for drinking the blood of the fallen enemies from Atiu. 'Whoever told you Mitiaro meant "Face on the Water" was not from Mitiaro and could not know our true history!' said a neighbor later.

There are as many histories of the Cook Islands as there are islands, but somewhere out at sea the HMNZS *Waikato* was steaming relentlessly toward us and the next morning, this first warship in over a century would land, not on a bloody raid from Atiu, but in peace from New Zealand. New history was about to be made.

I watched the children for a while, but it was evident the young men were edgy with me around. Not wanting to be perceived as admiring them, which, of course, I was, I withdrew and strolled back through the villages.

Spying a middle-aged couple seated in a yard plaiting palm fronds, I paused and greeted them: '*Kia orana.*' The woman smiled and responded, the man continued working, eyes downcast.

'Are these for the *umukai*?' I asked, pointing to the long, green boat-shaped containers the pair had finished. She flicked her eyebrows in assent. After some time had elapsed, she asked, 'Do you come to *umukai*?'

I replied that I would like to very much and asked what time it would be. She leaned toward her husband and spoke to him in Cook Islands Maori. He replied at great length.

'He says tomorrow', she responded.

I pointed to my watch and looked at her quizzically. 'What hour?'

She studied my watch gravely for a long time, then nodded. 'That one is like my brother's who stays on Rarotonga', she said.

I realized it was a silly question in the first place in a land where time is measured by sun, moon and seas, so I changed the subject.

'Could you please tell me where I might find Nga, the Girl Guide leader? I have a parcel for her from Miri on Rarotonga.'

The woman rose ponderously, indicated I was to follow her, and we walked down the track to another house. She went inside. Through the door, I could see a room heaped with small girls in bright blue uniforms, all sitting on the floor having a meeting. Reclining on a huge *tivaevae*-covered bed was a mountainous woman with gray hair, looking for all the world like an old engraving of a Polynesian queen holding court. It was a magnificent tableau.

A sturdy woman in her early twenties broke from the group and came out to meet me. This was Nga. She wore the spotless, carefully mended, white uniform of a Girl Guide leader. Like the uniformed children, she was barefoot. We strolled down the track.

'Please excuse me', she said, 'my family is in the bush getting food for tomorrow or they, too, would greet you.'

'Your English is excellent', I said admiringly. 'Did you go to school in New Zealand?'

'No. I have only been to Rarotonga', she said with a sigh. 'My little girl stays in New Zealand. Maybe someday, I go to see her.'

'Is she your only child?'

'No, I have two boys. They stay with me. My husband, he did not want any girls. He was not good to my little girl', she said, eyes haunted with sadness and some anger. I didn't know what to say.

'She stays with my uncle now. He came with my aunty from New Zealand to stay with me. They don't have any children. I told them they could have this one. They were so happy.'

A pair of small boys approached, heavily laden with taro root. 'Those are my boys.'

'What handsome children', I said admiringly.

She shrugged, 'I wish you could see my girl. She is so beautiful.' There were tears in her eyes.

I changed the subject, which was growing more painful by the minute. 'Will your Girl Guides wear their uniforms tomorrow?'

'Oh yes, we will all wear our uniforms. We will make a parade!' she said. 'Not just the Girl Guides, you understand, but the Boys' Brigade, the Girls' Brigade, the Boy Scouts, the Rangers *and* the Youth Club will march.'

'You have all those clubs on Mitiaro?'

'We have many more clubs on Mitiaro. Those clubs are the only ones who have uniforms', she explained.

People were returning now from the bush and the sea, heavily laden, gossiping. There was a festive air as the sun went down.

Throughout the night, every able-bodied member of that population (which Papa Raui said was 256, not 300 anymore) over the age of two worked. No hand was idle. There were heaps of *kai* or food: *taro*, breadfruit, *kumera* (sweet potatoes) and bananas to prepare and *poke* to be made. *Umus* or pit ovens smouldered throughout the night, loaded to capacity with vegetables, pigs, chicken and fish. At dawn, they were emptied and refilled with still more leaf-wrapped food.

The *umu* in the Pokoati backyard was a large empty oil drum, sunk in the ground to its top band. A bonfire in the bottom heated stones which were removed when they were ready with wooden sticks used as tongs. Then, a layer of food wrapped in banana leaves was placed inside followed by a layer of chestnuts that looked like fistsized rocks. This was followed by more packages of food wrapped in banana leaves. Then the hot stones were replaced and the remaining space packed with leaves as big as platters, followed by burlap, an old wooden hatch cover from a shipwreck, and finally, everything handy including a big bush knife.

A large section of corrugated iron was propped up on the seaward side under the thatch-roofed shelter to keep out the breeze. Several women reclined on mats throughout the night, dozing and alternately checking the *umu* and chatting cozily.

One of them, Mama Ivi, had the most startlingly beautiful Polynesian face I had ever seen. It was hard not to stare. Her long hair was pure white, drawn back from her face in a bun with loose ends trailing about her dark cheeks and neck like fibers of spun glass. Her teeth were perfect and of a white that outshone her hair. She wore a ragged dress, once white, now stained and filthy from the *umu*. The wide neckline had shifted, leaving one brown shoulder exposed. She transcended rags and age like some goddess, haunting and luminous, reclining on a thin, tattered pandanus mat in the firelight. I didn't see how her beauty as a young woman could possibly have surpassed what I saw then.

'I described her the next day to Nga. 'Who is that extraordinary woman? Is she an *ariki*?'

'Oh, that's just old Mama Ivi', Nga shrugged.

'Eevee', I repeated. 'We would say, "Eve". That really suits her. If I were an artist, doing a painting of a return to the Garden of Eden, I would ask your beautiful Mama Ivi to pose as Eve as an old woman.' She looked at me oddly.

Women, not preparing food and tending *umus* that night were busy in their villages by lantern light, some stringing great ropes of pink and cream *tipani*, fashioning crowns or *'eis* of chrysanthemums and other flowers, croton, *rauti* leaves and fragrant green *maire*. Others plaited mats, containers and decorative covers for the pillars of the verandahs or patched and ironed uniforms by firelight, intent and serious.

Despite all the activity, it was very quiet except for the generator. People spoke and laughed in hushed tones. There was no music. The only radio on the island was Papa Raui's shortwave link with Rarotonga.

Island women have their special ways of performing traditional tasks which link them with the past, the present and each other. With these go little jokes, rituals, snatches of song and impromptu dance. The object is not to meet a deadline, but to do the job together with your own people. There are no jobs for those who don't share the collected memories of the clan.

Feeling a bit like a *voyeur*, I retreated discreetly to bed and book. As if on cue, the noisy generator stopped and the lights went out. It was 8:30 p.m. The blackness that followed was so deep, it was shocking to the senses. I went to the window. Gradually, my eyes adjusted and I could see the glow of the benzine lantern in back by the *umu*. The women now seemed to be sleeping, curled gracefully like large cats in the shadows. The only sound came from the surf, booming on the reef.

I turned on my little flashlight, intending to finish the chapter. With exuberance, every moth on Mitiaro slammed into it. Latecomers piled up on pillows and bed, perching on my head and arms, waiting their turn to dive into that tiny sun. I gave up, switched it off and went into a brushing routine to which, fortunately, there were no witnesses but the surviving moths. Mitiaro's wags might well have translated it into a hilarious hula routine telling the story of this odd white lady who descended on their island from the sky for no conceivable reason whatsoever, then went into a fit over some tiny moths and beat herself senseless.

The next morning, I awoke to an eerie silence. The huge house was flooded with golden sunlight. My breakfast was laid out, but there wasn't a sign of habitation. Had the ship come while I slept? Was everyone down at the sea? I started for the front door. Suddenly, Mama Tai ran in from somewhere behind the house, made imperative 'sit and eat!' signals and hurried off to the kitchen to heat coffee. She seemed agitated.

'Where are all the people?' I asked. 'Is the *Waikato* here already?' She looked at me blankly. Why was it so quiet?

Through the kitchen, I could see several great rough wooden tables on the back verandah, heaped with bunches of bananas, loaves of white bread that came over on the plane with me from Rarotonga and tins of New Zealand butter. I sat down, mystified. Mama poured my coffee, then rushed out back again. She shouted several names, sharply. There was no reply. Finally, three women joined her. An animated conversation followed and the younger one of the trio left. The others walked over to the tables and proceeded to peel bananas. They did not look happy.

It wasn't hard to figure out what had happened. The excitement of the ship's pending arrival was too much for the girls who had worked hard yesterday and through the night. A genteel mutiny had obviously taken place. They had abandoned Mama Tai, who as CAO's wife was hostess in charge of the official reception tea for the HMNZS *Waikato* officers. They were down on the beach to see what was happening.

The excitement was contagious. My anti-military prejudices forgotten, I was exploding with anticipation myself. Impatient with the social obligation of a guest to finish breakfast, I wanted only to rush to the beach too, to see the Islanders in all their finery and uniforms when the ship arrived. Or had it arrived?

I looked again through the kitchen at Mama Tai. Her work crew had now shrunk to one. Faces set, the pair were up to their shoulders in bananas and bread, one peeling, one slicing. Their task looked formidable.

Brazenly, I joined them. Flouting the Mitiaro Code of Etiquette for Guests, I picked up a banana and started to peel. Mama tensed, face wincing in horror. 'Let me help. You'll never make it in time with only one!'

She turned to her friend and spoke in tense, fast Maori. Her companion knew English. 'Mama Tai say you go to ceremony!' she translated the order.

'Okay, I will, but first, let's get the sandwiches made. The ship's officers will be here soon. Suppose they arrive and there's no food?'

There was another consultation. I had made a good point. Mama Tai handed me a knife and a tin of New Zealand butter, indicating I should put down bananas I had not grown and start cutting off breadcrusts and buttering bread. I was imported, therefore I undoubtedly was the logical person to handle the imported food. Pleased with this equitable solution and my temporary status as 'one of the girls', I attacked the formidable stack of white bread. We did not work in the leisurely island way, we worked fast, assembly-line style. Mama Tai set the pace: decrust bread, smear on butter, deal banana slices, slap second buttered slice on top, chop once with machete, stack on platters.

Suddenly, an inexplicable rattling, evocative of a herd of stampeding power mowers, shattered the stillness. 'What is that?' I cried as the sound reached a crescendo. We stared at each other, somewhat frightened.

'Oh!' I yelped, recognizing it. 'It sounds like a helicopter! Could it be?'

The two women looked back at me with no understanding whatsoever. We continued our work. We had to. Mama Tai and her friend seemed able to accept the horrible clatter without understanding it. I did not have their self-discipline. Dropping my knife, I ran across the yard as far as the generator shed hoping to get a better view, but ironwood trees and coconut palms interlaced, blocking out most of the sky.

I went back to work, that the noise diminished, then stopped. Five minutes later, the racket started up again. This time it didn't stop abruptly, but gradually faded to nothing. 'Don't you think that sounded like a helicopter?'

'Maybe generator', said Mama Tai's companion. I listened a moment, suddenly unsure, but the generator thunked along with its normal, familiar racket.

Speculation about the possibilities of the scenes on the beach made it hard now to keep pace with the other two. If it was a helicopter, and I couldn't imagine what else it could have been, how were Papa Raui's people reacting? How could they have ever seen a helicopter out here in the middle of the ocean? This was going to be an exciting day on Mitiaro. I could feel it crackling like electricity in the humid tropic morning.

## 22

## HMNZS *WAIKATO* DAY

The last banana tucked discreetly between buttered bread slices, tea pretties in place, Mama Tai and I settled down in the shade on the beach with Mitiaro's senior contingent. We'd missed the opening exchange and parade. The woman next to Mama Tai began whispering in her ear while another behind me leaned forward, adding murmurs of her own. I looked inquiringly at Mama Tai. Her eyes slid past mine and locked on her husband, who was addressing the officers. She was frowning. Something was amiss, or was it only my imagination?

Papa Raui, immaculate in crisp white shirt and trousers, was ending his speech to a row of equally crisp white-uniformed ship's officers lined up at attention. Ranks of New Zealand sailors, boy-faces scrubbed pink, stood at ease behind their superiors, smart in spotless white tee shirts with square necklines bordered in dark blue, white shorts and sandals. The little CAO turned toward the massed Islanders and raised his hand in a signal for the music to begin.

The orchestra and chorus sat crosslegged on the sand, barefoot. The front row was splendid, neon chartreuse and orange flowers on royal blue; muu-muus for the women, shirts for the men, all alike. Neat white trousers completed the ensemble for the men. Those who did not possess these vivid uniforms sat in the back, dressed in tee shirts and shorts, spotless, patched, neat and proud. All were crowned with chrysanthemums and *tipani*.

The instruments consisted of two guitars, several handcarved wood and coconut ukuleles, a wooden slit-gong made from a scooped-out log, and a kettle drum. The latter was played bongo fashion with the palms of the hands by a serious-faced young matron. The group played and sang with all their might, needing no amplifiers to drown out the waves exploding on the reef and the constant applause of the palm fronds slapping briskly in trade winds overhead.

After a few bars, out came the dancing girls, plump and thin teenagers of all sizes, some with complexion blemishes; shyness was ill-concealed behind earnest fixed expressions and flickering smiles. The first number had a country-western rhythm. The words were bellowed in a fractured English nasal singsong, each girl singing as hard and loud as she physically could, holding nothing back. One line in English kept popping up in the Maori chorus: 'Welcome, welcome to you home.'

This troupe of Mitiaro maidens was costumed in new white tee shirts with 'Kia orana, Rarotonga' across the front over a picture of a dancing girl encircled with red hibiscus. Slightly green hula skirts of leaves shredded into coarse strips were worn modestly over white skirts or *pareus*. Strings of fern and pink *tipani* encircled their hips. They danced barefoot and graceful in the sand with admirable precision. No one made a mistake.

The next lot of girls swayed out in wide, faded-black halter tops, white *pareus* tied chastely around their waists (not at pubic hairline like their Tahitian sisters). Thick bands of giant fern leaves covered their midriffs, almost completely obscuring any stray flash of skin. They wore thick '*eis* of pink *tipani* reaching the ground, which they picked up and held out like gorgeous floral offerings as they danced and sang:

> If you ever take a notion
> That you like to see the island,
> Just take a steamer
> To Nukuroa Land.
> In Nukuroa,
> Dare de girls can do de hula
> In natives costumes
> And pretty '*eis*.
> And the ukuleles playing
> Beside the swinging and the swaying
> All the way to Nukuroa
> On a moonlights night.

It was so banal, so sincere, so downright sweet, my eyes filled with tears. I happened to glance across at the faces of the young sailors. To a man, they were plainly in love and melting away there under the palms. Most were in their late teens and early twenties themselves, and this was their first real South Seas island encounter. It was to be a day of mutual wonder for the young people.

On the white coral sands of the beach beyond them, among the birdlike outrigger canoes, perched a fat high-tech dragonfly. That mystery, at least, was solved. The clattering intruder of the morning's stillness was indeed a helicop-

ter. Beyond the reef the great white frigate, HMNZS Waikato, seemed to fill the
horizon, bristling with guns, radar antennae whirling. Between ship and breakers, Mitiaro men came surging forward at the oars of an unwieldy-looking rowboat. It was loaded to the gunwales with uniformed sailors, bailing with coconut
shells. A small sleek powerboat sped back toward the mother ship, apparently
unable to make the dangerous pass in the reef.

As the show ended, the rowboat landed. Its load of wet sailors disembarked
with remarkable dignity, a couple pausing to help the Mitiaro rowers launch it
back toward the breakers. Now, ordinary sailors and Islanders eyed each other,
milled about and made tentative efforts to get acquainted. The ship's officers
filed up to the big house for their offical tea with the CAO.

On the verandah, flooded with the magical golden light filtered through
sheer orange curtains, tables were laden with our thick white banana sandwiches, fruits of Mitiaro and tea. With little cash for sugar, flour and milk for
cakes and biscuits, the Islanders had managed a rich display anyway of the best
their island offered.

Unsure my presence was appropriate at the official reception, I slipped away
and returned to the shore instead to watch the suspenseful show of leaky row-
boats full of sailors surf the last hundred feet through the turmoil of the break
in the reef. Miraculously, they all seemed to land right side up.

Kiwi sailors now thronged Mitiaro's narrow beach, shiny-faced, restrained
and immaculate, even though drenched. They seemed more like English public
school lads on a field trip. A junior officer who had followed me back to the
waterfront from the house stared at me fixedly. 'Excuse me', he said. 'Do you, by
chance, speak English?'

'Me?' I was somewhat amazed. 'I not only speak English, I am the Official
Mitiaro Tourist.'

It was his turn to be astonished: 'Mitiaro has a tourist? But it's so remote!'

'Well, it's so very remote and small, it only has one', I said reassuringly.
Relaxing, the officer grinned. 'So, what do you think of Mitiaro so far?'

'I'm quite surprised! It's lovely! I've never seen a tropical island before outside the movies and frankly, I was disappointed that Mitiaro was to be my first.
From the briefing we got, I expected a scene of ragged, heartrending poverty
and desolation. The island was described as swampy, mostly uninhabitable and
the home of a rare species of eel which is prized by people who fancy eels.'

'Do you?' I laughed.

'Eels? I don't know as I've ever tried one', he replied. 'It might be interesting.'

'Great attitude', I grinned. 'To tell you the truth, I was really dreading the
invasion of three hundred sailors on such an isolated place, especially after what

I've seen of the French Foreign Legion in Tahiti.'

'What do you think, now?' he asked anxiously.

As if I, Mitiaro's tourist, were personally responsible for the welfare of Mitiaro's people, I pompously responded: 'From what I've seen so far of your crew, I'm impressed. But do be careful because, as you know, these people are very innocent, very gentle and almost too kind.'

'Not to worry. I think most of us are half afraid of them, we're so worried we'll do the wrong thing. We should be right though, now that we've had a most thorough briefing about deportment, not only from our captain, but by the Official Tourist of Mitiaro!'

'Point taken', I grinned.

'I understand lunch won't be served for at least an hour', he said. 'Since you're the Tourist, you must know of a decent place to swim? I want to do some diving.'

'I think it's all coral reef', I said. 'You don't want to go beyond that surf out there. It's breaking straight down on razor-sharp coral. You could probably swim through it and spearfish in the deep sea beyond, but you'd get your brains smashed trying to get back.'

'I noticed coming in, it looked a bit hostile. I thought perhaps there might be a swimming hole.'

'I don't know', I said. 'The kids seem to be quite happy just swimming here in the pass in the reef. You might walk along the beach for a ways and see if you can find one. You can't very well get lost.'

'Why don't you come along and we'll explore together?'

'Me? Don't be silly. You didn't come to a South Sea island to meet tourists. Why don't you ask one of those lovelies?' I asked, gesturing toward a group of teenaged girls. 'They'd probably welcome a chance to practice their English.'

'That's quite impossible, much as I'd like to. We've been prohibited from being alone or even out of sight with the local girls, even if they're in a group!'

Immediately forgetting that I, too, was not supposed to go out of sight, I told him to wait while I got into a bathing suit and *pareu*. As I changed in my room, I overheard Papa Raui and the captain talking on the verandah.

'Please', said the captain, 'do not hesitate to tell me what we can do to be of help to your island during this one day we are here. The machinery, medical staff and services of the *Waikato* are at your disposal.'

It didn't take the little CAO long to respond. 'Will you blast a wider passage through our reef, then? We've asked the government to do this for us many times, but they do nothing and you have now seen what it is like, going through our reef. We must do it every day when we go to fish.'

The skipper cleared his throat and said diplomatically, 'I'll do what I can, but it's too big a job for one day. What I can do is mention it in my report and hope for the best. I'm only a sailor, you know, not a politician.'

Chuckling with appreciation at my host's opportunism, I left the house, *pareu* tied chastely, hiding my bathing suit, clutching mask and snorkel. My officer was waiting and we rushed off down the beach like aging truant kids. Exuberantly, he grabbed my hand. Feeling about ten years old, I clutched his. It was great to have someone to explore this magical little island with, even for an hour, and I'd always had a secret dream of walking on some island beach hand-in-hand with some mystery man.

Ambitiously, we waded out to every large tidepool that looked big enough to lie down in. Most proved to be only inches deep. In desperation, we tried lying perfectly still on the surface of the deeper ones, actually succeeding in floating and drifting along with the narrow riverlike currents streaming over shallow chasms in the coral. Masks in place, we scanned the crevices. Aside from scattered black and white angelfish and sea urchins, there was little to see and we managed to scrape ourselves thoroughly on the coral rasps we couldn't clear. I thought of sharks, but obviously, if we could do no more than float in water inches deep, sharks couldn't get far either, no matter how enticing our blood smell must be.

Cuts stinging from the salt water, we finally got to our feet and picked our way back to the narrow beach and its kinder coral sand. We had traveled out of sight of the boat landing. Clouds of mosquitoes zeroed in on our bloody scrapes and cuts, putting the final lid on our expedition. Cursing, slapping, wincing and laughing, we returned to the boatlaunch area where a game of netball was ending between villagers and sailors. Cases of soda pop were piled up, probably a gift from the Navy. The *tapu* against beer and alcohol didn't seem to put any noticeable dent in the festive spirits of young or old.

As we approached, the log slit-gong drum chattered commandingly. It was time for the *umukai*. Served under a thatch-roofed shelter made for the occasion with palm log supports wrapped in mats woven from green palm leaves interspersed with flowers, the repast was lavish. There was pork, fish, chicken and eel and every delicacy the island offered plus a few imports from other Cook Islands such as pineapple.

There was no time to run up to the house and change my damp *pareu*. I sat down on the rough-hewn log bench amidst the sailors with my fellow explorer, dressed as I was. At least, I reasoned, I was properly covered.

When we could eat no more, my friend asked to see the 'tourist accommodations'. I took him up to the house and showed off my room, the wonderful shower arrangement and parlor, pointing out the fine needlework and beautifully carved tables. He was as enchanted with it all as I was. He took my hand again and we returned to the beach, me giggling deliciously at the sheer silliness of holding hands with a sailor. Me!

The departure process had already started when we rejoined the others. First, the Mitiaro rowboat would set out, loaded down with sailors, rowed by strong locals. Once through the reef and beyond, an open-sea transfer would be made to the warship's fancy motor launch. This was especially tricky because the launch was filled with Mitiaro Islanders returning from a tour of the *Waikato*. The passenger switch had to be done with great precision on heaving seas. A sailor would scramble into the launch at the exact moment an Islander scrambled into the Mitiaro rowboat. Everyone was wet and shrieking with laughter.

Then the launch would speed off to the frigate to deposit sailors and pick up Islanders; the Mitiaro rowboat would surf back through the reef, dislodge its load of locals and pick up more sailors to repeat the process. A wave of sadness engulfed me out of all proportion to the moment. My delightful companion would soon leave and it was unlikely I'd ever see him again. Had I known what my impetuous actions that day would cost me, I would come to wish we'd never met.

The crowd of sailors thinned to a handful. The last boat was nearly empty. A laughing mob of Mitiaro girls climbed aboard. I looked at them hopefully. They beckoned and made room for me.

Waiting for the right moment, the rowers shot through the pass in the reef during a pause between breakers. The *Waikato*'s launch awaited us with the last of the visitors from shore. The transfer was made with wild rocking and near-swamping as the last of the Islanders climbed on board and the officers and remaining sailors left us for their vessel. 'Don't forget to write to me in the States', I called to my friend.

'I promise!' he shouted back, but I knew he wouldn't.

As the strip of water widened between us and the ship's launch, all of us in the Mitiaro rowboat were weeping. Suddenly, one of the girls broke into a wild, lamenting version of 'Red Sails in the Sunset'. Others joined in. The effect was closer to that of an eerie wailing traditional chant or *himene* than the once-popular tune. Seaspray washed away our tears. Soon, the sound of crashing surf ahead drowned out the words. With oar handles disintegrating under the constant friction, the boatmen of Mitiaro rowed us back toward the pass in the reef, piles of sawdust growing under the oarlocks.

## 23

# BLACK TIARE

A wild searing loneliness, unlike any shades of lonely I had ever known, swept through me like a firestorm and I wondered – this then, must be what island women feel again and again over all the partings that come with all the meetings of strangers they've grown fond of. The smaller the island, the larger the loss. I don't know if that's true, but it sounded about right.

Though my heart was bursting with the pain of it, I recorded what I felt that night in my log because it was a new feeling for me and one I was unlikely to ever feel again with the same intensity.

I was lonely before, but it had no shape, no face, no name. When lonely is impersonal, there are many distractions. When it has an identity, it seems as if everything is a reminder. There is no place to hide. The stars are magnificent tonight, but I feel only that they will burn me if I stay out under them too long. They frighten me with their indifference.

The kittens I saw in the tree, the family on the mat eating together by benzine lantern, the girls walking along playing the ukulele and harmonizing softly – everything I see and hear now makes me poignantly aware that no one is here that I can turn to and say: 'See that? Hear that?' No one is here to make jokes with.

The sea has never looked so empty. Tomorrow, maybe, the pain will be less. I've only known you for a few hours, for God's sake. That's a small investment for such a big pain. Yet, I'm glad you were here and I'll try not to care that I'll never see you again. As it is, the relationship was perfect. There are no flaws. It's like a miniature work of art: frugal brush strokes from a Japanese master – a hint of form, some quick, perfectly proportioned lines, a well-placed blot or two. It's all there with exquisite restraint.

There is that one flaw, though, isn't there? I gave you my address though you hadn't asked and now I will never truly savor the perfection of this day and this tiny, exquisite, completed relationship for hoping that I'll see you again.

How can I dare to sit here in the dark and say, 'Is that all?' There was a beginning and it was funny and warm. There was a middle and it was rich with small adventures. There was a poetic ending. Love? Of course it was love, but it was only a small love, perishable as a *tiare Maori* – waxy white and fragrant today, black and withered tomorrow in the way of all flowers and all small loves. How dare I feel such loneliness?

The great ship *Waikato* is out there somewhere in the dark, moving powerfully through the sea toward Aitutaki.

Damn those hardcase Aitutaki girls with their *tango tango* hot pants! They'll be swarming all over those sailors like mosquitoes. They'll have a hard time being the gentlemen they've been commanded to be. It will be such a different sort of South Sea Island for them.

Will they forget their first one, plain, humble Mitiaro, when they see voluptuous Aitutaki with its wide turquoise lagoon, its impertinent little mountain and rich lush lands where everything flourishes?

Will they recall this brooding low patch of makatea called Mitiaro and laugh and say, 'The government handbook was quite right. What a poor island indeed!' when they see how much richer in material goods and foods Aitutaki is with its three village shops, movie shed, hotel, guesthouse and open-air takeway restaurant? Will they laugh at memories of the shy, shabby Cinderellas of Mitiaro when they meet the lusty party girls of Aitutaki, so ready to dance and play love games in the shadows?

Will my officer quickly forget this intense, awkward, aging, overeager Tourist of Mitiaro? My loneliness that's always with me has a face tonight and I hope I forget it soon because it's like a stone in my shoe, making me limp when I would run free.

## 24

# WHY THE NAVY HAD WET PANTS

Papa Raui sat with me at breakfast the next morning, relaxed and expansive. I was touched at this break with custom, grateful for the company. Beaming, he listened to my praises of the great *umukai* and entertainment.

'Yes, we are very pleased. The *Waikato* officers were extremely generous and gave us everything we asked for, including flour and sugar.'

'Well, almost', I said. 'You didn't get the hole in the reef blasted wider.'

'No, but soon they will take care of that, too. The captain also promised he would ask the New Zealand Department of Education to give us science materials for our school. We have none at all. They even fixed our island's power mower. It hasn't worked in years! We had to use our bush knives to cut back the grass like we did in the old days.'

'Imagine that! Didn't they need special tools?'

'Oh yes, very special. They could not fix it here on Mitiaro so they put it into their helicopter and flew it out to the ship so they could work on it in their machine shop. Many of our people were taken out to the ship in boats and they saw that machine shop. They can do anything on that ship of theirs. It is like an island.'

'Will they send the mower back to you when they return to New Zealand?'

'We already have it. It flew back to us on the helicopter in perfect working order after the *umukai*.'

'I wouldn't think they would have had the manpower on the ship to do repairs. Weren't all the sailors at the *umukai*?'

'Oh my, no. Mitiaro is too small for the entire crew', Papa Raui said. 'Those who couldn't come ashore for our *umukai* will visit Aitutaki today.'

'Poor guys', I said. 'I don't see how Aitutaki could put on half as fine a welcome as Mitiaro's. I was sad that I couldn't see your whole program. I missed the *Waikato*'s arrival and your welcoming speech and parade.'

'I thought you were there.'

'No, I stayed behind to help Mama Tai. We both missed it. Everybody was so excited, they ran off to see the ship before the sandwiches were made for the officers' tea.'

'That was very nice of you, but we don't expect our guests to do such things. ...'

'Well, I know that, but it was sort of an emergency.' He looked so upset, I changed the subject quickly. 'Was everyone surprised to see the helicopter? When I heard that noise, I knew it had to be one. That must have been exciting, eh? Had you ever seen one?'

'I knew what a helicopter was, but I never saw one before. You did not hear what happened? You did not know that I refused to receive that machine? You did not see the disgraceful way the captain and first officer of the *Waikato* first landed on our island?'

'No. What are you talking about?' I searched his stern features for a hint that he was joking. He was serious. Then, a strange story unfolded as Papa Raui Pokoati, the CAO of Mitiaro, told me how he singlehandedly stood off the initial invasion of the New Zealand Navy and exerted his power of authority over that of the mighty skipper of HMNZS *Waikato* himself. It was a heroic tale of the twentieth century fit to go down in Mitiaro's history and eventually into its rich mythology to be embellished and preserved in song and dance in celebration of the brave little CAO of Nukuroa.

It was approximately 8:30 a.m., 18 May 1979, a soft, warm tropical Friday morning. The dawn lavenders had faded from the big cumulus clouds piled on the horizon, leaving them white and sudsy in a pale blue sky. The entire population (with the exception of those too frail to rise from their mats and two banana sandwich makers) was massed on the crushed coral shore opposite the break in the reef, gazing seaward.

Out beyond the jade shallows and lazy line of morning waves foaming on the reef, HMNZS *Waikato* broke the usually empty horizon of this stretch of cobalt sea. Bristling with guns, its radar dish whirling, it stood offshore awaiting some signal of readiness.

Squadrons of smartly uniformed Boys and Girls Brigade members, Girl Guides, Boy Scouts, Rangers and Mitiaro Youth Club members stood at attention.

Dancers, singers and musicians fidgeted, making minute costume adjustments, tucking and patting at themselves and each other, securing flowers, repositioning *'eis*. The green and gold flag of the Cook Islands snapped in the trade winds. The moment of first contact had come.

Suddenly, there was a barely perceptible movement from the ship out at sea. As the dark brown eyes of the massed Islanders widened in amazement, a tiny mosquito-like object detached itself from the huge mothership and a faint clatter grew to a roar.

The 'insect' materialized; a machine unlike any ever seen by the people of Mitiaro – a machine whose name was not even known. It swooped over the sea. Abruptly, with a hideous chattering that drowned out all familiar sounds of Mitiaro's world, it dropped from the sky and landed on the shore, propellers hurling a fusillade of sharp coral chips into the scrubbed, expectant faces of the population. There was a brief violent whirlwind, then stillness.

It's a credit to the courage of Mitiaro's people that even the youngest did not cry out or run. As they stared shocked, shoulder to shoulder, a door opened in the machine and something resembling men like themselves emerged, dressed strangely in white helmets and jumpsuits like moon men they'd seen in the *Cook Islands News*.

It was the commander of the *Waikato* and two of his officers. Smartly, they removed their protective outerwear in unison like dancers. Helmets tucked under one arm, spines erect, heads up, they marched forward, white uniforms immaculate, coral crunching under precise blows from their heavily shod feet. Snapping to a halt, they stood at attention before Papa Raui Pokoati, CAO of Mitiaro, and his reception committee of Island leaders.

The men stared at one another across a silent, vast technological gulf. Confident, the officers smiled expectantly to put the Islanders at ease.

Papa Raui's face was stone-serious. His eyes blazed. Behind him, the musicians and uniformed organizations had recovered from the shock and the first strains of music trickled in rivulets through the silence. Papa Raui's right arm shot up, then chopped down. The music stopped. The marching teams froze in their tracks. The slapping of the flag, the rattle of coconut palm fronds and the rhythmic boom of the surf swelled and filled the silence again.

Something was wrong. The officers looked at each other questioningly. What special act was expected of them that they hadn't performed? Was their briefing deficient? What was the protocol here?

Papa Raui stood silent and forbidding, letting the strands of minutes snap off until tension grew so thin that one more minute lost would make it explode. Finally, he spoke and his voice was sharp and sure like the ring of a *pate* (wooden drum) beaten with a stick.

'It is not traditional to land on our shores on an official visit in this fashion!' His eyes, dark and blazing with all the pride and power of his great seagoing ancestors, bored into the blue eyes ranked before him.

'Return to your ship now in your machine. Come back to our shores in the small boat as men of the sea have always done. Only then can we greet the New Zealand Navy with the welcome which is traditional on Mitiaro.'

Like the well-disciplined men they were, the captain and his officers responded with matching dignity. Smartly, they marched down the beach to their helicopter, donned jumpsuits and helmets and withdrew in another whirlwind of flying coral chips to HMNZS *Waikato*.

Before long, a small motor launch could be seen separating itself from the mother ship. It sped toward Mitiaro. The boatmen of Mitiaro were waiting. With a lifetime of experience behind them, they shot through the treacherous opening in the reef in a weathered old rowboat, twice the size of their graceful canoes resting on the sand. Meeting the ship's launch halfway, they pulled alongside while the *Waikato*'s commander and officers came aboard in the tossing sea. Rowing with skillful strokes, the Mitiaro boatmen pulled toward the breakers to poise, now backstroking, watching for the right moment to surf through the treacherous opening in the reef. New Zealand and Mitiaro sailors alike bailed vigorously with tin cans and coconut shells. With a rush, they came ashore, this time with the surf as men of the sea have landed on Mitiaro for centuries.

Without further ado, the welcome ceremonies commenced, the barefoot, uniformed clubs paraded, speeches rose and fell from both sides, followed by singing and dancing. The celebrations had begun. The wet uniforms of the officers were dry even before the speeches ended.

As the festivities progressed, the helicopter flew back and forth from ship to shore. It was now a welcome guest in its own right with an openly admiring audience.

Boatload after boatload of sailors landed wetly through the reef passage in the only way appropriate for men of the sea. Their smart motor launch never came ashore. It sped them in as close to the maelstrom and jagged coral as it dared, wheeling saucily after each open sea transfer of passengers was made and roared back to the *Waikato*. Its return cargos were excited Mitiaro schoolchildren and adults, off for a tour of this great technological maritime wonder, while *Waikato*'s boyish sailors bailed and shot through the boiling reef passage in its humble, splintering old sister, rowed by laughing, proud Mitiaro sailors, to their first South Sea Island.

The New Zealand Navy had been challenged that day by the CAO of Mitiaro with words like the traditional brandished spears of his seafaring warrior ancestors. They had met that challenge with style and grace, winning Papa Raui's respect and admiration. It was mutual.

## 25

# THE SCARLET WOMAN OF MITIARO

Papa Raui set off for his inland plantations after breakfast. Again, I had to remain behind. There were no women available to accompany me. 'Perhaps you can come along and help pick string beans after lunch if one of the women is free then', he says, 'or if not today – maybe Monday.'

Resigned, I stroll aimlessly through the villages in the morning heat, calling 'kia orana' to women whose faces are now familiar. No one responds. Perhaps it isn't customary to speak aloud before 10 a.m. No, they chat aimiably in Maori to each other until I greet them. Then, silence; averted eyes. Something is wrong.

I meet a missionary named Nane on the road, a Rarotonga girl of about nineteen of extraordinary beauty and piousness who was educated in New Zealand. She's staying on Mitiaro to teach Bible classes and new himenes. Nane has a remarkable, melodious voice which must span four octaves. She greets me, a merry twinkle in her nearly black eyes.

'I'm so glad to see you', I say, relieved to find a familiar face that doesn't fog over when our eyes meet. 'What on earth's going on? Everyone I speak to pretends I'm invisible.'

'Yes, you are right. All is not well', Nane replies with unsmiling candor.

It wasn't the answer I expected. I figured she'd reassure me that everyone is still struck dumb with shyness. 'What on earth have I done? Was I too pushy yesterday, insisting on helping make sandwiches?'

She counters with a strange question. 'Was that man you were with yesterday your husband?'

'My husband? That officer? No. Of course not. My husband's in California. Why do you ask?'

She stares into space silently, trying to formulate the right words. 'You went off alone with him', she says finally. 'And', her eyes meet mine, then flick away, 'you took him to your room.'

'What? People are upset because I was friendly with an officer from the *Waikato*? Wasn't I supposed to be? Everyone else was friendly with the crew.'

'But you were different. You went to the bush alone with him. You took him to your room.'

'I didn't go to the bush with him. We went to the beach! And yes, I took him to my room – in broad daylight with twenty people in the house! I was showing him around. He wanted to see what your "tourist" accommodations looked like!'

Nane nods. 'I understand', she says with a fleeting look of relief. 'Mitiaro people are very old-fashioned, still. They hold fast to the laws the missionaries gave to them. Men and women do not go to the bush together, even if they are related. A woman must not even be seen crying at the grave of a man who was not her child, her father, her brother or her husband. This is the way of small islands.'

'Now I feel really stupid!' I say glumly. 'I knew that about Mitiaro before I came. I've tried to be sensitive – apparently, not hard enough. I suppose it was also the mark of a scarlet woman that I sat right down with my friend and ate a meal with the men.'

She flicks her eyebrows in assent and says, 'um'.

'Sadie Thompson lives again! God dammit! Excuse me, Nane. I would think, though, that at my age rules like that would no longer apply.'

'Who is Sadie Thompson?' she asks, curious.

'Oh, just a character in a story I once read by Somerset Maugham. She was sort of a ...', I search for a polite word for it to make up for cussing in front of a missionary, 'a harlot.' Good biblical word! 'She was run out of Honolulu, then got stuck in Pago Pago and had a merry time with the sailors there until ... nevermind, it's just a made-up story. I don't suppose you read any Maugham in school, did you?'

'No', she smiles. 'I was a Bible student in school and I am still a Bible student. There is so much to learn in the Bible, I could read it my whole life and never learn all it has to teach me. I study it and I study it. I have no time for other books. Do you read the Bible?'

'Not a whole lot. No. But I probably read too much and don't stop to consider when I'm in strange situations that they're real, not a story I can move through and still be myself without endangering anyone.' I sigh, deeply depressed. 'I just can't believe people thought an old lady like me was fooling around. You know, I'm old enough to be your mother!'

She laughs, bringing sudden color back to a tropical island that had turned black and white. 'Nobody in the Islands is ever too old for that!' I laughed then, too, as her words brought a sudden flashback of Widow Cameron of Aitutaki with her policeman.

'Never too old for a little tickle, eh?' I repeat the line I'd heard on Aitutaki. She smiles, wise as a grandmother, and we stroll on down the road.

'You don't seem like a missionary.'

'But I am very much a missionary. You must remember, I was educated in New Zealand. I've lived in your world as well as on my home island of Rarotonga and on isolated islands like this one. I have great understanding of how differently people can view events.'

We reach the large community meeting house. She pauses and we lean against the rail of the cavernous porch that runs the length of the building. On the other side, young women sit on mats spread on the wooden deck, laps heaped with magnificent *tivaevaes* in process. The color combinations are fearless. One stitcher embroiders huge turquoise flowers on a scarlet background. Others work in orange and purple, Honda yellow on royal blue and combinations one wouldn't think feasible. They sit in the lotus position with the wonderful constructions over their knees like psychedelic lap rugs as they embroider and chat. Off to one side, their seniors weave enormous mats of finely shredded pandanus fibers. Children play around and under everything. On this day, no one has to go to the bush to find food. There's plenty left over, enough to feed the whole population through Sunday.

The girls call out greetings to Nane, ignoring me. Now that I know the cause, I refuse to slink off. 'What is that pattern called?' I ask a young woman of about sixteen, working on an enormous yellow appliqué on hot pink. She doesn't reply.

Nane speaks to her sternly at some length in Maori. Finally, the girl looks in my general direction and replies flatly: 'Pineapple.'

'It's beautiful', I say. 'And yours', I turn to another. 'What do you call this gorgeous thing you're making?'

'It is *matirita*. I don't know how you say in English. Is a flower.'

'What a pretty child, too! Your sister?'

'My daughter', she replies. 'Tell the lady your name', she says, but the tot, who looks about five, wriggles under her teenaged mother's arm instead and wedges herself between her back and the wall. Everyone laughs.

'They're speaking to me again! What did you tell them, Nane? That I'm a nun?'

'Something like that', she says with a grin.

'Well, maybe you'd better mention that I don't eat children.'

She laughs. 'That little girl is very shy. She'll come around once she gets used to you.'

'What about my getting my *tivaevae* and joining them? Do you suppose that would be acceptable?'

'You are making one? I didn't know anyone but our people could make them.'

'I've never made one, but I want to learn. A woman on Aitutaki cut a pattern for me and I have the background cloth. I can sew, after a fashion. I just need someone to show me how to baste the pieces together. Maybe if I just meekly start working on a *tivaevae* too, your friends here will stop judging me like I'm some sort of philistine, trampling on customs they hold dear. I've got to do something and obviously, I can't go for a walk and explore the island by myself. They'll think I have a man stashed in the bush – maybe one of theirs.'

Nane looks sympathetic and gestures in the direction of the village with her chin. 'Nga can show you how to sew the *tivaevae*', she says. We set off, waving goodbye to the women.

'That girl I spoke to looks very young to have a child that old.'

'She's younger than I am, but she has two children by the policeman. His wife gave him a terrible beating right on the main street here in front of everybody the last time', she says conversationally.

'She isn't married to the father?'

'No. Most of those girls you saw sewing are single.'

'But there were so many children playing around. Where are their mothers?'

'Those girls are their mothers.'

'How can they get pregnant if men and women aren't allowed to be alone together?'

'Well, that one girl, she got her last baby when one of the police took all the Girl Guides camping in the bush.'

'Wait a minute!' I stop abruptly. 'You mean the scoutmaster takes the girls off camping and fools around with them? In my country, he'd spend the rest of his life in jail if the girls' parents didn't kill him first! And these are the same girls who won't speak to a woman visitor old enough to be their mother who makes friends with a man and shows him around in broad daylight?'

'They're related to each other, too', she says, relishing my indignation. 'That's one reason why his wife got so mad she beat him.'

I was speechless.

'When Papa Raui left the cabinet and came back to be our CAO, he had much work to do. Some people think he's too strict and they say he is, what you call it ... dick ...?' She searches for the word.

'Dictator?'

'Yes. A dictator. But me, I think he is strong and the only kind of a leader for this kind of an island. He doesn't allow the girls to go to the bush with the men unless they're a married couple. There's no drinking on this island anymore, either. They used to be drunk all day, all night. They wouldn't work the land. Then, Papa Raui brought electricity and cold beer to the island. Now, every week, each man is allowed to buy two tins from Papa. No one else is allowed to sell it. When they come to his house to buy their beer, they must be dressed in clean clothes and their faces must be shaved.'

'What about women? Do they buy beer?'

'No. Only men!'

'Odd', I muse. 'Don't the women like beer, too?'

'Sometimes, but it is the men who come to buy the beer. All week, Papa makes the men work very hard, but he is always fair. He never mistreats them.

'They're now building a road to the plantations they've cleared out of the bush in the interior. It's going to go all the way across the island to the lake. There are eels in that lake that are so good', she rubbed her stomach, 'that they are famous as far away as Rarotonga.

'Papa has taught these people to grow vegetables for the export market. When you leave Mitiaro next week, the first shipment of string beans will go on the plane with you to Rarotonga. It will earn much money for the people here. They will also be able to ship eels and dried bananas. They have a special way of drying bananas that makes them last a long time.'

'Dried bananas and eels I can understand, but do they eat string beans on Rarotonga?'

'Oh, yes. The people who have lived in New Zealand like them. When they grow enough, they will even ship string beans to New Zealand.'

'That's great! It's pretty hard to raise cash when you have nothing to sell but coconuts and fish, I guess.'

She flicks her eyebrows. 'Papa has plans for this island that will make the people rich! You know the *maire*? It grows in abundance back in the bush. There was a man here from Hawaii, a *papaa* like yourself and he told Papa Raui people would pay much money for *maire* in Hawaii. He said this is the finest he's ever seen!'

'But perfectly good *maire* grows in Hawaii. They call it *maile* and it's almost a sacred part of Hawaiian ceremonies. Why would they go over two thousand miles to Mitiaro for it?'

'I'm not sure', she says. 'Papa said he heard you can't get it in Hawaii anymore because some people now grow another plant in the bush they guard with guns. Everyone is afraid to go back there to pick *maire*.'

I laugh. 'Did he say what the plant is? *Pakalolo* or marijuana maybe?'

Nane looks blankly back at me and I change the subject. 'The people must have worked very hard making the villages so clean and neat for the *Waikato's* visit. There's not a bit of litter and every house looks immaculate. Even the curtains in the windows look new.'

That brings a ready laugh. 'This island is always like that since Papa Raui became CAO. Every month, there's a *tutaka*. Every month! Not every six months or year, like the rest of the Cook Islands, but every single month! You know the *tutaka*? It's like a competition to see whose gardens are most clean with no rubbish and no weeds. The houses must be clean, too, repaired and perfect, inside and out when the inspection committee comes.'

Before I can comment, we meet Nga on the road. The young matron greets us and the two Islanders lapse into their own language. Finally, Nga turns to me and asks if I brought my *tivaevae* along.

'I'll run get it', I say gratefully. Perhaps my painful rites of passage are over.

I spend the rest of the day humbly, sitting cross-legged on a mat in a far corner of Nga's immense coral cement house which has no furniture except for two great wood-framed beds in an alcove. The operation I was about to witness was not one for amateurs.

The Girl Guide leader spreads the white, double bed–sized cotton background on the bare coral cement floor, smoothing it with her strong brown hands. Deftly, she unscrambles the huge, navy blue design that was cut on the folds making multiple repeat patterns. This is to be appliquéd on the white in one piece. I had never seen it opened out before. 'Wow!' I gasp.

'Ah', she sighs. 'There it is. But I don't know this pattern. It's beautiful. Where did you get it? What is it's name?' There was excitement in her voice.

'It's called "butterflies and grapes". An old woman on Aitutaki designed it and cut it out. I don't know what inspired her. They don't grow grapes in the Cook Islands. I haven't seen many butterflies, either, for that matter. Maybe she's been to New Zealand.'

'Grapes?' Nga asks with a puzzled frown.

'It's a fruit. Looks sort of like *limu*', I say, referring to the seaweed that grows on the reefs, 'but the fruits are larger and come in colors of green, purple, red or dark blue. It grows on the land.'

'Beautiful', she says reverently.

'No more so than the beautiful patterns you make here on Mitiaro. I'm very impressed!'

'You are?' She looks at me thoughtfully. 'We are just simple people here. Most of us have not travelled, even to Rarotonga.'

Now, frowning, she bends to concentrate on centering the cutwork on the background, spreading it as smooth as possible on the pocked cement floor. Idle chatter ceases as the master begins to demonstrate the correct way to baste from the center outward, placing each temporary stitch with precision to keep the design anchored.

As she sews without so much as a pin to hold the parts together, she cautions me to watch the direction in which she bastes each time she starts a new quadrant out from the center. 'You must always sew in this same direction. That will keep it nice and smooth and flat.' I watch intently, hoping to God I can remember the direction. I do.

The really difficult part was done for me, the design cut by an artist of Aitutaki, the foundation secured by a craftswoman of Mitiaro to withstand the punishment of countless unfoldings and refoldings it will be subjected to as her student flounders with it alone, far from her island tutor. All I have to remember is one stitch and one direction.

Repetitive tasks like this – turning under a maze of frayed raw edges and encasing them in embroidery – are a part of the fabric of a woman's daily life in most of the Cook Islands and parts of French Polynesia. The magnificent folk-art bed coverings and shrouds were never intended to be made by one person, but by several on a verandah filled with family and friends, gossiping, dreaming, sewing, weaving and making in the midst of a village.

Taken out of context of the Islands, the *tivaevae* was to become a Project to be Completed in my other life, prodded on its way by patronizing queries such as: 'When exactly do you think you'll be finished with this *thing*?'

The appropriate formula reply I would adopt was invariably, 'When it's done!', delivered with a rather good imitation of the South Seas Eyebrow Shrug, guaranteed to be a *piripiri* (burr) in the seams of deadline-bound family and friends.

It took me three years to complete that *tivaevae*. Every crude stitch I took alone on my California patio in hours stolen from my so-called 'real' work connected me in my dreaming to a tropical Polynesian island, throbbing with color and chatter, four thousand miles away and three hours earlier in a parallel reality, out there in the Pacific.

# 26

# AND ON THE SEVENTH DAY ...

I awake determined, Sunday, to the predawn cacophony of roosters. On this day, I vow to get the hang of it! I will go an entire day without sin against custom. I had not come all the way to this remotest of islands to shock, to offend or to challenge local mores. Why was I there? I sorted it out again: I had come as a rogue researcher, penetrating the mai tai curtain to learn what Pacific Islanders were really like without harming them or myself in the process. Of particular interest to me were womens' lives, values and perspectives – and, in all honesty, wasn't I there for the adventure?

I hadn't expected to fall in love. These wonderfully self-possessed people of Mitiaro who didn't know the word 'poverty', who could transform rags into uniforms with a needle, bread and bananas into hors d'ouevres fit for an admiral and rough makatea into an airstrip with a teaspoon, these were people who could get under your skin and make you a love slave for life!

Oh, I still had fragments of loss inside when a glimpse of that empty sea reminded me of laughter and easy companionship gone beyond the horizon. Somehow, though, the flint-sharp edges of loneliness were quickly ground down by the currents of Mitiaro's lifestream to an insignificant scattering of pretty pebbles.

I spent a restless night trying to define my feelings and identity, which had gone fuzzy in the myopia of my dark chamber in the stillness that comes in isolated places when a generator shuts off. The quiet was unnerving. Even the waves were muted and lazy, dropping with small plops on the coral reef, then retreating with a sigh.

I ventured as far as the deserted verandah, barefoot and *pareu*-wrapped in the dark, and watched the night sky. Occasionally, a star would fall, leaving a cypher of light that glowed for an instant, then vanished. The Milky Way was a luminous veil of spun pearl filaments above the black silhouettes of the coconut palms.

I drifted back in time to the small girl called Diddy Boo I once was, who believed that if she spread her arms wide, she could soar up into the stars. I found myself holding on to a porch pillar as I had then when the illusion was so strong, I had to hang on tight to something connected to the earth until the threat of becoming airborne passed. Now I blinked away the fantasy, released the pillar and stared back at the stars with defiance. They only seemed to mock me for my failure to join them long ago when I could ascend with dreams that were light and strong as wings, not heavy and gnarled with skepticism, anxieties and contradictions.

During that long night, I came to some understanding of my inconsequential presence on this small island in mid Pacific. All that I was, my struggles, accomplishments, goals, possessions, meant absolutely nothing. The sum of my existence equalled what people saw as I stood before them on Mitiaro. Since I had no blood ties with anyone here, I had no history. My opinions were irrelevant. If I had any value at all, it was entertainment. The lessons to be learned were all by me. I was the one who was poor, needy and ignorant. They were the rich, the powerful, the competent, the survivors, the keepers of the land.

Now it was the Sabbath, Blue Laws Sunday, the legacy of the London Missionary Society to all the islands in the British Commonwealth, from Skye in Scotland to Mitiaro in the South Seas. This day was dedicated to the Lord: no playing, no working, not even cooking!

Despite its small population, Mitiaro has two churches, one for Catholics, the other for Protestants. The latter, of course, was the Cook Islands Christian Church, an LMS offshoot. Papa Raui had been a CICC pastor for twenty years, so it was to this sober coral limestone edifice we directed our steps. Mama Tai loaned me a hat so I wouldn't be a disgrace to the family. I would have been, had anyone searched my purse. Despite my solemn dawn vows of impeccable behavior, I slipped fresh batteries and a blank cassette in my small tape recorder and secreted it in my bag, microphone against thin woven sides facing outward for maximum pick up. I rationalized that this was in no way disrespectful. I only wanted to have a piece of Mitiaro with me forever through its music.

The a capella singing was of extraordinary power, with every member of that small congregation pouring forth massive *himene* harmonies as if each person, alone, must sing loudly and perfectly enough to catch the ear of God. I felt in that tiny church on Mitiaro what I had felt in churches of all sizes throughout Polynesia when this magnificent outpouring of musical worship exploded. The sound did not exist outside and apart from any individual. The rhythms, the tones seemed to come from the pulse of the brain, the wrists, the stomach, the guts, the very rotation of the earth. My body and mind were like an anvil, echoing sound vibrations outward, beaten out of my silence. It made no difference that in my ignorance of the language and music form, I had no song. I was given one and it resonated throughout my body, linking me to the others.

Somehow, two hours of preaching and singing in a language unknown to me passed like moments. If the sermon was banal, I was spared that annoyance and uplifted by the rise and fall of oration which, when skillfully done, can be thrilling as a song. It was a great performance, in any language.

The service over, I found myself abandoned with a blank Sabbath Day to fill. This was a challenge. No work allowed. Okay, writing would be considered work if I unzipped my typewriter and pecked away. What about writing in longhand? At least it was quiet. No, I decided that too might be viewed as some sort of labor. Starting the sewing on my *tivaevae*? Extremely sinful! Aimless walking about? Nope, not even during the week. Swimming or snorkeling? No, even if I could find a big enough tidepool to float in, I'd be seen and ostracized. I recalled something Nane had mentioned about a womens' meeting, but where?

Shyly, I walked down the lane to the meeting house where the women had worked on their sewing and weaving. A welcome sound of voices trailed off into the rising heat of the Sunday afternoon like vapors. Entering, I slipped into a seat, hoping I hadn't been noticed.

The entire female Protestant population of Mitiaro seemed to be present. There were mamas resplendent in dresses of green satin, chaste white or island prints, all crowned with marvellous white hats of *rito* woven from the unfurling newborn coconut palm leaf, some wearing beach sandals on broad, capable feet, most barefoot.

I had no sooner settled in my seat than a woman rose and welcomed me eloquently in English, instructing me to carry the love of the mamas of Mitiaro with me wherever I went in the world. Then she translated this into the local language for the sake of the older people present. A murmur of approval rose as the women nodded solemnly and glanced my way.

In the front of the hall was a large blackboard on which biblical questions were written in Maori. The group leader would read one aloud, then translate into English for my benefit. To the mamas, each one was an inspiration. One after the other would leap to her feet and deliver a spirited oration in response, accompanied by enough gestures for a hula.

Though obviously this was very serious business, each mama was also a comedienne, her pantomimes and inflections making her a scream in any language. We laughed ourselves into a rib-aching, gasping state interspersed with periods of attentive, sometimes apprehensive listening. The intensity of feeling communicated so powerfully, it didn't occur to me until later that I didn't understand a word that was said.

Once, a heavy woman leapt to her feet to challenge the statements of another. An impassioned argument followed, raising itself to a screeching crescendo. Suddenly, the challenger plopped sulkily back to her seat and the victor broke into a hula, hooting and wagging her considerable expanse of bottom at the vanquished to the shrieks of her delighted sisters.

My favorite mama must have been at least ninety. She had a rugged homemade cane which she alternately pounded for attention and emphasis, or waved madly back and forth to illustrate some point. Sometimes she cast fear into all of us. Frequently, she reduced us to hilarity.

There was no question that this was a religious exercise of great scope and depth. Mitiaro women just seemed to have an unlimited capacity to enjoy whatever it was they were doing.

The biblical debates went on into the afternoon. Finally, they gave way to a *himene* practice. There was a break while messengers went home and told the men it was time. Nane had brought new *himene*s to Mitiaro. Would she hand out song sheets? How were these complex harmonies and counterpoints taught?

As the expanded group settled in the great meeting house, men on one side, women on the other, I soon found out it must have been learning by telepathy. There was no printed music, no piano, no pitch pipe, nothing but the sketchiest of examples picked up instantly by a people who simply seem to know things without visible evidence of formal teaching. The men would listen to a few snatches from Nane. Then they'd pour forth a thunderation of rhythmic grunts and chanting. Then the rich middle harmonies of the women would join in, incised by the nasal keening counterpoint of the old women.

Nane would listen attentively from her seat amidst the women, respectfully apart from the male leader up front by the blackboard. Both would follow the music, then suddenly, the sharp tap-tap-tap of a stick against the floor would stop the *himene* abruptly. Vocal corrections and adjustments would be made by example. The song would pick up again from the beginning.

As familiarity freed up the singing, Nane's voice separated itself from the rest, fluttering free and playful in a birdlike descant weaving in and out of the high notes, then plunging through the middle range to the very bottom, ending in harsh notes as deep and guttural as those of the men. She seemed totally unaware that her range was extraordinary. She evoked memories of the great Peruvian singer, Yma Sumac.

Remembering my tape recorder, hidden in my bag along with extra cassettes, I pulled it out and held it up, catching the attention of the male leader. He tapped for silence and asked me in English if what I held was a recording machine. I replied in the affirmative and asked permission to record their practice. At first, he was reluctant, wanting me to wait until the group had reached perfection. I managed to convince him that it would be of value to record the learning process leading up to the final result. I promised him copies of the tapes so he could study them. I waited in suspense while the group discussed this new development. Most had never seen a tape recorder. I passed it around.

Finally, permission was granted and I set it up in the middle of the room without further ado. Five minutes later, everything stopped. I must play what I had recorded. I did. A breath of astonishment swept the room, punctuated with laughter and the little machine was accepted as a working member of the music workshop.

Nane walked beside me after the meeting. 'You have one of the most remarkable singing voices I have ever heard', I said. 'You could be another Kiri Te Kanawa. Are you going on to study voice in New Zealand?'

The young woman stopped walking and stared at me, wide-eyed. 'Me? I am not a singer like that Maori woman in New Zealand. Oh, I have heard of her, but to sing like that takes many years of study overseas.'

'Well then, you should go to New Zealand and get started', I said briskly. 'With all that natural ability, you should be eligible for all kinds of scholarships.'

'I cannot go overseas to study. My life is here. I'm the youngest in my family. I have been chosen to stay home and take care of my parents in their old age.'

'But Nane, is that what you really want to do? You could have such a wonderful future if you'd get more education. You'd be more use to your parents that way.'

'I have a wonderful future here in the Cook Islands. My parents are the dearest thing I have. It is my joy on earth to be chosen to stay behind and help them.'

It was said so matter-of-factly and with such sincerity, I felt ashamed of my defective value system. Again, I was struck dumb, tears stinging my eyes. I turned aside. 'I'm going to look in on the Village Council meeting', I said gruffly. 'Papa Raui said I might if I was interested. Do you know where they meet?' This girl, young enough to be my daughter and old enough to be my great-grandmother, led me down a dusty path, baking in the afternoon sun, to a small house.

Inside, men and women crowded together on mats or old wooden benches, heads bowed, listening intently. Someone beckoned me and made room for me on a bench and the scolding continued, because that's what this meeting seemed all about. First, Papa Raui would lambaste the women for lopping off the tops of young coconut trees to make hats. He translated some of his admonitions for my benefit. 'You kill the trees', he shouted. 'You are not careful when you cut the young leaves. If you take the time to do it properly, the tree will not die. You know the correct way to cut the leaves. Too many hats. We need coconut trees, not hats!'

Then Tiki Tetava Ariki, who lived in the house next to the CAO's, scolded everyone present for throwing drinking coconuts in the road after they'd drained the contents.

Next, Papa Raui spoke again, now in a quieter tone, reminding the men that they must be neatly dressed when they come for their beer on Friday. A few squirmed noticeably and stared glumly at the floor. Finally, he proclaimed a new law, effective Wednesday, three days hence. 'Every man, woman and child, aged fourteen to sixty-five must plant twenty coconuts a month or be fined!' The group heard out the new edict in silence, only the flexing of eyebrows indicating that it had been heard and digested. There was no discussion or argument.

As the sun descended into the sea, I strolled back to the Pokoati home, tired but stimulated, to find Mama Tai very sad. Her face bore traces of crying, heaps of family photos around her. She beckoned me to sit down beside her on the sofa. Papa Raui joined us. 'She is missing all of her nine children', he explained. 'She is longing especially for Tungane, her daughter in Rarotonga, and her granddaughter. There hasn't been a letter in some time. She is growing worried.'

I looked at the strong face of a laughing young woman with a bushy Fiji-style haircut, her arm around a little girl of about seven: a modern young woman, far from Mitiaro's humble but complex life, rendered glamorous by black-and-white photography.

'Maybe a letter will come on the plane next week', I said. We nodded together. Mama Tai offered a weak smile and a strong sigh, got to her feet ponderously and shuffled off to the kitchen to prepare the evening meal. I think she was crying for her children again.

## 27

# FACE ON THE OCEAN
# WITH MY TEARS

Monday, I'm finally allowed to sit with the women on the porch of the meeting house. I join them on a large mat, back against the cool coral limestone wall, legs pretzeled, nonchalantly spread my *tivaevae* over my knees as they do and take up my needle and thread.

Immediately, everyone stops sewing to watch. Does the *papaa* even know which end of the needle the thread goes into? To everyone's satisfaction, I prick myself repeatedly and find it almost impossible to poke the thread through the hole in the needle. I pretend not to hear whispers in Maori of 'I told you so!' At least, I'm affording them some sort of amusement with my fumblings. Finally, the thread connects with the hole by some fluke and I'm threaded up. 'Ah!' I say, and start in, from the center out, as Nga had demonstrated.

I amaze them. They sit, needles suspended, watching. The strange, useless *papaa* is performing an approved woman's function. Tupu on Aitutaki had taught me well, though a nagging teacher she was. I am using an embroidery stitch they recognize to attach my design to the background. Perhaps my stitches are not small and neat as theirs are, but they aren't bad for a beginner. The comedy show is over, there is nothing left to watch. The women resume their work.

Minutes tick away. Contentment spreads through me like the morning sun as I focus on the repetitive task. Even children seem to have forgotten I am from the wrong side of the reef and climb on my work and me with as much disregard as if I were a rock or an old tree trunk. I strain to understand the gossip, wishing foreign languages came more easily to me.

My reward for appropriate behavior comes after lunch. Papa Raui has found a woman willing to leave her duties in the village to accompany me for the rest of the afternoon. Now, he can take me inland, show me the plantations and perhaps even the lakes.

We bump along the track in the Pokoati Honda through deep jungle growth. Soon, the scenery changes to one of orderly coconut groves and well-tended vegetable plots. The good rich smell of healthy growing things fills the air. It's incredible that such lush gardens can be wrested from the makatea. Papa Raui has even worked out an efficient irrigation canal network.

Men are working hard, some hacking coconuts in half with bush knives for copra, others weeding or harvesting. Papa stops the Honda and we walk the rows, admiring the first crop of magnificent, rich dark green string beans, the long thin variety not much wider than spaghetti. Some are almost six feet long. The makatea evidently agrees with them. 'Can I help pick them?' I ask. He un-successfully smothers a smile.

'Have you ever picked string beans before?'

'No. I've never even seen them growing. But you can show me. I learn fast.'

Amused at his tourist's strange idea of a good time, he shows me how to tell mature beans from unripe and I get to work, my female companion who speaks no English nearby. It's hard labor in the high humidity under a fierce equatorial sun. I'm soon drenched with sweat, mosquitoes feeding on me with whining tenacity.

Papa Raui strides off down the rows, stopping here and there to check the progress of the men, pausing to pick a few beans as he goes. This is his first harvest. It goes to Rarotonga on tomorrow's plane, then onward to New Zealand. Undoubtedly, it will fetch a good price. This is a historic crop, marking Mitiaro's entry into the export market and the world of cash economy. The little CAO finally rejoins me, timing it just before I pass out. He's as fresh and vital as if he's just risen from a good night's rest. There's not a drop of sweat on him, the clothes on his wiry, hyperactive frame look newly laundered and pressed, and he carries a mountainous bag of beans he's picked along the way.

With infinite tact, he adds my modest haul to his after singling out individual beans for close inspection and an educated tasting. 'Good, good', he says with pride. 'They will pay much money in New Zealand for such beans.'

We drive on, leaving the plantations behind, now bouncing over trails that seem to disappear periodically. Finally, Papa Raui stops the car. We're as close to the lake as the Honda can get, but there's no sign of water, just a snarl of bush. My female companion and I set out on foot.

The terrain is rugged. We slog through foul-smelling, mud-masking, razor-sharp makatea coral ridges, which make short work of my zories. One is speared off and sinks from sight in black ooze. The other is sliced in half. I continue, now barefoot, groping with my toes before putting my weight into each step, trying to find smooth plateaus between the hidden, vicious blades of dead coral. I can almost feel infections spreading through my open mosquito bites and coral cuts. There's nothing to be done about it now. I must see the lake.

My female companion strides on ahead, bare feet seemingly impervious to the mud-filled gulleys bristling with razor blades and shifting boulders. Finally, she turns to wait for me, puzzled that I'm having such a hard time. 'How much farther is the lake?' I ask. She replies in Maori. I don't know what she says, but the exchange gives me a few minute's rest. The heat is terrific. I slip, lurch and stumble onward. The mystery lake of this South Sea Island will not come to me, I must go to it.

The jungle suddenly gives way to a sea of mud. We have arrived. I gasp. Before me is the most unremarkable body of semi-liquid ooze I have ever seen. There's a thin line between whether or not it's a lake or a mud puddle. Away out toward the center is a patch of what seems to be deeper water, judging by a pattern of ripples. This, then, is where the famous eels of Mitiaro rule. It's a fitting setting. Great gnarled trees grow on the perimeter of the lake; monstrous apparitions with heavy fluted roots. This is the *utu* (*Barringtonia sepciosa*) tree which thrives in makatea, its thick, twisted branches interlocking overhead, great leaves blotting out the sun. A few spidery yellow flowers are scattered here and there among the tree roots. The *utu* blooming season is past, its nutlike poisonous fruit ripe. Mature nuts are still occasionally pounded up and spread on the water to stupify fish for an easy, if unsporting, catch. The poison apparently has no effect on the fish's edibility. In the old days, it was said, the nuts were made into poisonous drinks to get rid of troublesome people.

As we bump back past the plantations to the house, I ask Papa Raui where he got the training to do so much for his island. 'Were you educated overseas? You seem to know such a variety of things like civil engineering, farming, psychology, administration and didn't you say you'd been a pastoral minister for twenty years before you went into politics?'

'I didn't even go to school until I was twenty years old', he said. 'Yes, you are right, I did study overseas, but not in New Zealand or Australia. I went to Rarotonga. There was no school on Mitiaro when I was a boy.'

'Why did you wait until you were twenty?'

'There was no money to send me away to school. I was hungry for education. When I got to Rarotonga, I went to school with the little children because I wanted to learn to read and write so badly. At first, they laughed to see a grown man sitting in the school with little children. I paid no attention. This was the only way I could get education: to be humble, work hard and pay no attention when people made fun of me.'

Seeing my fascination, he told me his story.

The young Raui worked diligently and learned his reading, writing, arithmetic and even English in a relatively short time. He entered the missionary college in Tutakimoa, over the bridge behind the Rarotonga Library and Museum, graduated and was ordained as a CICC Minister.

Over the years, he kept adding new studies through extension courses, such as psychology. Now married, he found he couldn't earn enough money to take care of his increasing family the way he wanted to, so he left the church and went into business on Rarotonga. When the Cook Islands achieved self-government in 1965 he was elected as a Cook Islands Party (CIP) member of Parliament by his Mitiaro constituency.

Sure of Mitiaro's loyalty, Sir Albert threw development assistance to Demo stronghold islands in an effort to attract CIP support. When Mitiaro was left out of the planning for interisland air service, Papa Raui protested. Sir Albert suggested he go home and build his own airport.

Furious, with tears of disappointment on his cheeks, Papa Raui sailed to Mitiaro on the interisland cargo boat, organized his people and the rest is history. Weeks later, Cook Islands Airways flew over Mitiaro. The pilot was amazed to see the airstrip nearly completed. He reported to Rarotonga. Sir Albert resignedly sent the grader to Mitiaro on the boat. The machine tidied up for a few hours and the first plane landed.

Raui had hoped in vain that the grader could be left on Mitiaro for a week or two to clear a road inland, but Sir Albert's son was standing as a candidate in a byelection on Mauke. The grader was needed to make a display of government support for Mauke's development.

Angry, but resigned, Raui and the people of Mitiaro sighed and started chipping away again. They had cleared an airfield from the jungle and leveled it from dead coral, they could eventually get a road done too. But the last straw was in the trade winds.

In 1977, a year after the airport was completed, Sir Albert flew to Mitiaro to take a little holiday. At first, he was welcomed to the Pokoati home, but he brought a supply of liquor with him and, to his host's horror, proceeded to drink under his roof. Now, this was against vows Raui had taken as a CICC minister, which he pointed out politely to the premier. The latter continued to drink anyway. Papa Raui, patience wearing thin, moved Sir Albert and his hooch to the Community House, where he made his premiere as comfortable as possible with furniture and a bed from the big house.

Raui explained, with many apologies, that he didn't want to shock me, but matters went from worse to intolerable and since he'd told me that much, he'd tell me the rest. I assured him I did not shock easily and he got on with the worst of it. He sent a couple of men over to guard the premiere, who promptly slipped one of them money with instructions to go get him a young girl. The villager reported to Papa Raui, who told him angrily to return the dirty money. He did and Sir Albert, who was by then well into his cups, went berserk and smashed bottles and everything he could get his hands on in his rage. Papa Raui decided that night he could never respect such a man again, withdrew all support from Sir Albert and resigned from the CIP.

He continued in politics a bit longer in the vain hope of reforming the political system the Cook Islands had adapted from the British model. He founded the Unity Movement with supporters and disenchanted politicians like himself. It was called a 'movement' because its purpose was to end party politics forever in the Cook Islands. Papa Raui hoped to validate it with legislation that would specify that members of Parliament must serve all their constituency members equally, not just those in the same party.

Though a scattering of Unity Party candidates stood for office in subsequent elections, none ever won and the idea of a political 'party' to end political parties became something of a joke. Political parties had come to stay in the Cook Islands. After all, there had to be something to replace intertribal warfare besides rugby and the land courts.

My toy 'P-38' Cessna Mixmaster was due at noon Tuesday, the following day. I didn't think I could part with this island that had come to mean so much to me without a disgraceful display of uncontrollable weeping, but Mitiaro has a knack for keeping visitors off balance. My departure was something of a circus.

Depressed and sniffling, I dragged my last bag to the verandah and prepared to load the car for my sad trip to the airport. Suddenly, Nga appeared, agitated and out of breath. 'Are you not coming to the *umukai*?'

'*Umukai*? What *umukai*? The plane comes in an hour. I have to get to the airport.'

'No, no, you must come to the *umukai* we have prepared for you and my uncle who is also leaving.'

'But there isn't time! I'll miss my plane!'

'The plane will not leave without my uncle. He is a very important man!'

Papa Raui intervened at that point. 'You must go. The *umukai* is our way of saying goodbye to you.'

I followed Nga through the villages, grimly, glancing at my watch. Entering her house, I saw that a long, low plank table now presided where she had basted my *tivaevae* together. The large room was filled with people.

It was only 11 a.m., but the humid heat was almost unbearable indoors. I was feeling sick from that and the pent-up grief I had walled up inside to keep it from spilling over onto my inevitable departure. The last thing I wanted to do was eat. But eat we must.

A huge, greasy banana leaf full of eel was offered to me as I sat down. A pig lay dead before me in the middle of the table, eyes staring, huge chunks of its body torn off and distributed on banana leaf plates. A wave of born-again vegetarianism engulfed me. I could not eat something that was looking at me.

There was fish aplenty, but it too was intact and staring. Reacting quickly, I reached for the *rukau* and heaped my banana leaf with the spinachlike young taro leaves steeped in coconut cream. 'Just a wee bit of the eel', I said, thankful it was headless. It was delicious and I found my appetite returning in spite of my sadness. I piled on taro and fish but had taken only a few bites when Papa Raui pulled up outside with his Honda and trailer piled high with boxes and people.

We drove off after farewell embraces all around. I tried not to look back, not to think that I would never see these kind people, this beautiful plain jane of an island again. I made conversation desperately, yearning to hang on to some relationship with this paradoxical face on the sea. Maybe we could form a cooperative and I could help the ladies market their magnificent *tivaevaes* overseas. They were folk art of a kind never seen in the outside world. That would surely help Mitiaro's economy. Papa said he'd think about it, but the women never made them for sale. They had all they could do to keep up with the needs of their families overseas in New Zealand.

Inanely, I babbled about the evident problem of single women and too many babies. Did Mitiaro have any birth control measures available? Yes, there was a dresser, a sort of practical nurse, on the island who gave shots of some sort to married women with too many children for their husbands to support one more.

'What about some of these very young girls who get pregnant. Some of them can't be any more than twelve. Can't they get shots?'

He glanced in mild surprise that I'd noticed such a thing. 'I agree with you', he said slowly. 'It is a problem here, but those girls have no husbands. Only the married women are entitled to the shots.' Our arrival at the airfield put a stop to any arguments I was ready to launch.

A good-sized crowd had already assembled, though no one had passed us on the road. Mitiaro's mamas were already putting the finishing touches on the tea things on the lace-covered table under the thatch-roofed shelter for the pilot and incoming passengers. A few youngsters strummed beautiful handcarved ukuleles that had cardboard frets strung with fishline.

The little plane came swiftly out of nowhere, breaking into my reveries with its buzzing engines fore and aft, jolting me back to the twentieth century and another reality. I must not give way to the sobs that filled my throat.

As I walked toward the plane, I noticed Papa Raui and the young pilot in heated discussion, gesturing and glancing my way. Curious, I drew closer, welcoming any distraction.

'Papa Raui wants me to bump you so we can take his string beans', the pilot explained, his brows furrowed. 'I told him I wasn't expecting the shipment this flight. He didn't radio ahead and I don't have room. He thinks they'll spoil if he has to leave them for a week.'

'Leave these beautiful string beans? This is the very first harvest! I helped pick a few myself. You can't leave these precious beans to rot. Papa and his people have worked so hard. Can't you give them a break? How else are they going to make any money here?'

'I'd like to help him out, but there simply isn't room', the pilot retorted. 'The plane is full.'

'I'll stay behind and leave next week then', I said hopefully. 'The beans can have my seat.'

'No, no! Don't even consider it!' He took me aside. 'Raui must learn that arrangements have to be made in advance for shipping! We cannot ask a tourist to give up a seat.'

'You sure can ask me', I said stubbornly.

The pilot glared at me, annoyed. He was adamant. I, not string beans, must go to Rarotonga today because my ticket said so.

With a breaking heart, I left this humbling, tiny 'face on the ocean' which I'd finally come close enough to see and flew off to gemlike Rarotonga, for which I'd soon cry too.

*Epilogue*

# DEATH OF THREE HEROES

### Papa Raui Pokoati

Papa Raui died 25 March 1981 of pneumonia and heart failure in the Rarotonga Hospital. He was sixty-nine. Four flights were chartered to carry his body and family to Mitiaro, where he was buried.

His daughter, Tungane, moved back to the island to care for her mother and opened a small guesthouse.

In the years that followed, the population dropped to 249. Mitiaro acquired electricity, a wider boat passage blasted through the reef, video and crime. The only school was upgraded but, in May 1992, an arsonist torched it. The principal's office, home science classroom, library, staff room and resource room were destroyed.

Mitiaro being the island that it is, the staff and all seventy-six pupils took things into their own hands. They held a march to raise funds to rebuild their school. A reception committee of parents and friends waited for them beside the road. The children and teachers gave speeches and 'passed the hat'. They raised a staggering NZ$3,200, which comes to about NZ$12.85 from each man, woman, child and baby on this 'face on the ocean'.

### Pa Ariki

Within a year of her marriage in 1979, Pa Ariki's husband was knighted by Queen Elizabeth. This further complicated the protocol of a marriage of politics and nobility, especially to the outside world, which now saw quite a bit of this jet-setting couple. She objected to being called 'Lady Davis' as strongly as she had to being addressed as First Lady. 'The Queen of England is not referred to as a duchess because her husband is a duke. A queen is a queen', she said. She finally accepted the moniker Pa Ariki Lady Davis to humor journalists overseas.

Her palace was not rebuilt during her lifetime. When we got together, now as friends and confidantes, during my intermittent visits to Rarotonga, she spoke of tensions building up in her marriage, of her need to have a place of her own from which she could minister to the needs of her constituents, of the growing frustration of her Takitumu people with her increasingly arrogant husband.

Shortly after becoming prime minister by default, Davis rammed a constitutional amendment through the Legislature increasing government's term from four to five years. Petitions to stop the amendment were ignored. He did not take kindly to anyone disputing his decisions.

As his ruling style seemed to grow more lone and arbitrary, opposition wags nicknamed him Sir Papadoc after Haiti's Duvalier. The nickname was gleefully picked up by the media in New Zealand. When one of his arbitrary schemes threatened Takitumu itself, his queen rose up against him with all the power of forty-seven generations of *arikis* coursing through her veins.

The crisis came in March 1986, when the prime minister announced his government's approval of a $25 million, 300-room resort hotel project to be constructed in the middle of Muri Lagoon and connected to the land by a causeway. It was not only the first the community had heard of it, it was the first his wife had heard of it.

Muri Lagoon is the crown jewel of Takitumu and of Rarotonga, past and present. It is a constant source of food for the people, and the pass through its reef at Avana is the most historically significant spot on the island. According to local history, it was through this pass that the final wave of Polynesian explorers and navigators came in their great double sailing canoes from Raiatea and Samoa, then, years later, set sail to colonize Aotearoa (New Zealand). Shock gave way to action. Preliminary meetings were held. Letters to the editor peppered the local newspaper like buckshot, inhibited only by the requirement that letter writers' real names be published.

The prime minister was quoted in the *Cook Islands News* as denying that his wife had no prior knowledge of the resort project. 'She [Pa Ariki] doesn't oppose it ... the Ngatangiia people have the habit of changing their minds every five minutes. They've known about it for two months', he claimed.

Pa retorted: 'I strongly oppose Government's proposed project. We the people of Takitumu, especially people of Ngatangiia, didn't know about it two months ago. The PM was quite wrong when he said my people are in the habit of changing their minds every five minutes. ... When it comes to an issue which concerns people on a major project of this kind, I am not in the habit, neither are my people, to go back and eat our spittals!'

Meetings were called in Takitumu with traditional leaders and villagers. Pa described Muri Lagoon as 'the kitchen of my people.' The broad, shallow body of water with its three reef islets is a source of fish, shellfish and *rori*, a sea slug prized for its flavor and nutritional value.

There were other factors, too, that disturbed the queen and her people. Despite promises that the resort would provide jobs and additional business for local shops and farmers, as well as hefty lease revenues, the community feared the impact of a large influx of foreign holidaymakers. Dire predictions snowballed: the resort would bring an invasion of drug pushers, pornographers and Sabbath-breakers lurching around the peaceful village lanes in bikinis; the lagoon's islets would be invaded by nude sunbathers creating havoc for passing fishermen.

The member of Parliament for Ngatangiia addressed a mass meeting of his constituency to clarify government's position. Pa Ariki thanked him for coming to his people to explain and to hear their opinions, but warned: 'You're going to take away something that God meant us to have ... you're taking away many things that my ancestors believed in. ... I myself, personally, will die a slow death with it. [Muri Lagoon] is the foundation of Pa-ma-Kainuku and the Takitumu People.'

Finally, the prime minister himself was forced to face his royal wife, her associate chief and her people in a public meeting. The session was long and explosive. They listened with courtesy as he described the projected economic benefit to Takitumu and the neighboring districts. The pros and cons were dissected by all sides. Finally, Pa and Kainuku Ariki announced their decision. It was an unequivocal '*no*' to the project. The people's continued free use of the lagoon for food and enjoyment outweighed the monetary benefit from any resort.

Sir Thomas imperiously overruled their decision.

A spokesman from the district cried out: 'Pa Ariki and Kainuku Ariki are respected and highly regarded by their people and to have their decision disrespectfully ignored by Government is insulting, to say the least. In days gone by, such an insult would not be tolerated!'

Pa Ariki rose. The room fell silent. Stretching out her right arm, she pointed her index finger at her husband. Her voice rang out clear and pure: 'Let it be known that Pa-ma-Kainuku voiced their opposition and the consequences of this will be on your head!' Her warning reverberated through the hushed crowd.

The silence elongated. Tension mounted. Suddenly, the prime minister rose to his feet and called the whole resort project off. But the relief and elation were short lived.

The next day, Sir Thomas changed his mind again and publicly reaffirmed his decision to approve the $25 million resort. Events that followed on Easter weekend made newspaper, radio and television headline news in New Zealand and throughout the Pacific, bringing shock and shame to the people of the Cook Islands. The unthinkable had occurred and now the whole world knew. Pa Tepaeru Ariki, the Queen of Takitumu, had been beaten up, allegedly by her husband. The latter did not show up at his office the following Monday, nor did anyone seem to know where he was. Days went by with no word of Sir Thomas.

Geoffrey Henry, then leader of the opposition in the Cook Islands parliament, called for the prime minister's resignation: 'He is no longer fit to be called an honourable member of Parliament, nor is he any longer fit to be the PM nor a Knight of the Commonwealth. There is only one honourable course of action left the PM – he must resign.

'Of concern to me', he continued, 'is the fact the woman involved is no ordinary woman, nor is she a housegirl or servant nor is she just the wife. She is a traditional chief of the land, the President of the House of Ariki, the First Lady of the Land. In days gone by, a mere attempted assault upon a chief, whether provoked or not, would have had fatal consequences. I have much sympathy and respect for Lady Pa. She has stood loyally by her husband with considerable courage and dignity. She could have easily left him.'

Henry called on the prime minister to cancel his scheduled trip to New Zealand for a conference with Prime Minister David Lange. 'Why must he travel to Wellington and exacerbate the shame of Cook Islanders there when the [domestic violence] incident is commanding primetime viewing and listening in New Zealand?'

The prime minister cancelled his trip, but Henry's plea had nothing to do with it. As it turned out, the nation's controversial leader, who stands at well over six feet and weighs more than two hundred pounds, was a bit under the weather. He was reported 'recovering from wounds he suffered in the recent domestic row which saw him cut around the ear, the leg and on his chest. It was reported yesterday that Sir Thomas required several stitches to the wounds and has spent the past ten days recovering after being treated and moving out of his private home to the PM's official residence. ...

'It is understood there have been no complaints to the police about the attack. On Radio New Zealand, Sir Thomas had said that reports about the fracas have been exaggerated. He said he would rather not talk about what happened.

'His wife, Pa Tepaeru Ariki, said the whole incident has grown out of proportion.'

A neighbor living down the road from the couple reported privately that had the cut in the groin been a half-inch higher, 'Sir Thomas would be a soprano in the Ngatangiia Church Choir!'

The resort? The financing supposedly forthcoming from a mysterious California-based Korean–Malaysian company fell through, and the allegedly giant corporation, which the author discovered was operating out of a small suburban bungalow in Long Beach, vanished.

The prime minister and his queen made peace and Rarotonga was again basking in the admiration of visitors who found it 'unspoiled, with people of unsurpassed friendliness.'

I saw Pa for the last time a few months after the Easter Weekend Massacre. It was 9 August 1986 in Fiji. She and Sir Thomas were there for the annual South Pacific Forum Meeting of heads of governments. We met for tea in the lush tropical gardens of the Suva Travelodge. A mob of reporters milled about the lobby and grounds hoping to catch a delegate for a private interview.

She looked deeply tired. We embraced. 'I guess you're still married to that guy', I said.

'Still the same company. No changes', she sighed. We spoke of mutual friends and of the fact that we were getting fat – we spoke of everything except 'it', which I had no intention of bringing up.

Suddenly, she reached across the table and took my hands in hers. I looked at her inquiringly. Was something wrong? Yes, something was terribly wrong and she needed my help in putting it right.

'You know you can count on me, Pa', I said. 'What's wrong?'

'It is important to me', she replied gravely, 'that you know what happened to the prime minister. The media exaggerated. They did not tell the truth.'

'Pa, please, you don't have to ....'

Releasing one of my hands, she raised her finger for silence. My eyes were riveted on her face. She spoke dramatically, with great conviction:

'The prime minister rolled on his knife in his sleep. That is how he was wounded.'

I swallowed hard and watched her for the slightest familiar hint of mischief. There was no twinkle in those sad brown eyes. She wanted to be taken seriously.

'Pa, does he often sleep with his bush knife?'

'I don't know', she said. 'I think he may have had a bit too much to drink. It was an accident and he did it to himself.'

'I want to be sure I understand what you're saying. He almost cut his ear and his testicles off and slashed his chest by rolling on his machete in his sleep?'

'Yes, Mel. That is what happened.'

A deep weary sadness came over me. 'I wish you hadn't told me that, Pa. You didn't have to tell me anything and I would never have asked. It's your very private business. The truth is between you and Tom.'

'That is the truth, Mel. I want you to write about it in one of your stories. Promise me that you will.'

I promised, but I didn't see how I ever could without making people laugh. She was a kind, gracious, fiercely loyal woman as well as an extraordinary queen. She left me a note repeating: 'My dear friend, no it is still the same company – no changes at all. See you when I return. Great meeting you again, Mel. God bless. Regards, Pa.'

I never saw her again. She died suddenly four years later, 3 February 1990, in Auckland. She was there on an official visit as queen, accompanied by her husband, who was no longer a prime minister. He'd been stripped of his office in 1988 by Parliament via a vote of no confidence. It was unanimous. Members of a Cook Islands dance team touring California when the news came reacted with cynical jubilation. 'They should've of shot him', said one male dancer.

Her body was flown back to Rarotonga, arriving on the 3:50 a.m. Air New Zealand flight on 9 February. Thousands of Islanders wept as the plane doors opened and Pa Ariki, the brave Queen of Takitumu, returned home for the last time.

A prayer service was held on the tarmac and the funeral cortège began its slow pre-dawn journey down the road through the columns of eighty-foot coconut palms, their fronds silent, for once, beside the still black waters of the lagoon. Turning inland, the procession wound through the fields to her husband's A-frame house in Takitumu, where we had held our first interview. Her body lay in state there most of the day.

That night, the bones of her ancestors rattled in their graves as the wailing chants of the *apare* rent the night as has been customary for royalty since ancient times. The next morning, pallbearers carried her Cook Islands flag–draped casket to a hearse. The procession moved slowly down the road a short distance to the Baha'i Centre at Muri Lagoon, where a special ceremony was held. The cortège then continued, pausing for services at churches around the island. Guards of honor were made up of childrens' organizations of Takitumu.

The government, now led by Prime Minister Sir Geoffrey Henry, chartered the local airline and flew the *arikis* in from all Outer Islands that had airports to bid farewell to their president of the House of Ariki.

She was buried at Kake Ra, Ngatangiia, next to the Ngatangiia Primary School on the lagoon side of the road. The opening hymn and prayer were offered by members of the Cook Islands Baha'i faith. The Cook Islands Christian

Church conducted the remainder of the service. At the end, the haunting Cook Islands National Anthem was played – the anthem she had composed with her husband in the happy first years of their marriage.

Her wishes for a humble grave and simple marker, where her grandchildren and great-grandchildren could play and know her memory, were ignored. A mighty white cement monument about the size and shape of a container vessel crate was erected to the gallant queen who fought for her tribe against resort developers and her own husband so that even the poorest of her people would always have access to their lagoon and food.

A simple bronze plaque faces the road: Pa Tepaeru Te Upoko Tini Ariki, born 14 August 1923, died 3 February 1990: Thy paradise is my love; thy heavenly home, reunion with me. Enter therein and tarry not. — Baha'u'llah.

Thus ended the reign of the forty-seventh Pa Ariki, who did not have to marry a politician to become a first lady. She was born a first lady, she lived as a first lady, and she died a first lady.

Her surviving children include her sons, Taitairariki, George and Malcolm, and daughters Mahinarangi, Bambi, Suiabel, Marie, Elizabeth and Memory.

Her only Cook Islands–dwelling child, Marie Napa, was the choice of the people of Takitumu to succeed her mother. Married to a planter and son of an *ariki* of the Tinomana line of Arorangi, she came from a life of hard work, but no training for chiefdom. She picked and packed pawpaws and other produce for export to New Zealand, developed a nursery business for flowers and orchids, held down a day job, first with the Tourist Authority, later in a local bank, raised a family and devoted the rest of her time to her church. Therein lay a conflict. Marie Napa was a Jehovah's Witness who went door to door passing out *The Watchtower*, admonishing her neighbors to change their ways and repent. Her husband too is a devout member.

Her religion prohibits involvement in political activities or the taking of secular titles. Like her late mother, Marie was faced with a choice between religious convictions and a title. Her mother defied the Island and kept both but swore if a choice were forced on her, she would chose her religion over her title and people. Marie chose the title after much soul-searching and left her church. She was invested with full traditional pomp as the forty-eighth Pa Tepaeru Te Ariki Upokotini Ariki on 27 June 1990.

Family land was cleared beside Muri Lagoon by the new Pa and her husband for the long-awaited Palace of Takitumu in 1992. The Maori Queen of New Zealand planted the first coconut tree; the author, a mango in the late Pa's memory. Convicts from the ever-growing population of the Arorangi Prison dug the hole.

Down the road, resorts encroach on the shores of the Lagoon to accommodate the increasing mobs of visitors as they escape to the South Seas for a brief visit to 'heaven while you're still on earth'.

### Pouvanaa a Oopa

Marcel Oopa died in a cancer hospital in Paris in 1961 with his father at his side. Pouvanaa had been taken from his prison cell for the death watch only after intense lobbying by his Tahitian supporters.

Seven years later, Francis Sanford, a leader in French Polynesia's autonomist movement, was finally able to negotiate Pouvanaa's pardon and release. The *metua* had then served ten years of his harsh sentence and was partially paralyzed.

According to Bengt and Marie-Thérèse Danielsson in their book *Poisoned Reign*, Sanford sent an urgent letter advising the French government that Pouvanaa had only a few days to live and that if he died in exile, the news would have an 'explosive effect on the Polynesian people.' According to the Danielssons, the letter ended with an ultimatum: 'Pouvanaa must be returned alive to Tahiti before 1 December 1968.' Doctors were sent to examine the old freedom fighter. They confirmed what Sanford said: Pouvanaa was dying.

Four days later, a bulletin from the official French news agency, AFP, was released announcing that 'General de Gaulle had signed a decree pardoning Pouvanaa and abrogating his banishment in commemoration of Armistice Day. The decision can be viewed as a humanitarian measure, particularly appropriate as the beneficiary is a veteran from the 1914–18 war.'

Just before dawn, 30 November 1968, a jet aircraft landed at Faaa on the island of Tahiti. Thousands met it. The doors of the plane opened and a feeble old man emerged. Barely able to walk, the 72-year-old Pouvanaa was carried in triumph by his friends to a waiting car bedecked with flowers. He raised his hand occasionally to thank the people for the flowers they threw, but he seemed in a daze. The road from the airport at Faaa to Papeete was carpeted with *tifai-fais* in a display of love and respect from the women.

The Town Hall was overflowing. He sat through an exhausting program of speeches, music and song. His own speech was faltering and brief. He thanked God for his deliverance and called on the people to unite and work together. He then demanded a retrial. His closest friends walked with him from the Town Hall to his house. Very little had changed there since he had been taken away ten years earlier. The Danielssons described the scene, in the center of the sparsely furnished living room stood a table covered with a cloth, on which lay a Tahitian-language Bible. 'Next to it stood the only comfortable chair, in which Pouvanaa sunk down. He bowed his head and closed his eyes. It was obvious to all of the reverently silent onlookers that he had reached the limit of what he could endure.'

But Pouvanaa a Oopa was not ready to die yet. He regained enough strength to stand for and win a seat on the Territorial Assembly again. Though frail and confined to a wheelchair, he fought for an end to nuclear testing in the Tuamotus and continued doggedly to battle for autonomy and a retrial to clear his name. Despite deteriorating health, his mind remained keen. He was still the honored *metua* of his people, who deferred to him on important issues and accepted his decisions as absolute. From the French, however, he never got a retrial. He never got justice. He died in 1978 at the age of eighty-one.

Pouvanaa a Oopa's fifty-year struggle for his people's freedom and independence was grotesquely whitewashed for future generations with a 3 million franc monument. It is possibly the ugliest piece of public art in the Pacific. It would be hard to top Danielsson's adjective, 'hideous', in describing the bust of Pouvanaa on a stone stele near the waterfront in Papeete.

Erected to placate his supporters three years after the old freedom fighter's death, the text on the plaque at the base of the monstrosity is unsurprising. It praises Pouvanaa as a war hero and proclaims him a hero to his people because he persuaded the French administration to employ more natives, increase welfare handouts and return some land rights to their rightful owners.

Pouvanaa's true story is stronger than the bronze and stone of his false monument. It will endure, as long as *te aho maohi* tell it to their children.

# REFERENCES

Carter, John, ed. *Pacific Islands Yearbook,* 15th edn. Sydney: Pacific Publications, 1984.

Clairmont, Leonard. *Tahitian–English, English–Tahitian Dictionary.* California: Edward Dew, 1958.

*Cook Islands News,* various editions. Published on Rarotonga.

*Cook Islands Politics.* New Zealand: Polynesian Press in association with the South Pacific Social Sciences Association, 1979.

Danielsson, Bengt, and Marie-Thérèse Danielsson. *Moruroa Mon Amour.* London: Penguin Books, 1974.

———. *Poisoned Reign.* Sydney: Penguin Books, 1986.

Earl, The, and the Doctor. *South Sea Bubbles.* New York: D. Appleton, 1872.

Ellis, William. *Polynesian Researches, Society Islands.* Rutland, Vermont: Charles E. Tuttle, 1969. From Ellis's journal, 1817–1825.

Frisbie, Florence (Johnnie). *Miss Ulysses from Puka Puka.* New York: Macmillan, 1948.

———. *The Frisbies of the South Seas.* New York: Doubleday, 1959.

Frisbie, Robert Dean. *The Book of Puka Puka.* London: John Murray, 1930

———. *Island of Desire.* Boston: Country Life Press, 1944.

Gill, Rev. William. *Gems from the Coral Islands; or, Incidents of Contrast between Savage and Christian Life of the South Sea Islanders.* Philadelphia: Presbyterian Board of Publication, 1857.

Hall, James Norman. *The Forgotten One.* Boston: Little Brown, 1952.

Henry, Teuira, recorded by J.M. Orsmond. *Ancient Tahiti.* Honolulu: Bernice P. Bishop Museum Bulletin No. 48, 1928.

Langdon, Robert. *Tahiti, Island of Love.* London: Cassell, 1959.

*Maps of the Cook Islands.* Government of the Cook Islands Survey Department.

Neale, Tom *An Island to Myself.* New York: Holt, Rinehart and Winston, 1966.

# REFERENCES

*Pacific Islands Monthly*, various editions. Published in Australia and Fiji.

Quill, Frank. *Milan Brych, the Cancer Man*. Australia: Publishers House, 1981.

Savage, Stephen. *A Dictionary of the Maori Language of Rarotonga*. 1962; rpt. Institute of the South Pacific, Fiji, in association with the Ministry of Education of the Cook Islands 1980.

'Statistical Bulletins' (Various). Government of the Cook Islands.

*Te Rau Maire, Poems and Stories of the Pacific*. Rarotonga: M.C.D., Rarotonga; Institute of Pacific Studies, University of the South Pacific, Suva; South Pacific Creative Arts Society, Suva; University of Victoria, Wellington and University of Auckland, 1992.

Webb, Frederick W. *Parliamentary Handbook of the Cook Islands*. Rarotonga: Government of the Cook Islands, 1983.

Wilkes, Owen. 'Dirty Work in the Cook Islands'. *New Zealand Monthly Review*, September 1987.